Traditional Chinese Tales

Traditional Chinese Tales

Translated by

CHI-CHEN WANG

COLUMBIA UNIVERSITY PRESS

New York : 1944

First printing February, 1944
Second printing May, 1944

Foreign Agent: Oxford University Press, Humphrey Milford, Amen House, London, E.C. 4, England, and B. I. Building, Nicol Road, Bombay, India

MANUFACTURED IN THE UNITED STATES OF AMERICA

To Wang-Chen Chihling

Preface

Here in these twenty tales the reader will find practically all the themes of traditional Chinese fiction except that of the historical romance and the realistic novel. The supernatural predominates, probably because it is easier to paint creditable portraits of ghosts and demons than of men—to paraphrase the dictum of an early Chinese art critic. In fact, traditional story tellers scarcely attempt to delineate character or analyze motive at all; incident and moral are about the only things that interest them.

As far as form is concerned, traditional tales are of two types, both represented in this volume. The first type is written in classical Chinese (roughly the kind current in Confucius' time) by and for the literati. It is characterized by extreme brevity and economy of expression, often to the point of incomprehensibility. The second type is written in the vernacular and had its origin in the oral tradition of professional story tellers. The earliest written versions of tales of this type were probably set down by the more literate story tellers to be used as prompt books. It is probably because of this oral beginning that tales of the popular type are apt to be diffuse and repetitious, for it was through these apparent faults that the story teller was able to overcome the hazards that beset the spoken word, to say nothing of the disadvantage of having to contend with an audience that kept drifting in and out.

C.C.W.

Columbia University
July, 1943

Contents

Hsü Yen's Strange Encounter or Lovers within a Lover

Wu Chün

469-520

In the Eastern Chin period (318-420) Hsü Yen of Yanghsien was passing through the Suian Mountains. He met a student lying by the roadside who complained of pains in his feet and asked Yen if he would carry him in his goose cage. Thinking that the stranger was only joking, Yen said that he would. Thereupon the student crawled into the cage and settled down comfortably beside the two geese. He did not seem to grow any smaller or the cage any larger; nor did Yen find the cage any heavier when he picked it up.

When Yen stopped under a tree to rest, the student came out of the cage and asked Yen if he would like to have some refreshments. When he said that he would, the stranger spat out a bronze box with all kinds of rare delicacies in it. All the utensils were made of bronze and the foods were all delicious beyond anything that Yen had known. After the wine had been around a few times, the stranger said to Yen: "I have a woman with me that I should like to have join us." "Fine," Yen said, and thereupon the stranger spat out of his mouth a girl of about sixteen, gorgeously dressed and extraordinarily beautiful.

After a while the student became drunk and fell asleep, whereat the girl said to Yen: "Though I am married to this student, in reality I love another man and have him with me at all times. Since the student is asleep I should like to entertain my lover a while, if you would promise not to tell."

Yen promised, and the girl spat out of her mouth a handsome

young man of about twenty three or four and introduced him to Yen. Suddenly the student stirred, whereupon she spat out a brocade screen and put it between him and her lover. Then she went behind the screen and joined the student.

The young man now said to Yen: "Though this girl loves me, yet she does not entirely fill my heart. So I too have a woman with me and I should like to take this opportunity to see her. Pray do not tell." Yen promised and the youth thereupon spat out of his mouth another girl about twenty years old and drank and jested with her for a long while.

But presently there came the sound of the student stirring, and the young man said: "Those two are waking up!" and forthwith took the girl he had spit out and put her back into his mouth. Then the girl that had been with the student came out and, saying that the student was about to get up, swallowed the young man and sat alone with Yen. Then the student said to Yen, "I am sorry to have slept so long and left you sitting alone. It is getting late. I must take leave of you." So saying he swallowed the girl and all the utensils except a large tray, which was about two feet in diameter and which he gave to Yen, saying, "I have nothing except this to offer to you as a memento of our meeting."

In the T'ai Yuan period (376-396) Yen was an imperial archivist. Once he used the tray for serving refreshments to Chang San, secretary in attendance, who ascertained from the inscription on it that it was made in the third year of Yung P'ing (A.D. 60) of the Han dynasty.

The Ancient Mirror

Wang Tu

FL. 585-625

Mr. Hou of Fenyin of the Sui dynasty (581-618) was a remarkable man, whom I, Wang Tu, served as my master. Just before his death he gave me an ancient mirror with the intimation that its possession would ward off evil spirits of all kinds. I accepted the gift and treasured it. It was eight inches in diameter, with a knob in the form of a crouching ch'i lin.[1] Around the knob were ranged four symbolic animals—the tortoise, the dragon, the phoenix and the tiger—each in its proper quarter. Outside there were the Eight Diagrams and beyond these the twelve zodiacal animals. At the outermost periphery were twenty-four characters which resembled in style the Li script but which could not be found in any of the dictionaries. According to Mr. Hou they symbolized the twenty-four solar periods. When held up to the sun, the designs and characters on the back appeared distinctly in the reflection; [2] when tapped, the mirror gave out a resonant note that reverberated all day. It was clearly a mirror of no ordinary quality, and what wonder that it should have been treasured by such a worthy man as Mr. Hou and looked upon by him as a spiritual object. Once Mr. Hou explained the story of the mirror to me: "I have heard that the Yellow Emperor once cast fifteen mirrors, the first of which was fifteen inches in diameter, corresponding to the number of days that the moon requires to grow. Since each succeeding mirror is one inch smaller in diameter, this must be the eighth in

[1] A fabulous animal of auspicious omen, comparable to the unicorn.

[2] A quality actually possessed by a certain type of bronze mirror, of which there is one in the American Museum of Natural History.

the series." Though the time of the Yellow Emperor [3] was remote and there is no written record of these mirrors, yet one must give due credence to the view of such a worthy man as Mr. Hou.

In ages past Mr. Yang was blessed through the acquisition of a jade ring, while Mr. Chang died with the loss of his sword. Now these are disturbed times and I have been deeply saddened by events; the empire is aflame with strife and there is no place where one can live in peace. And on top of all these troubles I have, alas! just lost my mirror. I shall, therefore, set below all the marvels connected with it, so that those who come by it in future generations may know its origin.

I acquired the mirror in the fifth month of the seventh year of Ta Yeh (611) from Mr. Hou, whose death occured on my return to Hotung after I was relieved of my post in the Censorate. On my way back to Changan in the sixth month of the same year I passed by Changlopo and stopped at the inn of Cheng Hsiung. Cheng had recently come by a bondmaid, a very pretty girl named Parrot. As I took my mirror out to look at myself and tidy my clothes, I was observed by Parrot, who immediately fell on her knees and knocked her head on the ground until blood came from it, crying the while, "Spare me and I shall go away!" I summoned my host and asked him about the strange behavior of the maid. Said my host: "Two months ago a man came with this maid. As she was very sick, he left her here, saying that he would come back for her. He hasn't reappeared yet. That's all I know about her." Suspecting that she was an animal spirit of some sort, I approached her with the open mirror, whereupon she said, "Spare me, and I will resume my original form." "Tell me about yourself before you do," I said, covering up the mirror, "and I will spare you." The maid then kowtowed and said: "I am a thousand-year-old fox that used to live under an old pine before the temple of the Guardian Deity of Hua Mountain. I have incurred the penalty of death because of my transformations. I was seized by the Lord of Huashan but I escaped and fled to the region between the Ho and the Wei. There Chen Ssu-kung of Hsiakuei adopted me as

[3] Traditionally given as 2697-2597 B.C.

his daughter and treated me with kindness. Later I was married to Chai Hua of the same region but as I could not live in accord with him, I ran off and traveled in an easterly direction until I reached the Hancheng district where I was captured by Li Wu-ao, a very fierce and violent man. He forced me to travel with him for several years until he left me here. Unfortunately the sacred mirror has been turned upon me and makes it impossible for me to conceal my true form."

"Since you are an old fox," I said, "is it not your intention, in assuming the human form, to harm people?" "I have assumed the human form so that I can serve men, not harm them," she said. "However, it is offensive to the gods for animals to masquerade under human form. I shall surely have to pay with death." "I am willing to spare you if it is possible," I said to her. "I am grateful for your kindness," she said, "but having once encountered the all-revealing rays of the mirror, it will be impossible for me to continue in my assumed form, and I who have so long gone under the shape of man cannot endure the humiliation of going back to my original form. I only pray that you put the mirror back in its case so that I can drink and be merry for a last time before I die." I said to her, "Wouldn't you escape if I put the mirror back into the box?" She said, smiling, "Did you not, sir, offer to spare me? It would be ungrateful of me to vanish after you cover up the mirror. Moreover, the mirror has deprived me of power of transformation; I only wish to have a brief moment of joy before death overtakes me."

Thereupon I put the mirror back in its case and had wine brought for her and summoned my host's neighbors to join the feast. The maid was soon intoxicated. She rose and danced and sang the following song:

O magic mirror, magic mirror!
Alas, my life, alas, my life!
Since I cast off my own form,
How many dynasties have risen and fallen?
Though life is indeed sweet,
It is vain to mourn death.

So why cherish only this world?
Why cling only to this life?

Having finished the song, she bowed again and then changed into an old fox and died, to the astonishment of all those present.

On the first day of the fourth month, eighth year of Ta Yeh, there was an eclipse of the sun. I was then at the Censorate and was resting in one of the chambers when the sun began to grow dark. Soon I was informed by the clerks that the eclipse was a severe one. When I rose and took the mirror out to tidy myself, I found that it had grown dim and lost its usual brilliance, and I realized that the mirror was so made that it corresponded to the mystery of light and darkness, for otherwise how can one explain the fact that it also should be without light when the Great Luminary was in eclipse? Before I had done marveling at the phenomenon, the mirror brightened, and with it the sun also began to shine; and when the sun had recovered completely its luminosity, the mirror too shone with its former brilliance. I noted thereafter that whenever the sun and moon were in eclipse. the mirror grew dim.

On the fifteenth of the eighth month of the same year my friend Hsueh Hsieh called on me to show me a bronze sword that he had previously acquired. It was four feet [4] in length, and the blade was of one piece with the handle, which was decorated with dragon and phoenix, while the blade was embellished with patterns like tongues of fire on one side and with patterns like ripples of water on the other. It shone with a dazzling light and was evidently no ordinary sword. Hsieh said, "I have observed a remarkable thing about this sword. If you place it in a dark room on the fifteenth of the month when the moon is full and bright, it will radiate rays of light to the distance of several rods. I have had this sword for some years, and since you long for the sight of strange things and ancient objects as the hungry crave for food and the thirsty crave for drink, I should like to demonstrate this phenomenon to you tonight." I was overjoyed on hearing this, and as

[4] The ancient Chinese foot measure varied from eight to ten inches of the English system. It is divided into ten *ts'un* or inches.

it happened to be a clear night we shut out all the light from one room and stayed there to make the test. I also took my mirror and placed it by my side. Presently the mirror shone forth with a light that brightened up the room like day, but the sword along side of it gave no light at all. Hsieh was greatly astonished and said, "Please put your mirror back into the case." I did so and it was not until then that the sword radiated some light to a distance of only a foot or two. "So," Hsieh said, sighing, "even with magic objects there is also a difference in quality and the inferior has to yield in the presence of something superior." Thereafter, whenever the moon was full, I would bring out the mirror and place it in a dark room so as to watch its radiance; it never failed to light up the room to a distance of several rods. But if the moonlight should be allowed to penetrate into the room, then there was no light from it, which showed that it could not stand up against the brilliance of the Great Male and the Great Female.[5]

In the winter of that year I was appointed member of the Institute of Historiography and set myself the task of writing a biography of Su Cho. It happened that I had an old servant of seventy by the name of Pao Sheng who had once been in the service of the Su family. He had a fair knowledge of history and some appreciation of literary composition. When he saw the draft of Su's biography he fell into an uncontrollable fit of grief. When I asked him the cause, he said, "His Excellency Su treated me with kindness and generosity when I was in his service. I grieve now because what he prophesied has come true. For, sir, the magic mirror that you have was once given to His Excellency by Miao Chi-tzu of Honan and he greatly treasured it. In the year of his death, he was constantly in a state of melancholy, and once, summoning Miao Chi-tzu to him, he said, 'My death is not far off and I wonder what will happen to this mirror after my death. I want now to divine it by the milfoil and should like you to witness it.' He then commanded me to bring the milfoil sticks and having cast them and read the pattern, he said: 'Ten years after my death, the mirror will be lost to my family, no one knows where. But the presence of a

[5] The sun and the moon.

spiritual object is always indicated by some supernatural sign. I note that of late there have been emanations of an auspicious nature in the region of the Ho and the Wei, and that these emanations coincide with the message of the milfoil. The mirror will probably be recovered in that region.' 'Will it be found by some man?' Chi-tzu asked. His Excellency examined the milfoil again and then said, 'It will first come into the possession of a man by the name of Hou and then pass into the hands of a man by the name of Wang. After that it is impossible to tell.'" Pao Sheng, the servant, wept after giving this recital. I inquired of the Su family and found that it was indeed as Pao Sheng had said, and that the mirror vanished after Mr. Su's death. Therefore I appended this incident to Su's biography. I had this in mind when I wrote: "Mr. Su had a surpassing skill in the art of divination and was able to put it to his own use."

On New Year's Day of the ninth year of Ta Yeh a Buddhist monk from the Western Regions came to our house to beg and was received by my brother Chi,[6] who, impressed by his uncommon appearance, invited him into the house and set food before him. After a while the monk said to Chi, "It appears that you have in your house, charitable patron, a unique mirror. May I have the honor of gazing upon it?" "How do you happen to know, Master of the Law?" Chi asked. "I have some instruction in magic," the monk replied, "and I am thus able to detect the presence of spiritual emanations. For the past two years I have noted a jade-green light emanating from your mansion by day and a saffron light when the moon is shining and I know it for the work of a magic mirror. I have come on this auspicious day in the hope of looking at it." Chi brought out the mirror, whereupon the monk took it in his hands and danced with joy. Then he said to Chi, "This mirror has several magical qualities that you may not be aware of. If you paint it with a gold ointment and spray it with pearl dust, its rays will penetrate the wall. And if you smoke it with incense of gold and wash it with liquid jade before you apply the ointment and pearl dust, it will enable you to see the inner

[6] Wang Chi, the poet. Died A.D. 644.

organs of man. The only pity is that it provides no cure for the ailments that it enables you to diagnose." Before he went away, he left some of the ingredients required for the tests, which all turned out as he said. The monk was never seen again afterwards.

In the fall of that year I was sent from the capital to serve as governor of Juicheng. In front of the governor's yamen there was an ancient jujube tree, several rods in circumference and untold centuries old. It had been the custom for the new governors to make sacrifices to this tree, for failure to do so had invariably brought disaster. As I was of the belief that the malign spirits were born of man's imagination, I was inclined to discontinue the sacrifice, but the clerks and officers all begged me to follow the former custom, and unable to refuse them, I complied. Then I thought to myself that the tree might indeed harbor some evil monster which had grown in magic power as no one had been able to destroy it. Therefore I secretly hung the mirror among the branches of the tree. That night around the second watch I heard a rumbling sound like thunder in front of the yamen. When I rose and went out to look, the sky was darkened by a storm and there was thunder and lightning that shot around and up and down the tree. In the morning a huge serpent with purple scales and a red tail, green head, and white brow, and the character for "king" patterned on its forehead, was discovered dead of numerous injuries under the tree. I took down the mirror and had the serpent burned in the public square. I also had the tree cut down and in doing so the trunk was found to be hollow down to the ground and to have traces left by the serpent. After this no malign spirits troubled the district.

In the same winter I was ordered to the Hopei Circuit to supervise dispensations from the government granaries; there was then a famine in the land and the people suffered greatly from hunger and disease, particularly in the regions of Pu and Shan. Among my officers there was a man by the name of Chang Lung-chu, a native of Hopei, whose entire household, numbering more than a score, was stricken with sickness. Taking pity upon them, I went to his house with my mirror and left it with Lung-chu with the instruction that he should uncover it at night. When this was done the sick all rose from their beds with their fevers completely gone. They said that Lung-chu had come into the room with a moonlike object in his hand and that its light had chilled them like ice and driven away their fevers. Since it did not occur to me that this service would cause the mirror any harm, while it might save a multitude of people, I instructed Lung-chu to take the mirror and turn its magic emanations on the other people in the district who were afflicted, but that night the mirror made a strange, chilly, and penetrating noise and did not stop for a long while. In the morning Lung-chu came to me and said, "I dreamed last night that I was visited by a man with the head of a dragon and the body of a snake, wearing a red hat and a purple robe. He told me that his name was Purple Gem and that he was the spirit of the mirror. 'I have come to you,' he said, 'because I have just been of assistance to your household. Please tell Mr. Wang for me that the people have been visited with sickness as a penalty of Heaven and that he should not make me cure them contrary to the Higher Will. Moreover, the sickness will pass of itself in a few months; why should he set me this task?' " I complied with the request, and indeed in a month or so all those who were stricken gradually recovered, just as the spirit of the mirror had said.

In the tenth year of Ta Yeh my brother Chi resigned from his position as assistant magistrate of Liuho and decided to embark upon a tour of the mountains and rivers of the empire. I tried to dissuade him from the project as there were signs of disturbed times to come, but in vain. He asked me to lend him the mirror for his protection. This I gladly did. He was gone for a long time and did not return to Changan until the sixth month of the thirteenth year of Ta Yeh. "The mirror was indeed a marvelous object," he told me and went on to tell of the wonder that it had wrought and of the animal spirits that it had exposed.[7] "Then," he concluded, "I met the retired scholar Su Pin of Lushan, a man of profound erudition and with a gift for prognostication of things to come. 'A

[7] I have omitted these incidents as they add nothing to the magical prowess of the mirror.

magical object such as your mirror,' he warned me, 'will not for long remain in the midst of men. The world is now in turmoil and you should return to your native home while you still have the mirror for your protection.' I agreed with him and started northward. But in Hopei I tarried for a while until one night I dreamed that the mirror came to me and told me that it was about to leave the world of man and that it would like to have a last meeting with you. It begged me, therefore, to return to Changan as soon as I could. In the dream I granted its request, and on waking up the following morning and reflecting upon the situation, I immediately set out for Changan. Now that I am with you, I have fulfilled my promise. I am afraid, however, that you will soon lose possession of this marvelous object." After some days my brother returned to Hotung, and then on the fifteenth day of the seventh month, the thirteenth year of Ta Yeh, there came from the case in which the mirror was kept a mournful sound. At first it was low and remote but it soon grew in intensity until it was like the roar of dragons and the growl of tigers. It was some time before this sound subsided. When I opened the case to look, the mirror had vanished.

The White Monkey

Author Unknown

7TH CENTURY

Toward the end of the Ta T'ung period (A.D. 535-545) of the Liang dynasty, the Emperor sent General Lin Ch'in on a campaign for the pacification of the southern frontier. He led his armies as far as Kueilin and there defeated the armies of Li Shih-ku and Chen Ch'e. Ou-yang Ho,[1] one of the generals under him, reached Changlo in the course of his marches and conquered all the mountain tribes in the region. Ho's wife was very beautiful and had a very white skin, and one of his lieutenants said to him, "Why have you, General, brought a beautiful woman to a place like this? For there is a spirit here that is in the habit of seizing young women, especially if they are beautiful. You must be on your guard and protect your lady well."

Ho became anxious and that night he surrounded the house with troops and concealed his wife in a secret chamber, guarded over by more than ten maids. The night was dark and there was a wind blowing, but nothing happened as late as the fifth watch. Then when the attendants had grown tired and had dozed off they were suddenly awakened by some noise and found that Ho's wife had vanished. The door was locked as before, and no one could imagine how she might have left the room. To search for her then was out of the question, for the house was surrounded by precipitous mountains and it was impossible to see beyond the distance of a foot, but when a search was made after dawn there was no trace of her to be found.

Ho was exceedingly grieved and swore that he would not leave

[1] Father of the great calligrapher Ou-yang Hsün A.D. 557-645.

the region until he had found his wife. He went out daily in all directions and forded rivers and climbed mountains in search of her, and one day, more than a month later, he suddenly came upon an embroidered shoe lying in a thick growth of vines and brushes, which, though wet and discolored from the rain, he recognized to be one of his wife's. This made him redouble his efforts. He selected a group of thirty strong men, armed with weapons and provided with food, so that they could pass the night in the caves and eat out on the open and thus avoid having to interrupt their search. About ten days later they espied, when they were about two hundred li from their quarters, a mountain to the south of them, which was more heavily wooded than any they had seen. On their approach they found that it was surrounded by a deep stream, which they crossed on an improvised raft. They caught glimpses of red among the bamboos on a sheer cliff and heard voices and laughter. When they pulled themselves up by the overhanging brushes and vines, they found a well-laid-out park of trees and rare flowers and a fine lawn as soft as a carpet. It was so quiet and still that it was unlike anything on earth. To the east there was a stone gate and under it there were more than a score of women at play, all costumed in fine silks and singing and laughing. They all stopped and stood still when they saw Ou-yang Ho and his men, and when the latter approached, the women asked what had brought them. Ho told them, whereupon they looked to one another and said, "Your wife has been here more than a month. She is now sick in bed, but we shall take you to her." Ho followed them into the gate and found within three spacious halls carved out of the cliff, with thick mattressed beds along the walls. His wife was lying on a stone couch covered with a heavy mattress, and in front of her were set out all kinds of delicacies. Ho approached her, but when she saw him she motioned him to go away.

The women said, "Your wife and ourselves are all captives here. Some of us have been here as long as ten years. There is a supernatural being living here who is mighty in strength and whom a hundred armed men cannot subdue. You must go away before he comes back. If you will bring two jars of fine wine, ten fat dogs, and a quantity of strong hemp strands, we shall help you to destroy him. He always comes home at noon,[2] so do not come too early. We shall expect you in ten days."

After saying this they urged him to go away without delay, which Ho did. Then he secured the strongest wine that he could get and the dogs and hemp, and went back as he had agreed. "He is fond of wine," the women told him, "and often gets very drunk. When he does, he always tries to show off his strength. He will ask us to bind his hands and feet to the bed with silk and will then burst the bonds with a mighty heave. But once we bound him with three thicknesses of silk and he was not able to break free. We shall conceal the hemp strands in the silk and bind him thus; surely that will secure him. His body is as hard as iron, but there is an area of a few inches under his navel that he always keeps well protected. This must be the spot which will not stand up against weapons." And then pointing to a cave at one side, they said, "That is the food store. You can hide there and wait for your chance. We shall place the wine by the flowers and scatter the dogs among the trees and then summon him to his death feast."

Ho hid himself as directed and watched with bated breath. At noon he observed something flutter like a piece of white silk on a neighboring mountain and then come flying in his direction and enter the cave. Presently a man emerged with the women. He was over six feet tall, had a beautiful beard and was dressed in white and carried a staff. At the sight of the dogs, he started with pleasure and pounced on them and tore them to pieces, sucking the blood and eating the flesh until he was full. In the meanwhile the women poured out wine in jade cups and coaxed him to drink. After the effect of the wine became evident, they took him into the cave, which soon resounded with laughter and frolic. After a long while the women came out and beckoned Ho to come forth. This he did and went into the cave with his weapon. There he saw a huge white monkey bound to the bed by his four feet; he was struggling to get free, his brows knitted and his eyes flashing

[2] Further on the monkey is said to vanish from his cave home shortly after noon. Such inconsistencies are typical of traditional Chinese tales.

like lightning, but in vain. Ho and his men all struck at him with their weapons but the blows fell on him as on iron and stone, and it was not until they succeeded in striking a blow under his navel that the blade penetrated and brought forth a gush of blood.

Thereupon the monkey cried, "It is heaven that has destroyed me, not you. Mark, however, that your wife is pregnant. Do not kill the man child that she will bear, for he will serve under a sage emperor[3] and bring honor to your family." After saying this, the monkey died. Ho searched through the cave and found a vast store of precious objects and rare foods; hardly a thing treasured by man was missing. In addition there were several cases of rare perfumes and a pair of swords, as well as the women already mentioned, who were all of surpassing beauty. They told Ho that as their beauty waned, they were carried off by the monkey to they knew not where, that the monkey carried on his depredations all by himself and was without accomplices of any kind, that he wore the same white robe all the year round without regard to the season and that his body was covered with white hair several inches long. They told him too that the monkey used to read wooden tablets inscribed with writing that looked like ancient seal characters or charms which were unintelligible to them and which he carefully put away under the stone steps after reading. On clear days he sometimes danced with his swords, which he swung so rapidly that they flashed around him like lightning, forming a circle of light like the moon. He ate irregularly, was fond of fruits and nuts but had an especial weakness for dogs, which he would kill and suck the blood from. He always vanished like a gust of wind shortly after noon but never failed to return at night; he was able to travel a distance of several thousand li in the course of the afternoon, and was always able to get immediately what he wished. At night he would go from bed to bed until he had made the complete round, never sleeping at all himself. They said that although his conversation was elegant and erudite, it was evident that he was but some kind of ape. That year when the trees were just beginning to shed their leaves he had one day said to them, with an air of

[3] Allusion to Emperor T'ai Tsung, actual founder of the T'ang dynasty.

sadness: "The gods of the mountains have lodged complaints against me and the penalty will be death. I must beg the more friendly deities to intercede for me, so that I may escape the penalty." Then last month just as the moon began to wax, he made a fire on the stone steps and burned all his books of wooden tablets, and said with a sigh: "I have lived a thousand years but I am without an heir. Now that I am about to have a son, I have to die." He looked around at the women and wept bitterly for a long while before he went on. "This mountain is quite inaccessible and has never been visited by men. I have never seen any woodcutters around but there are numerous tigers and wolves and other wild beasts to keep them away. If anyone should come to do me harm, it will be by the Will of Heaven."

Ho returned to his quarters with the women and the precious things and sent back those women who could still remember where their homes were. When his wife's time came, she gave birth to a son who resembled his real father in appearance.[4] Later Ho was executed by Emperor Wu Ti of the Ch'en dynasty, but his good friend Chiang Tsung, who had taken a liking to the boy because of his surpassing wit, took him under his care. When the boy reached manhood, he did indeed become famous for his literary accomplishment and his calligraphy.

[4] Ou-yang Hsün was described as homely and apelike in appearance.

The Disembodied Soul

Ch'en Hsüan-yu

FL. 2D HALF OF THE 8TH CENTURY

In the third year of the T'ien Shou period (692) Chang Yi of Chingho settled in Hengchow, where he served as an official. He was of a quiet disposition and had few friends. He had no son, only two daughters; the older of these died in her childhood, while Chien-niang, the younger daughter, grew up to be without equal in virtue and beauty. Yi had living with him his sister's son, Wang Chu, a talented and handsome youth, and he so esteemed this nephew that he said more than once that he would some day give Chien-niang to him in marriage. On their part, Chu and Chien-niang had a secret passion, of which Chien-niang's parents had no knowledge, so that when Yi later promised Chien-niang in marriage to the son of one of his colleagues, the maiden became saddened and the youth, too, quite unhappy. On the pretext that he must go to the capital to attend the civil service test, Chu begged leave to go thither, and Yi, after trying in vain to detain him, gave in to his wishes and sent him off with handsome presents.

Nursing a secret sorrow in his heart, Chu took leave of his hosts and embarked on his journey. By the end of the day he had covered a distance of some li and found himself among the mountains. At midnight, still unable to fall asleep, he suddenly heard rapid footsteps on the bank and, investigating, found Chien-niang running barefooted after his boat. Chu was beside himself with surprise and happiness. He took her hands in his and asked how she came to be there.

"I cannot forget you even in my dreams," she said, weeping. "But now they are about to force me to marry someone else. As

I know that you too have not changed, I have resolved to give up my very life to repay your faithfulness. I have therefore fled from my parents' house and come to you."

Chu was overcome with joy by his unexpected good fortune. He hid her in the boat and resumed his journey that very night, traveling thereafter by double stages until he reached Szechwan a few months later. There they lived for five years, during which she gave birth to two sons. Though she had not sent word to her parents, she was always thinking of them. "I have come to you against the wishes of my parents," she said weeping to him one day, "because I cannot be unfaithful to you. Now it is five years since I have beheld the loving faces of my parents. There can be no place in the universe for such an unfilial daughter as I." Touched by her piety, Chu said to her, "Do not fret, I shall take you there," and set out with her for Hengchow in fulfillment of his promise.

When they arrived at their destination, Chu went ahead to Yi's house to make his apologies but Yi said, "What preposterous talk is this! for has not my daughter been sick in her room these last five years?" "But she is now in the boat," Chu said. Yi was greatly astonished and sent one of his domestics to the boat to see if it was true. There indeed was Chien-niang in the boat looking well and contented. When she saw the servant she asked him how her parents were. The servant was perplexed and hastened back to report to his master.

Now when the girl lying sick in her room heard of the extraordinary occurrence, she rose from her bed, did her toilet, and changed her clothes. There was a smile on her face as she went out to meet the other Chien-niang, but never a word did she speak. Then before the very eyes of all those present, the two girls joined and became one, wearing the two sets of garments that the separate forms had worn.

Because of the bizarre nature of the event, Yi's family kept it secret, but it got to be known among some of his relatives. The couple lived forty years longer. Both their sons passed the examinations and became assistant magistrates.

I, Hsüan-yu, used to hear of the story in my youth. There were many versions of it, and some held it to be fictitious. Toward the end of the Ta Li period (766-791) I happened to meet Chang Chung-hsien, the magistrate of Laiwu, and learned from him the strange circumstances which I have related. Chung-hsien is Yi's cousin and is acquainted with all the details of that strange story.

The Magic Pillow

Shen Chi-chi

FL. 750-800

In the seventh year of K'ai Yuan (719 A.D.) a Taoist priest by the name of Lü Weng, who had acquired the magic of the immortals, was traveling on the road to Hantan. He stopped at an inn and was sitting and resting with his back against his bag when he was joined in a very genial conversation by a young man named Lu Sheng, who wore a plain, short coat and rode a black colt and who had stopped at the inn on his way to the fields. After a while Lu Sheng suddenly sighed and said, looking at his shabby clothes, "It is because fate is against me that I have been such a failure in life!" "Why do you say that in the midst of such a pleasant conversation?" Lü Weng said, "For as far as I can see you suffer from nothing and appear to enjoy the best of health." "This is mere existence," Lu Sheng said. "I do not call this life." "What then do you call life?" asked the priest, whereupon the young man answered, "A man ought to achieve great things and make a name for himself; he should be a general at the head of an expedition or a great minister at court, preside over sumptuous banquets and order the orchestra to play what he likes, and cause his clan to prosper and his own family to wax rich—these things make what I call life. I have devoted myself to study and have enriched myself with travel; I used to think that rank and title were mine for the picking, but now at the prime of life I still have to labor in the fields. What do you call this if not failure?"

After he finished speaking he felt a sudden drowsiness. The innkeeper was steaming some millet at the time. Lü Weng reached into his bag and took out a pillow and gave it to Lu Sheng, saying,

"Rest your head on this pillow; it will enable you to fulfill your wishes." The pillow was made of green porcelain and had an opening at each end. Lu Sheng bent his head toward it and as he did so the opening grew large and bright, so that he was able to crawl into it. He found himself back home. A few months later he married the daughter of the Tsui family of Chingho, who was very beautiful and made him exceedingly happy. His wealth increased and the number of luxuries with which he surrounded himself multiplied day by day. The following year he passed the examinations and thus "discarded his hempen coat" and joined the ranks at court. He was made a member of the imperial secretariat and had the honor of composing occasional poems at the emperor's command. After serving a term as inspector of Weinan, he was promoted to the Censorate, and made secretary in attendance. In the latter capacity he took part in the drafting of important decrees.

Then followed a succession of provincial posts, in one of which, as the governor of Shensi, he built a canal eighty li in length, which brought so many benefits to the people of the region that they commemorated his achievement upon stone. Next he was made governor of the metropolitan district. In the same year the Emperor's campaigns against the encroaching barbarians reached a critical stage, and when the Turfan and Chulung hordes invested Kuachou and Shachou and menaced the region of the Ho and the Huang, the Emperor, in his search for new talent, made Lu Sheng associate director of the Censorate and governor-general of the Hosi Circuit. Lu Sheng routed the barbarians, killing seven thousand men. He conquered nine hundred li of territory and built three cities to guard the frontier. The people of the frontier region built a monument on the Chuyen Mountain to commemorate his exploits, and when he returned to court he was received with triumphal honors and was made vice-president of the Board of Civil Service and then president of the Board of Revenue. No name carried so much prestige as his and he had the universal acclaim of popular sentiment, but these incurred the jealousy of the other ministers at court, and as a result of their slanderous attacks he was banished to a provincial post. Three years later, however, he was recalled to court and for more than ten years, with Hsiao Sung and P'ei Kuang-t'ing, he held the reins of government. Sometimes he received as many as three confidential messages from the Emperor in one day and was ever ready to assist His Majesty with his wise counsel.

Then again he fell victim to the jealousy of his colleagues. They charged him with conspiring with frontier generals to overthrow the dynasty and caused him to be thrown into prison. When the guards came to arrest him, he was stricken with terror and perplexity and said to his wife and sons: "Back in Shantung we have five hundred acres of good land, quite sufficient to keep us from cold and hunger. Why should I have sought rank and title, which in the end have only brought calamity? It is now too late to wish that I could again ride back and forth on the Hantan road as I once did, wearing my plain hempen coat!" Thereupon he drew his sword and attempted to kill himself, but was prevented from doing so by his wife. All those implicated in the plot were executed but Lu Sheng escaped death through the intercession of one of the eunuchs in the confidence of the Emperor. His sentence was commuted to exile to Huanchou. In a few years the Emperor, having ascertained his innocence, recalled him, made him president of the Imperial Council, and gave him the title of Duke of Yenkuo.

He had five sons, all of whom were gifted and were admitted into official ranks. They all married daughters of influential families of the time and presented him with more than ten grandchildren. And so he lived for over fifty years, during which he was twice banished to the frontier wilds only to be recalled to court, vindicated, and given greater honors than before. He was given to extravagance and was addicted to pleasures. His inner apartments were filled with dancers and beautiful women, and innumerable were the gifts of fertile lands, mansions, fleet horses, and such treasures that the Emperor bestowed upon him.

When advanced age made him wish to retire from court life, his petitions were repeatedly refused. When at last he fell ill, emissaries sent by the Emperor to inquire after his condition followed upon one another's heels and there was nothing left undone that eminent physicians could do. But all was in vain and one night he died, whereupon he woke up with a start and found himself lying as before in the roadside inn, with Lü Weng sitting by his side and the millet that his host was cooking still not yet done. Everything was as it had been before he dozed off. "Could it be that I have been dreaming all this while?" he said, rising to his feet. "Life as you would have it is but like that," said Lü Weng. For a long while the young man reflected in silence, then he said, "I now know at last the way of honor and disgrace and the meaning of poverty and fortune, the reciprocity of gain and loss and the mystery of life and death, and I owe all this knowledge to you. Since you have thus deigned to instruct me in the vanity of ambition, dare I refuse to profit thereby?" With this he bowed profoundly to Lü Weng and went away.

Jenshih, or the Fox Lady

Shen Chi-chi

FL. 750-800

Jenshih was a supernatural creature of the female sex. Wei Yin, a retired provincial governor, was the ninth of his family and a grandson of the Prince of Hsin An on his mother's side. As a young man he was unconventional and was fond of drinking. He had a boon companion called Cheng Liu (I do not recall his personal name) who married one of Yin's cousins. In his youth Cheng was trained in the warlike arts and was as fond of wine and women as Yin himself. Being poor, he attached himself to his wife's family. He and Yin were on intimate terms and one was seldom seen without the other.

In the sixth month of the ninth year of T'ien Pao (A.D. 747) the two friends were one day riding through the streets of Changan on their way to the Hsinshangli quarter to attend a party, but as they reached a point south of Hsuanping, Cheng suddenly recalled some matter that he had to attend to and so he begged his friend to excuse him and promised that he would meet the latter at the party later on. Yin went toward the east on his white horse while Cheng rode to the south on his donkey. Inside the northern gate of the Shengping quarter he encountered three women walking on the street, among whom there was one dressed in white whose beauty arrested his attention. He followed them on his donkey, sometimes riding a little distance ahead and sometimes just behind them, and was several times on the point of accosting them but did not do so for lack of courage. Finally the encouraging glances of the one in white emboldened him and he said to them, "Why are you ladies, beautiful as you are, going about the streets of Changan on foot?"

"What else can we do," said the one in white, "since no one has offered us his mount?" Cheng answered, "My shabby beast is hardly worthy of the honor of bearing such a beautiful lady as you, but I gladly offer it to you and walk behind you myeslf." They looked at each other and laughed. The other women, too, encouraged him and soon succeeded in putting him at his ease. Cheng followed them east and it was dark when they finally reached the Loyuyuan quarter. They stopped before a house with a mud wall around it and a carriage gate through the wall; inside, the buildings were neat. As the woman in white went in, she asked Cheng to wait outside a while before he entered, and left one of the women, who was evidently her maid, to keep him company. The maid asked him his name and where he lived, which he told her, and then he in turn asked her who the woman in white was and was told that her name was Jenshih and that she was the twentieth of her family.

In a little while Cheng was invited to go in, which he did after securing his donkey to the gate post and putting his hat on the saddle.[1] A woman around thirty years old came out to meet him; she was, he found, the elder sister of Jenshih. Inside candles had been lit and a feast spread out. After a few cups of wine, Jenshih, having changed her dress, came out herself. They drank heartily and became very merry. When the night grew late, Cheng retired with Jenshih and thus had an opportunity to marvel at the beauty of her form and the exquisite texture of her skin, and to grow intoxicated with her song and laughter and the grace of her carriage, all of a quality one would hardly think possible in the mortal world. Before dawn, Jenshih said to him, "It is time for you to go, for my sisters and myself are attached to the *chiaofang*[2] and must be at our posts early in the morning." Cheng went away, after having agreed on another meeting.

The gate to the quarter was not yet open when he reached it,

[1] It is difficult to tell whether "hat" is a corruption or whether some unknown custom of the time did require one to leave one's hat outside. Such problems are frequently encountered in traditional tales, especially of the "literary" type.

[2] A government bureau founded in the early part of the seventh century. It had charge of musicians and dancers. Often used in the sense of the courtesans' quarter.

but the Tartar baker who kept a shop nearby was already up and was building the fire in his oven by the light of a lamp. He went inside and engaged the baker in conversation while waiting for the gate to open. Pointing in the direction whence he had just come, he asked, "Who lives in the house around the bend to the east?" The baker answered, "It is only a deserted yard; there is no one living there." "But I have just come from there and saw signs that it is occupied," Cheng insisted, whereupon the baker seemed to be struck with a thought and said, "Ah, I know now. There is a fox in there that has been bewitching men. She has been seen three times recently. Do you happen to have met her?" Cheng blushed and evaded with a "no." He went back to look at the place and found the mud wall and carriage gate as before but when he peeped in he saw nothing but wild bramble and grass and occasional patches that still showed signs of former cultivation.

When he returned home, his friend Yin took him to task for not having kept his engagement. Cheng made up an excuse but said nothing to him of his extraordinary encounter. He could not, however, forget Jenshih, for he was enamored of her beauty and longed to see her again in spite of his present knowledge.

Then some ten days later Cheng suddenly came upon her in a dress shop in the West Market district that he happened to go into. She was accompanied by the same maid whom he had met. Cheng called to her, but Jenshih avoided him by stepping into a near-by crowd. Cheng kept on calling to her and following her. Only then did she stand still and said with her face averted and concealed behind a fan, "Since you know me for what I am, why do you seek me still?" Cheng answered, "What harm is there, even though I know?" "I am ashamed," she said, "and find it hard to face you." "But how could you bear to abandon me, since I long so much for you?" Cheng said. "How dare I avoid you?" she said; "it is only that I feared that I would revolt you." Cheng swore his love and became all the more insistent. Thereupon Jenshih turned to face him with her fan drawn aside and showed herself to be as beautiful as ever. "There are many women just as desirable as myself," she said to Cheng. "You have not met them, that's all. Do not embarrass me by behaving as if I were the only one." When Cheng begged her for another meeting, she said, "The reason why our kind incur the revulsion of mankind is that we draw upon men's essence and thus harm them. In this, however, I am different from my kind. If you do not detest me, I shall be willing to serve as your handmaid the rest of my life."

Cheng was more than glad at the proposal and they fell to discussing plans for setting up house. "East of here," Jenshih said, "there is a house on a quiet street for rent; you can recognize it by a big tree that rises above the wall. It will suit us well. Just before you met me the last time you were with a man on a white horse who left you and rode east. Is he not a cousin of your wife? You'll find that he has furniture stored away that you can borrow."

Cheng found the house described and then went to Wei Yin to borrow furnishings, for it happened that one of the latter's uncles was away on an extended mission and had stored away all his household things. Yin was incredulous when Cheng told him the purpose of his request and described the beauty of Jenshih. "For," said he, "your face being what it is, how could you capture the heart of a woman as beautiful as you say?"

He sent, therefore, one of his confidential servants with the curtains and beds and other articles of furnishing that he readily lent Cheng, so that he could verify the latter's claim. Soon the servant returned, panting and covered with perspiration. "Is there a woman?" asked Yin, "and how does she look?" "It is indeed a strange thing!" the servant answered, "for I have never seen anyone so beautiful." Now Yin had numerous relatives and had, moreover, met many beautiful women in his time. So he enumerated four or five of the most beautiful among them and asked his servant how Jenshih compared with them, but to each name the servant invariably answered that she could not compare to Jenshih. Finally he named the most beautiful woman he knew, the sixth daughter of the Prince of Wu and one of his wife's cousins, but again the servant answered that she was no match to the lady he had just seen. "How could there be such a beauty in the world!" Yin exclaimed.

He ordered water to be brought and bathed himself, put on his best clothes and set out for Cheng's new house. There he found that his friend had just gone out. When he went inside he saw only a boy servant engaged in sweeping the yard and a maid at the door. He asked the boy about the object of his visit, but the boy denied that there was anyone else in the house. Not satisfied, Yin went into the room and in looking about him he caught a glimpse of a red skirt under the door to the inner chamber. He pressed forward and found Jenshih hidden behind a screen. When he brought her to the light and looked at her, she was even more beautiful than the reports had described her. He was so enamored of her that he became maddened and tried to force himself upon her. She would resist him as long as she could and then would say that she would let him have his will, but when he relaxed his hold on her she would struggle against him as before. After this had happened a few times Yin exerted all his might against her and she, feeling exhausted and knowing that she could no longer resist him, ceased to struggle. However, there had suddenly come into her face such a look of misery that Yin was prompted to ask, "Why do you appear so unhappy?" "Because," she said with a long sigh, "I pity Cheng Liu!" "Why do you say that?" Yin asked, and she answered, "Cheng Liu has a stature of six feet like the rest but he cannot protect a woman! He is hardly worthy of the name of man! Moreover, you, sir, are rich and have known many women just as beautiful as I, while Cheng Liu is poor and has only myself to gladden his heart. Could you, sir, who have more than enough to fill your heart, bear to rob him who has so little? I pity him because he is poor and dependent upon you for the clothes he wears and the food he eats. It must be because of this that you take such liberties. If Cheng Liu had but some chaff that he could call his own to live upon, things would not have come to this pass."

Yin was by nature a generous man and a loyal friend. When he heard what Jenshih had said, he immediately let her go and apologized for his mad behavior. Presently Cheng Liu returned and the two friends grinned at each other for joy, one for his own good fortune and the other for the happiness of his friend.

Henceforward Yin supplied all her wants and never stinted anything that struck her fancy. He visited her every day. They took great pleasure in each other's company and in their intimacy but they never exceeded the bounds of propriety. Realizing how much he loved her, Jenshih said to him one day, "I am grateful to you for your love and kindness and I wish I could repay you, however unworthy I am. Though I cannot give myself to you because I am pledged to Cheng Liu, yet perhaps there are things that I can do to show my gratitude. As I am a native of Changan and come from a family of professional entertainers, I have many cousins much favored by men, besides many acquaintances in the profession. If there is any one among these that you have desired in vain, I shall undertake to bring her to you."

"That would be wonderful," Yin said, and asked her if she knew of a certain milliner by the name of Chang whom he had seen and liked. "She is one of my cousins," Jenshih said. "It will be easy to get her." And indeed in about ten days she brought her to him. When after a few months he grew tired of her and sent her away, Jenshih said to him, "It is so little trouble to secure women of the market place. I should like to have an opportunity to exercise my abilities in a more difficult task. If there is any one that you fancy but have put out of your mind because she is inaccessible, name her, and I shall try my best." Yin said, "While visiting the Chien Fu Temple with some friends during the Clear Bright Festival, I observed, at a musicale that General Tiao Mien was giving, a *sheng* player of striking beauty. She was just about twice eight and had not yet done up her hair. Do you know her?" Jenshih answered, "She is the general's favorite and her mother is one of my cousins. I can get her for you." Yin bowed to her in gratitude.

Thereafter she began to visit the Tiao mansion frequently and when about a month later Yin asked her how she was progressing in her scheme, she asked him for two bolts of silk for a bribe. These he gave to her, and two days later as Jenshih and Yin were at dinner, an old servant from the Tiao house came with a black horse to fetch her. When she was told of the presence of the messenger, she said to Yin, smiling, "Success is at hand." For she had caused the general's favorite to be afflicted with an illness that neither the needle nor simples could dispel, and when she heard that the girl's mother and master were distraught with anxiety and were about to consult a fortune teller, she bribed the latter to suggest that the patient must be moved to her own house before she could get well. So at the examination of the patient, the exorcist said that she was subject to a certain malign influence in her own house and that she must be moved to a certain distance southeast of where she lived. When the girl's mother and the general located the spot indicated by the exorcist, it turned out to be the site of Jenshih's house. The general asked Jenshih to let his favorite stay a while in her house. Jenshih pretended to refuse, pleading that her place was small and unsuitable, and affected reluctance when she finally yielded at his importunities. The girl and her mother were escorted to Jenshih's house and there she almost immediately recovered. After a few days Jenshih secretly took Yin to her and brought about their union. But after a month the girl showed signs of pregnancy, and her mother, becoming frightened, took her back to the general's house, and there the affair ended.

Some time later Jenshih said to Cheng Liu, "Could you raise five or six thousand cash? If so, I can make it possible for you to reap a large profit." "I can," Cheng Liu said, and when he managed to borrow the money, Jenshih said to him, "Go to the market and look for a horse with a mole on its left haunch. When you find it, buy it and hold it until you can sell it at a profit." Cheng went to the market and there encountered, indeed, a man with a horse for sale that had a black hair mole on its left haunch. He bought it and returned with it much to the amusement of the brothers of his wife, who laughed at him and said, "It is a worthless horse. What are you going to do with it?"

Soon afterwards, Jenshih said to Cheng, "Now the time has come to sell the horse. You should get thirty thousand for it." At the market a man offered him twenty thousand for the horse but

Cheng would not sell it, much to the astonishment of people around. "What merits does the horse have," they exclaimed, "that one should offer so much for it and the other refuse to sell?" As Cheng rode back to his house, the prospective buyer followed him and raised his offer again and again until it reached twenty-five thousand, but Cheng refused and said that he would not sell for a cash less than thirty thousand. In the meantime his wife's brothers called him a fool to refuse, but Cheng stuck to his position and finally got his thirty thousand. Being curious to know why the buyer should have paid such a high price, Cheng trailed him and asked him about it. Then he found that the buyer was an officer in charge of the imperial stables at Chaoying and that he was about to vacate his post. A horse with a mole in the identical place as the one he had just bought had died three years previously. As the horse was valued at sixty thousand cash he would not only stand to gain thirty thousand if he could substitute a horse of that description in the official register, but could also pocket the money he had saved on feed over those three years. The horse was therefore cheap at the price he paid for it and it was for that that he had bought it.

Once, her clothes having become worn, Jenshih asked Yin to get her some new dresses. Yin offered her some silks, but Jenshih refused them, saying that she preferred to have garments ready made. Yin called in a merchant by the name of Chang Ta so that he could ascertain from Jenshih just what she wanted. When Chang Ta saw her he was so struck with her beauty that he said to Yin, "A lady of such beauty could not be found outside the Emperor's palace or the mansion of some great nobleman. If you have indeed kidnapped her, you should return her at once so as to avoid the terrible consequences of detection." From this one can imagine how striking her beauty must have been. She never sewed but always bought ready made clothes, a circumstance that neither Cheng nor Yin could understand.

A year or so later Cheng received an order to go to Chin-cheng on a military mission. Now Cheng had been able to spend only the day with Jenshih since he was married and had to return to his wife at night, and he had been regretting the fact that he could not always be with Jenshih. So he asked Jenshih to accompany him on the mission. This she showed a reluctance to do, saying, "The mission will only take about a month. I would rather that you make provision for my needs and let me wait for your return."

Cheng repeated his request several times but Jenshih was adamant. Finally Cheng asked Yin to use his influence, which the latter did, at the same time asking her why she was so stubborn in her refusal. After a long while Jenshih said, "It is because a fortune teller once told me that it is unlucky for me to journey westward that I do not wish to go." Because of the urgency of his desire, Cheng thought nothing of her fears, but laughed as did Yin and said, "How could one as intelligent as you are permit yourself to give in to such superstitious fears!" "But should the fortune teller's predictions be true," Jenshih said, "I would have died without any benefit to anyone." "But how could that be?" the two men said and continued to importune her. Finally, she yielded. Yin lent them horses and went to see them off as far as Linkao, where they drank some farewell cups and parted.

They reached Mawei the next day. Jenshih rode ahead on a palfrey, followed by Cheng on his own donkey and a maid servant still farther behind on her mount. It happened that for the past days some dog trainers from around the West Gate of Mawei had been running their hounds on the bank of the River Lo and as Cheng's party rode by, the hounds suddenly rushed out on the road from the grass. At the sight of the dogs, Jenshih fell to the ground and resumed her original shape and ran in a southerly direction, pursued closely by the hounds. Cheng followed them and called to the dogs but he could not stop them. After about a li the fox was captured by the dogs. With tears in his eyes, Cheng took out some money and redeemed the carcass and buried it, marking the spot with a wooden tablet. When he returned to where he had left the horse, it was grazing by the roadside. On the saddle he found the clothes that Jenshih had last worn and on the stirrups were her shoes, cast off by her in the transformation as a cicada might have cast its larvae shell. On the ground he found her jewels, but otherwise there was no trace of her. The maid, too, had vanished.

At the conclusion of his mission he returned to Changan. Yin was delighted to see him and asked him if all was well with Jenshih. "She has passed away," Cheng answered, his eyes wet with tears. Yin also grieved when he heard the sad news and asked him what had brought about her death. "She was killed by some dogs," he answered. "But how could dogs, however fierce they may be, kill a human being?" Yin asked. "But she was not human," came the answer. "Then what was she?" Yin asked in astonishment. Then Cheng told him the story from beginning to end, much to the wonder and amazement of his friend. The next day they rode together to Mawei, where they distinterred and examined Jenshih's remains and wept most grieviously over them. Later when they indulged in reminiscences of Jenshih the only thing they could recall about her that marked her from other women was that she never made her own clothes.

In after years Cheng rose to be a superintendent and became very wealthy. At one time he kept more than ten horses in his stables. He died at the age of sixty-five.

During the Ta Li period (766-780) I, Shen Chi-chi, lived at Chungling and used to see something of Wei Yin. I learned, therefore, all the details of that extraordinary story. Later Yin became a censor and concurrently governor of Lungchou, where he died.

The story shows that there is no lack of virtue even in the animal world. Able to protect her chastity in the face of violence and to remain faithful to her lord to death, she was superior to many of her sex among mankind today. It is a pity that Cheng, a man with little subtle insight, cared only for her beauty and nothing of her true character. If he had been a man of learning and profundity, he would have been able, through his life with her, to learn something of the principles that underlie Nature's mysterious transformations, and the line that marks the mundane world from the world of the spirit, and to preserve for us in worthy language her great love; he would not have been satisfied with the enjoyment of the mere beauty of her outside form. What a pity it was, alas!

In the second year of Chien Chung (781) I was appointed to a post in the southeast and made the journey with General Pei Chi; Sun Cheng, the assistant prefect of the metropolitan district; Tsui Hsu of the Board of Revenue; and Assistant Counselor Lu Chun, who all happened to be going to that region, and also the Counselor Chu Fang, who was on a tour of the empire. While we floated down the Ying and crossed the Huai we spent the long evenings in telling one another of the strange things we had heard. When the company heard the story of Jenshih they all sighed in wonder and amazement and said that I should preserve this remarkable event in writing. It was at their request I wrote this record.

The Dragon's Daughter

Li Ch'ao-wei

FL. 9TH CENTURY

In the Yi Feng period (676-678) there lived a student by the name of Liu Yi. He had been unsuccessful in the examinations and was about to set out for his native home on the banks of the Hsiang when he recalled that he had a fellow countryman living in Ching-yang and decided that he would call on him to bid him goodby. Six or seven li from his destination, his horse was frightened by a flight of birds and ran for six or seven li before it stopped. There he saw a woman tending sheep by the roadside. The circumstance struck Li as somewhat odd and he paused for a better look at her. She turned out to be of extraordinary beauty, though she was sad of mien and dressed in drab clothes, and she was looking about her intently as if expecting some one.

"What troubles you that you look so sad?" Yi asked her.

For a moment she was silent but in the end she replied weeping: "It is kind of you, sir, to take an interest in an unfortunate woman, for though I must continue to bear the grievous wrong which I have suffered, it will afford me some measure of relief to unburden myself. I am, sir, the youngest daughter of the Dragon King of Lake Tung T'ing and was married by my parents to the second son of the King of the River Ching. My husband turned out to be a dissipated rake and of late, under the bewitchment of some maid, has begun to neglect and abuse me. I complained to my parents-in-law but they dote on their son and would do nothing. When I repeated my complaints, they too turned against me and banished me out here to this tedious task." At this point she was overcome with grief and wept for a while in silence. Then she continued: "How far away is Tung T'ing! Vast is the space that intervenes and unbridged it is by letters and messages! Though my heart is breaking and my eyes are worn out from longing, there is no way to make known my sorrow to my parents. I understand, sir, that you are returning to the Wu country. Since you will pass the Tung T'ing region, I wonder if you would be kind enough to carry a letter for me?"

"I am a man who likes to be of assistance to those who require it," Yi answered. "Your story stirs my blood and agitates my breath; my only regret is that I do not have wings so that I can fly there at your bidding. It is not, therefore, a question of whether I would. However, the waters of the Tung T'ing are deep and I am bound to the dusty earth. How am I to deliver your message? I fear that I shall not be able to communicate with your people because we live in different elements and that I shall only disappoint you in the end if I accept your command now, unless, of course, you have a way of making this possible."

"You are indeed very kind," the girl answered, still weeping. "If through you I should succeed in getting word to my parents, I shall be grateful till death. There is of course a way which makes Tung T'ing as accessible as any metropolis."

Yi begged her to tell him how this could be accomplished and she continued:

"On the north shore of Tung T'ing there is a giant orange tree dedicated to the tutelary god of the region. When you find it you should take off the sash you are wearing and tie around your waist something else [1] and then knock on the tree three times. Some one will answer your knock and if you follow him you will find the waters of Tung T'ing no barrier to your progress. When you see my parents I beg you to describe to them what I have told you and omit nothing, for I cannot tell everything in a letter."

"I shall carry out all your wishes," Yi said.

The girl then took a letter from under her coat and gave it to Yi, looking sorrowfully the while in the eastward direction of

[1] The failure of the author to name what that something is demonstrates how perfunctory Chinese writers often are about essential details.

Tung T'ing. She was so sad and wept so bitterly that Yi was profoundly moved. As he put the letter in his bag he asked her,

"What do you do with the sheep that you are tending? Do the gods also slaughter beasts for food?"

"These are not sheep," she answered, "but rain makers."

"What are rain makers?" he asked.

"They cause such things as thunder and lightning."

Yi looked at the sheep again and found that there was indeed something forbidding about their eyes and also the way they scampered about and grazed, though they were no different from ordinary sheep in size or in the texture of their wool and the shape of their horns.

"Since I am your messenger," Yi again said, "I hope you will not avoid me should we meet another day."

"Not only would I not avoid you," she answered, "but I shall treat you as if you were my kin."

Then Yi took leave of her and went east. When he looked back again after a score paces, the girl and her sheep had vanished. That evening he arrived at Chingyang and took leave of his friend. A month later he reached his native place and after greeting his family set out to make inquiries in the Tung T'ing region. There on the north shore he found indeed a giant orange tree and after changing his sash, he knocked three times on the tree and waited. Presently a man in warrior's clothes rose from the waves and asked him what he wished, and when Yi told him that he had come to see the Dragon King, the warrior opened a path in the water and bade Yi follow him.

"Close your eyes," he cautioned, "and you'll be there in a few moments."

Yi did so and was soon at the Dragon King's palace. There he found one imposing building after another and all kinds of strange plants and marvelous trees. The warrior took Yi into a huge hall and asked him to wait there. Yi asked what place it was and was told that it was known as the Ling Hsü Hall. Looking about him, he found in the hall all the things that the mortal world esteems. The pillars were made of white jade and inlaid with emeralds; the couches were made of coral and the screens of crystal; the lintel was studded with the purest glass and the rainbow beams decorated with amber. It was a vast and unique place that beggared description.

For a long while the Dragon King did not appear and when Yi asked the warrior where his lordship might be, the latter answered that he had gone to the Tower of the Mystic Pearl to hear Taiyang Taoshih[2] expound *The Book of Fire* and that he would be back soon.

"What is *The Book of Fire?*" Yi asked, and the warrior answered:

"My lord is a dragon and presides over the element of water. He can with a drop of that element drown out the mountains and valleys. Taoshih is a man and presides over the element of fire. He can with a tiny spark destroy the Ahfang Palace.[3] So though they are both powerful in magic, they make use of different elements. My lord has therefore gone to him to hear him expound the principles of fire."

Just then the gate to the palace opened and a man wearing a purple robe and holding a green jade tablet in his hand came in, followed by numerous attendants. "That is my lord," the warrior said, jumping up, and going to the Dragon King to announce Yi. "Are you not a man from the mortal world?" the Dragon King asked, looking at Yi, and on being answered that such was the case, he and Yi saluted each other, and after both had been seated he said to Yi: "Our realm is remote and our people unenlightened. To what do we owe the honor of your visit to this inaccessible realm?"

To this Yi answered: "I am a fellow countryman of Your Majesty. I was born in this the land of Ch'u and have visited the land of Ch'in to promote the advancement of my learning. Recently I had occasion to ride by the River Ching and there I encountered Your Majesty's beloved daughter tending sheep in the fields. It was more than I could bear to see her buffeted by the wind and be-

[2] Deity presiding over the sun.

[3] A palace reputed to be several hundred li in circumference, built by Ch'in Shih Huang Ti in the third century B.C.

spattered with rain. I asked her the cause of her distress, and she told me that she had come to this pass because of the neglect of her husband and the indifference of her parents-in-law. Her tears were so copious that it would have moved the heart of any man. She entrusted me with a letter to be delivered to Your Majesty, and it is for this that I am here." He took the letter out and presented it.

After reading it, the Lord of Tung T'ing covered his face with his sleeves and wept, saying, "It is because of my oversight that a helpless child of the inner chambers has been subjected to such abuse. You, sir, are only a stranger and yet you have come to her assistance in a moment of distress. I shall never forget your kindness." After saying this he wept and sighed for a long while, and the attendants too all shed tears. Then he gave the letter to a eunuch and bade him take it into the inner palace. Presently lamentations rent the air in that direction. The Dragon King was startled and said to his attendants: "Go inside and tell them to suppress their cries so that Ch'ien T'ang will not know what has happened."

"Who is Ch'ien T'ang?" Yi asked.

"My beloved brother. He was in charge of the Ch'ien T'ang river but had to resign."

"Why don't you want him to know?"

"Because he is mighty in strength and violent of temper. He was the cause of the nine-year flood in the time of Yao.[4] Recently he had a disagreement with some of the celestial generals and in his anger he uprooted five mountains. In consideration of my slight virtues of the past Shang Ti forbore with him and gave him no worse punishment than imprisonment. Though he is incarcerated in these parts, his influence is still felt in the region of Ch'ien T'ang, where people daily await its manifestation."[5]

Before the Dragon King had finished speaking, a terrific noise suddenly rent heaven and earth and rocked the palace to its foundations. It was followed by the appearance of a red dragon of over a thousand feet long, its eyes flashing lightning and its mouth spout-

[4] Legendary ruler 2356-2255 B.C.

[5] Literally translated: "He is still incarcerated here; therefore the people of Ch'ien T'ang wait for him day after day." Cryptic allusion to the famous bore of the Ch'ien T'ang estuary on the coast of Chekiang.

ing blood. Around its neck was a golden lock and attached to the lock was the jade pillar to which it had been chained. It was surrounded with the noise of thunder and darts of lightning bolts and in its wake followed sleet and snow, rain and hailstones. In a brief moment it had disappeared into the distant sky. Yi was so frightened that he fell prostrate to the ground, but the Dragon King raised him to his feet, saying,

"Be not afraid, for he will do you no harm."

It was a long time before Yi recovered from his shock. He begged permission to go, saying, "I should like to leave while I am still alive, for I am afraid that I shall not be able to survive the commotion attending his return." But the Lord of Tung T'ing assured him that his return would be in quite a different manner and begged Yi to stay so that he might fulfill the duties of a host. Wine was served and host and guest drank to each other.

Presently a gentle breeze rose and a patch of bright cloud appeared in the sky, followed by the sound of sweet music and the twinkling of a myriad jewels. Then amid the sound of merry laughter and excited talk a beautiful lady covered with bright ornaments entered. When Yi looked closely at her, it was no other than the girl who had asked him to carry a letter for her. In a moment she had vanished into the inner palace, leaving behind only a lingering perfume.

"The prisoner of Ching has come," the Lord of Tung T'ing said to Yi. He excused himself and followed his daughter into the inner palace. Presently the sound of grievous complaining came from within.

After a while the Lord of Tung T'ing returned, accompanied by another man in a purple robe and carrying a jade tablet. The stranger differed from the Lord of Tung T'ing only in that his features were more commanding and his manner more spirited.

"This is Ch'ien T'ang," the Lord of Tung T'ing said to Yi. The latter rose and saluted Ch'ien T'ang, who returned the salutation and said to Yi:

"My niece was the unfortunate victim of the abuses of a heartless boy. You, sir, have gone to her rescue in her distress and have made known to us the wrong done to her. If it had not been for you, she would have become merged with the earth of Chingyang. I cannot, sir, begin to thank you for your great kindness."

Still in awe of the terrible creature though he was now in a more benign form, Yi could only bow and profess his unworthiness. Then Ch'ien T'ang turned and said to his brother: "After leaving the Ling Hsü palace at the hour of *ch'en,* I arrived at Chingyang at *ssu;* I fought my battle at noon and returned here at *wei.*[6] In the meantime, I had gone up to the Ninth Heaven and reported the affair to Shang Ti. Knowing the wrong against us, he forgave me my past offense as well as my present deed. However, I am ashamed that in my outburst of rage, I took no time to ask your leave and frightened our guest."

"How many did you kill?" the Lord of Tung T'ing asked.

"Six hundred thousand."

"Did you harm the growing grain?"

"To the extent of eight hundred li of land."

"Where is the heartless young man?"

"I have eaten him."

"The action of the heartless young man is truly reprehensible," the Lord of Tung T'ing said with a frown, "but your action, too, is rather hasty. It is fortunate that Shang Ti in his omnipresence saw the wrong done to us and forgave you. Else I would have to bear the responsibility of your hasty act. Henceforward, you must not be so rash."

That night Yi was lodged in the Palace of Congealed Light. The next day he was banqueted in the Palace of Frozen Blue, where were gathered friends and relatives of the dragon kings. Dances were performed and the dragon kings each sang a song, to which Yi responded.[7] When night came Yi again spent it in the Hall of Congealed Light and on the following day he was invited to another banquet on the Terrace of Pure Brilliance.

When Ch'ien T'ang began to feel the effects of wine, he assumed a haughty air and said insolently to Yi: "Have you not heard that

[6] The fifth to the eighth hour, respectively, of the twelve-hour day.

[7] Omitted in this translation.

hard rock can be split asunder but not kneaded like clay, and that a proud man can be killed but not subjected to humiliation? I have something in my mind that I should like to say to you, sir. If you grant my wish, then shall we tread the clouds together; if not, then let us both be covered with earth! What do you say, my friend?"

"I should like to hear your proposal," Yi said.

"I have in mind," said Ch'ien T'ang, "the wife of the late son of Chingyang and the beloved daughter of Tung T'ing. She is gentle of nature and refined in quality, and is greatly esteemed by all the nine relations. It was her misfortune to be married to an unworthy man and to suffer humiliation at his hands. However, that is now past. I propose now to entrust her to you, kind and generous one, and thus unite your family and ours. Moreover, this proposal makes it possible for the recipient of favors to render her gratitude and the dispenser to receive his due. Do you not think, sir, that this is the best ending that can be devised for so auspicious a beginning?"

At these words Yi rose with dignity and laughed with scorn, saying, "Little did I think that the Lord of Ch'ien T'ang would behave in so childish a manner! I have heard, my lord, that you have once, in your indignation, devastated the nine provinces and smote the five sacred mountains, and I have seen with my own eyes how you broke the golden lock and, with the jade pillar still dangling from your neck, flew to the distress of your niece. I thought that surely there was no one in the world that could approach you, my lord, in courage and righteousness. For you have shown in the past the distinguishing qualities of the great heroes of antiquity: when your indignation was aroused, you did not let the fear of death stop you; when your heart was moved, you did not hesitate to give up your life. Why is it that in the midst of harmonious music and joyous company you should suddenly forget the principles that have guided you in the past and seek to impose your will upon others by force? It is certainly something that I have never expected from you!

"If I had encountered you, sire, over the billowy waves or among forbidding mountains, and you had, with your scales shining and tendrils darting, and your body enveloped in cloud and rain, threatened me with death, I would have merely looked upon you as an insentient beast and resigned myself to your claws without regret. But you are now wearing hat and robe and speaking the language of propriety and righteousness. You have practiced to the best of your ability the five virtues and have fulfilled all the subtle requirements of right conduct. In these things you have so demeaned yourself as to surpass many of the famed worthies of mankind, to say nothing of the creatures of the rivers and seas. Yet now you propose to make use of the lumpish mass of your body and give in to the violent side of your nature, and, under the influence of wine, threaten to enforce your will upon others. Is this the way of justice? If indeed such is your intention, then though I am so tiny that I can find ample haven under one of your scales, I shall not hesitate to match the courage of an incorruptible heart against the spirit of unhallowed violence! I await, sire, your majesty's decision."

Ch'ien T'ang was completely vanquished by Yi's courageous speech, and he apologized, saying, "I have been confined all my life in these palace precincts and have never heard such righteous discourse. When I reflect on the rash absurdities of what I said, I realize how unforgivable it was for me to have spoken thus to a man of enlightenment and courage. I hope you will, sir, forgive me and not hold it against me."

That night they again had a joyous feast and Yi and Ch'ien T'ang became fast friends.

The next day Yi begged leave to return to his home. The consort of the Lord of Tung T'ing gave him a banquet in the Hall of Submerged Scenes, at which all the ladies and attendants of the inner palace were present. The consort of Tung T'ing said, weeping, to Yi:

"We are greatly indebted to your kindness, sir. Now, before we have a chance to show adequately our gratitude, you have to leave us." Then she commanded her daughter, the girl Yi had encountered on the plain of Chingyang, to come forward to thank him. She expressed doubt that they would meet again.

Though Yi had refused Ch'ien T'ang's proposal at the banquet the day before, he was now not without regrets and showed it plainly on his face. After the banquet, he took his leave amid a general gloom in the palace. The number and variety of unique presents that Yi received were beyond description.

Yi left the Dragon King's palace the way he came. When he was back on the shore of Tung T'ing there were more than ten porters waiting for him, with the presents that he had received. They accompanied him to his home and then went away. Yi went to a jewel shop in Kuangling and sold some of the presents. Before he had disposed of one hundredth part of his treasures, his wealth had already reached millions, and he became richer than any family in the region east of the Huai.

He married a daughter of the Chang family. She soon died. He again married, this time a daughter of the Han family, but she, too, died after a few months. He moved to Chinling to live. He was depressed by his widowerhood and often thought of marrying again.

Sometime afterwards a matchmaker told him about a daughter of the Lu family who had been recently widowed. The betrothal was duly arranged and the wedding, one of the most elaborate that Chinling had ever seen, soon followed. A month or so later, Yi was suddenly struck by the resemblance between his new wife and the Dragon's daughter and remarked to her about it. Her only response at the time was, "What an extraordinary story!" But after the birth of their first child, she confessed to him that she was indeed the Dragon's daughter.[8]

"I have not told you the truth before," she said, "because I knew you had no fancy for beautiful women, and I tell you now because I know you are grateful to me for having borne you a child. A woman is of little worth by herself; I have, therefore, entrusted my fate to our common bond. I wonder if I am right and I fear that I may not have correctly read your thoughts.

"When you undertook to carry my letter on the plain of Chingyang, you said, 'Do not avoid me if we should happen to meet on Tung T'ing.' Did you then entertain the possibility of our union

[8] This paragraph is slightly abridged.

today? Later, when my uncle proposed to give me to you in marriage, you steadfastly refused. Did you do so because the prospect was really repulsive to you or was it because of your anger at the way he broached the subject? Please tell me."

"It seems to be fate," Yi answered. "When I first saw you on the bank of the Ching, I was indignant at the treatment that you were receiving, but aside from a desire to be of assistance to you in your distress I had no other thought. When I said that I hoped that you would not avoid me when we met later, it was only a chance remark. When Ch'ien T'ang sought to coerce me, I experienced nothing but anger and indignation. For how could I think of such a thing as to take some one else's wife after causing, though indirectly, the death of her husband? That would cast doubt on the unselfishness of my motive when I offered my assistance. This was the first reason for my refusal. Then I have always prided myself for holding steadfast to truth and justice; I could not bow myself before force and do things against my heart. This was the second reason. It was because of these reasons that I was so outspoken at the farewell feast and paid so little heed to the possible consequences.

"However, I was not without regrets when I saw, at our leave taking, that you were yourself distressed because I was going away. I could not help then wishing that things were otherwise. Now in marrying you as a daughter of the Lu family [9] I am relieved of my scruples. From now on let us live in happiness always and entertain no fear and suspicion."

Yi's speech touched his wife deeply, and for a long time she wept. Then she said, "Do not think that, because I am of a different race, I am without the sense of gratitude, for it is my desire to repay your kindness in some way. Now the dragon's life is ten thousand years; I shall share it with you. I shall also endow you with the power to be at home in water as well as on land. I can make all these things possible for you; do not think I am indulging in mere talk."

[9] It is not explained by what stratagem or magic the Dragon King accomplished this ruse.

Together they visited Tung T'ing, where he was entertained with wonderful feasts too numerous to mention. Later they lived for forty years on the shore of the Southern Sea, where the inhabitants were all amazed at Yi's retention of his remarkably youthful appearance.

In the K'ai Yuan period (713-741) the Emperor, having become interested in the art of long life possessed by the immortals, sent emissaries all over the empire to seek out men versed in the secrets of immortality. To avoid a summons to court, Yi and his wife returned to Tung T'ing and for more than ten years no one knew where they were.

Toward the end of the K'ai Yuan period, Hsueh Ku, a cousin of Yi, was on his way to the Southeast, after having been relieved of his offce as mayor of the metropolitan area. One day as he was crossing Tung T'ing, a mountain suddenly appeared out of the distant waves. The boatmen became uneasy, saying, "There is no mountain in that direction as far as we know. We are afraid that it must be a mirage created by some water sprite."

Presently the mountain drew near and a gaily decorated boat sailed forth from the mountain and headed straight in Ku's direction. When it came within hailing distance, a man shouted to him, saying, "Mr. Liu has come to pay his respects to you." Recalling suddenly his cousin, Ku got into the boat and was soon at the foot of the mountain. There he found a palace constructed much in the same fashion as found among men. In the palace he found Yi, with musicians ranged before him and such a marvelous array of pearls and gems behind him, as are never found in equal splendor in the world of man. In speech Yi had grown wiser and in appearance younger.

He met Ku at the foot of the steps and said, taking his hands, "It has been but a twinkling since we last met, yet how gray your hair has already become!" Ku answered, laughing, "You are now, elder brother, an immortal while I have become a mere bag of rotted bones. Such is fate." Yi then brought out fifty pills and gave them to Ku, saying, "Each of these pills will give you an additional year of life. Come again when you have exhausted them. Do not tarry too long in the world of man, where you only fret and vex yourself to no purpose."

After a joyous feast, Ku took his leave. Nothing has been heard of Yi since. Ku used to tell his friends about his encounter. Four decades later Ku too disappeared.[10]

[10] A short paragraph of the author's comment has been omitted from the translation.

Huo Hsiaoyü

Chiang Fang

FL. FIRST HALF OF THE 9TH CENTURY

In the Ta Li period (766-779) Li Yi of Lunghsi passed the examinations at the age of twenty. In the following year, having been duly qualified, he went to Changan in the sixth month to await the selective tests held by the Board of Civil Service, and there found lodgings in the Hsinchang quarter.

Yi was of a good family and was gifted in literary matters from youth. He was renowned above his contemporaries for his pretty verses and neatly turned lines, which won even the admiration of those with long established reputations. He had a good opinion of his own qualities and thought that he must find a lady worthy of his talents. He looked extensively among the courtesans but for a long time had no success.

There was at that time a matchmaker in Changan by the name of Pao and known as Shih-yi-niang. She had been a bondmaid but had won her freedom more than ten years previously. She was sociable by nature and clever of tongue and hence a great favorite wherever she went. There was not a single house of any consequence where she was not a visitor and she was universally acknowledged the past mistress of the profession wherein hints and stratagems play a most conspicuous part. To her Yi had confided his wish and had won her loyalty both by his earnestness and by the generosity of his presents.

One afternoon a few months later as Yi was sitting in the southern pavilion of his lodgings he suddenly heard an urgent knocking at the gate, followed by the announcement that Pao Shih-yi-niang had come to call. He went out to meet her and asked what had brought her there. "Have you been having nice dreams?" Pao said, laughing. "You should, for I have found a lady for you who is like a goddess in exile in this mortal world and who, moreover, cares nothing for wealth and jewels but only for talent and romance. She is exactly suited to you, Shih-lang." [1]

On hearing this, Yi became light of body and spirit and jumped for joy. He took Pao's hand in his and thanked her, saying that he was forever her willing slave. When he asked the lady's name and where she lived, Pao answered, "She is the youngest daughter of the late Prince Huo by his favorite handmaid Chingchih, and her father doted upon her. Her name is Hsiaoyü. When the prince died, her brothers paid scant consideration to her because of her lowly origin, but gave her some money and sent her out of the palace with her mother. Few know that she is the daughter of a prince, but her beauty and carriage are such as I have never seen in my life, and in such matters as music and verse and calligraphy she can boast accomplishment in all. A few days ago her mother asked me to look out for a nice young man who would be suited to her in nature and accomplishments, and I told her all about you, Shih-lang. She too has heard of your reputation and was greatly pleased with my proposal. They live in the Ancient Monastery Lane in the Shengyeh quarter. I have made an appointment for you for tomorrow at noon. If you go to the head of the lane at the appointed time, you will be met by a maid servant named Kueitzu."

After Pao's departure, Yi began his preparations for the meeting. He sent his page Chiuhung to his cousin Mr. Shang, a counselor to the prefect of the Metropolitan District, and borrowed from him a black charger with a bridle of gold. That evening he bathed and trimmed his face and put on his best clothes and was so excited at his prospects that he slept not at all that night. In the morning he put on his hat and studied himself a long while in the mirror for fear that he might prejudice his cause by not presenting himself at his best. The noon hour was almost upon him before he realized it and so he ordered his horse and

[1] Tenth young master.

rode at a gallop to the Shengyeh quarter where at the appointed place he found a maid servant waiting, who asked him if he was not Li Shih-lang. He dismounted and handed the reins to the maid and hastily went inside the gate. There he was met by Pao, who said jokingly to him, "What manner of young man are you that you come unannounced into people's houses?" Thus bantering with each other, they went inside the middle gate, where he found four cherry trees in the court and a parrot in a cage hung in the northwest corner. When the parrot saw Yi, it called, "There is someone here! Lower the screen!" Yi was startled but as he was hesitating whether to advance farther, Chingchih came down the steps to meet him. She invited him inside and made him sit down. She was a little over forty years old but was still comely and had a charming manner of speech. "I have heard of Shih-lang's talents and accomplishments," she said to Yi. "I am glad to see, now that I have seen your person, that in your case the man is more than worthy of the reputation. Now I have a daughter, who, though lacking in proper instruction, is at least not without a measure of comeliness and will make a suitable mate for a gentleman like yourself. I have repeatedly spoken of my wish to Pao Shih-yi-niang and I am now happy to have my daughter enter your service 'with basket and broom.' "

"It is an unexpected honor," Yi answered, "for a clumsy and mediocre man like myself to receive your condescension. If you should be so good as to bestow on me your choice, my gratitude to you will transcend this life."

A feast was set out and at Chingchih's command, Hsiaoyü emerged from a chamber to the east, and Yi went up to salute her. Her presence was as dazzling as a forest of gems and jade trees, so bright were her eyes and so bewitching her glances. As she sat down beside her mother, the latter said to her, "This is the author of the lines of which you are so fond, 'When the wind stirred the bamboo without the screen, I thought it was the sound of my old love coming.' [2] What a pleasure it must be for you to

[2] A conceit much affected by Tang and later poets. Compare, for instance, with the quatrain on p. 78.

meet a poet whose verse you are forever humming to yourself." Hsiaoyü bowed her head with a smile and said in a whisper, "It seems that sometimes a man's face falls short of his reputation. How is it that a man of genius is not always handsome?" At this Yi rose and said with a bow, "It has always been true that a woman loves talent while a man admires beauty, for by thus complementing each other they achieve both." At this remark mother and daughter exchanged glances and laughed.

After a few rounds of wine, Yi begged Hsiaoyü for a song; she refused at first but finally yielded when her mother also urged her. Her voice was clear and resonant and her rendering skillful and full of surprises. They wined and feasted until darkness fell, when Pao conducted Yi to the western compound and ushered him into a suite of quiet and richly furnished rooms, where she left him with two maids to wait upon him.

Presently Hsiaoyü arrived. She was gentle in speech and ingratiating in manner, and carried herself with grace even as she undressed for the conjugal bed. They let down the curtains and laid their heads on the pillow, and enjoyed a state of blissfulness which, Yi told himself, could not have been surpassed by meetings on the Mountain Wu and the River Lo.

But in the midst of this happiness, Hsiaoyü suddenly wept and said, looking at Yi, "Since my mother has been a dancer, I know that I am no proper mate for you. Now you have taken me under your protection because you love me for my beauty; I fear that as my beauty wanes, you will transfer your affections elsewhere and discard me like an autumn fan. When I think of how I shall then be like a wisteria vine with nothing to lean upon, I cannot help grieving in the midst of our happiness."

Yi was overcome with emotion when he heard this confession. Pillowing her head on his arm, he said to her, "In you I have fulfilled the aspirations of my life and I swear that I shall never abandon you, though my bones be shattered and my body torn to pieces. Why have you said such a thing? Please get me a piece of silk so that I may solemnize my oath in writing."

Thereupon Hsiaoyü dried her tears and had one of her maids

bring Yi brush and inkstone and pull back the curtain and hold up the candle while he wrote. In spare moments from playing the pipes and plucking the strings, Hsiaoyü had devoted herself to verse and exercises in calligraphy and she had writing materials which had been used in the prince's palace. Now she brought out an embroidered case and produced from it a piece of rare writing silk and gave it to Yi. Being gifted in such matters, he dashed off a composition in short order. He called upon the mountains and rivers to be witnesses to his love and the sun and moon to testify to his fidelity, and was so sincere and earnest in every word that no one who read him could remain unmoved. After he finished writing, he had the document put in Hsiaoyü's jewel box. Henceforward they lived in joy and harmony, like a kingfisher transporting with its mate in the clouds. For two years they were together day and night.

In the spring of the third year, Yi qualified himself in the Board examinations and was appointed assistant magistrate of Chenghsien. In the fourth month, as he was about to set out for his post, he gave a party at Tunglo, at which most of his friends and relations at Changan were present. It was at that time of the year when spring was still in evidence and summer just beginning to exhibit its luxuriant beauty.

After the guests had gone, Hsiaoyü, her thoughts preoccupied with the approaching separation, said to Yi, "Because of your fame and talents, many are the families that are eager to draw you into marriage ties. Moreover, your parents are still living and they will not allow you to leave vacant your private room. I am certain that you will on this journey acquire a good mate, thus making your vow but so many empty words. However, I have one small wish which I should like to have gratified and I wonder if you would be willing to grant it."

Yi was surprised by the tenure of her speech and said, "What offense have I committed that you speak like this? Please state your wish and rest assured that I shall carry it out."

Hsiaoyü said, "I am now eighteen and you twenty-two. There are still eight years before you reach the prime of your life. What

I ask is that you give me these eight years of happiness before you make your choice of your life's mate among the many noble families that are eager to have you. That would not be too late. When the time comes I shall abandon this world and take up the cloth. If I could but have this wish I shall live without regret the rest of my days."

Yi was so moved that he could not restrain his tears. "I shall never forget my oath to the end of my life," he assured her. "How could I have such thoughts of betrayal as you have just imputed to me when it is my firm belief that love like ours cannot end with this life? I implore you to admit no doubt but to wait for me and be confident that our separation will not be a long one. For as soon as I am settled down at Chenghsien I shall send for you. That should not be later than the eighth month at the latest."

A few days afterwards Yi took leave of Hsiaoyü and journeyed east to his post. Some ten days later he secured leave to visit his parents at the eastern capital. There he found that his mother had made an engagement for him to marry Lu-shih, one of his cousins. As his mother was a strict and resolute woman, Yi did not dare to voice his opposition but went meekly to the Lu family and carried out the confirmation rites.

Now the Lu family was a great one and had been accustomed to receive large sums as betrothal presents. As Yi's family was poor, it became necessary for him to extend his leave so that he could visit his friends and relations far and wide in order to borrow the money required. This took him across the Kiang and the Huai and into the following summer. Because he was ashamed of his betrayal of Hsiaoyü, he sent no message whatever and, furthermore, enjoined their mutual friends and acquaintances not to divulge to her his movements.

On her part Hsiaoyü made diligent inquiries but in return she received only falsehoods and evasions. She consulted fortune tellers and called in mediums of all sorts, but it was all in vain and after more than a year of sorrow and anxiety she fell into a long, lingering illness. For though Yi's messages had been entirely cut off, her hope and longing never changed. The expenses she incurred in order to get news of her lover put a severe drain on her resources, until at last she was forced to sell piece by piece her treasured jewels. These she disposed of largely through Hou Ching-hsien, a merchant in the West Market who sold goods on consignment. Once when Hsiaoyü's maid was on her way to him with a jade hairpin, she encountered an old jade craftsman on the road. When the latter saw the hairpin that was in her hand he came up to her and said, "I made this pin years ago for the youngest daughter of the Prince Huo when she reached the age of tying up her hair. I remember it well because the prince gave me ten thousand cash. Who are you and how have you come by this pin?"

"My mistress is the daughter of the prince," answered Wan Sha, the maid. "Her fortune has suffered a decline and she has given herself to an untrustworthy man. It is now more than two years since he went to the eastern capital and he has sent no message whatever in that time. In her unhappiness my mistress has languished and fallen sick. She has asked me to have this sold so that she might engage some one to find news of him."

On hearing this sad tale, the jade worker wept, saying, "What a pity that the daughter of a noble family should come to such misfortune and suffer such unhappiness. Old as I am, I cannot remain unmoved by such vicissitudes of fortunes as you have just told me." He then took her to the mansion of the Princess Yen Hsien and told the latter Hsiaoyü's sad story. The princess was also deeply moved by it and for a long while she sighed deeply and wept. She gave the maid one hundred and twenty thousand cash to take to her mistress.

As the Lu family was living in Changan at the time, Yi secured leave and went thither in the twelfth month for the wedding after he had secured the necessary sum for the betrothal present. He rented a house in a remote quarter of the city so that his presence in the city might not become generally known.

Now there was among Yi's intimate circle a certain Tsui Chiuming. He was Yi's cousin and a faithful and loyal friend. He used to be a frequent visitor at Hsiaoyü's house in her happier days and took part in the gay festivities there. Now he continued to visit

Hsiaoyü in her misfortune and to bring her whatever news he had of his cousin. Hsiaoyü on her part often made presents to him of provisions and clothes. Tsui was naturally grateful to her, so that when Yi arrived in Changan he went immediately to her and told her of his presence.

"How could he be so cruel as not to let me know!" Hsiaoyü said, sighing. Through their mutual friends and acquaintances she sent word to Yi begging him to come to her, but to all these importunities Yi turned a deaf ear. He was ashamed of himself for his faithless conduct and did not have the courage to face her, especially in view of the fact that she had fallen seriously ill because of him. He went out early in the morning and came home late at night in order to avoid her emissaries. On her part, Hsiaoyü never gave up her longing for another meeting with him; she wept day and night and neglected food and rest until her illness was so aggravated by her grief and anxiety that she was unable to leave her bed. Her plight gradually came to be known all over Changan and all who became acquainted with her story were deeply moved and were as filled with admiration for the constancy of her love as they were outraged by the heartlessness of her lover's conduct.

It was then in the third month when spring outings were the order of the day. Yi and five or six of his friends went to the Chung Ching Temple to look at the mutan peonies that were then in bloom. As they strolled along the western verandah and composed impromptu verses for the occasion, one of Yi's intimate friends, Wei Hsia-ching by name, said to him:

"How sad it is that Hsiaoyü should be languishing alone in her sickroom when the weather outside is so glorious and the trees and flowers are so beautiful! You must be indeed a hard man to abandon her like this. It is not right. You really ought to think the matter over and do something about her."

As Wei was thus upbraiding his friend, a young man with handsome features loitered near by and listened. He wore a yellow robe and was carrying bow and pellets. Suddenly he came up to Yi and saluted him, saying, "Are you not, Sir, Li Shih-lang? My ancestors came from Shantung and I am distantly related to you through marriage. Though I am not cultivated in the literary arts, yet I admire men who are and have longed to meet you of whose reputation I have heard so much. It is a great pleasure, therefore, to meet you today. My house is not far from here. I have a band of musicians and eight or nine beautiful dancers and more than ten fine horses. All these I place at your disposal, if only you would honor my house with your presence."

Yi's friends were all impressed with the offer and readily agreed to adjourn the party to the stranger's house. They got on their horses and went off with the stranger, but after a while their journey led them to the Shengyeh quarter and Yi grew uneasy as it was near where Hsiaoyü lived. He made some excuse and was about to turn back when the stranger seized his reins, saying, "Surely you would not deny me the honor of your presence now that we are but a few steps from my house?" He ignored Yi's protestations and urged him on. At the head of the lane where Hsiaoyü lived Yi became panic stricken and made another desperate attempt to break away, but the stranger frustrated him by ordering his servants to seize him and force him into Hsiaoyü's gate, which he locked immediately. Then he shouted, "Li Shih-lang is here!" The announcement brought the sound of rejoicing inside which could be heard out where Yi was.

The night before Hsiaoyü had dreamed that a man in a yellow robe had carried Yi to her. Then he ordered Hsiaoyü to take off her shoes, whereupon she awoke and thus interpreted the dream to her mother: "The word 'shoe,' being homophonous with the word for 'accord,' symbolizes that Shih-lang and I will be reunited. However, the taking off of the shoes can only mean that he and I will be separated again. The dream then portends that I shall see him again but that I shall die soon afterwards."

In the morning she asked her mother to dress her hair for her. The latter would not consent at first, thinking that her mind was disordered because of her long illness, but finally had to humor her because of her insistence. Her mother had just finished doing her hair when Yi suddenly arrived. For some time past Hsiaoyü had found it necessary to have assistance even to turn over in bed, so wasted was she by her long illness, but at the announcement of her lover's arrival she rose unassisted, changed her clothes, and went out to meet him, as if assisted by some supernatural power.

She met Yi in a silence which did not conceal her sorrow and her sense of injury. From time to time she cast a glance at him and so weak and emaciated was she that she seemed hardly able to bear the weight of her clothes, and so sad and touching was her mien that all those present found it impossible to hold back their tears. Then suddenly a feast consisting of scores of courses was brought in from the outside, which upon inquiry was found to have been ordered by the stranger in the yellow robe.

After the company had taken their seats, Hsiaoyü looked steadily for a long while at Yi and then pouring a libation from her cup, delivered the following denunciation of her faithless lover: "I, a poor woman, have been the victim of a cruel fate; you, a man of standing, have been faithless of heart. Though still young and unfaded, I shall die of grief; though my mother is still living, I shall not be able to attend her. Farewell, farewell, Shih-lang. And as you have been the cause of my untimely departure for the Yellow Springs, so will I, as an unhappy ghost, plague you and all those who try to take my place." Then dashing the cup to the ground and putting one hand on Yi's arm, she gave a long wail and died. Her mother raised her body and put it in Yi's arms, but for all Yi's loud lamentations she did not come back to life.

Yi put on mourning for her and lamented for her bitterly night and day. On the eve of her burial, Yi suddenly saw Hsiaoyü come to him in the mourning room. She was as beautiful as she used to be in her happier days and was dressed in a skirt of pomegranate red, a purple gown, and a shawl of red and green. Standing beside the curtains, her hand playing with her embroidered sash, she gazed at him and said, "Since you have deigned to attend my wake, you cannot be entirely without feelings for me. I shall be grateful to you in the other world." Then she vanished.

The next day she was buried in Yusuyuan near Changan. Yi escorted the procession to the place of burial and did not return until all the rites were performed. A month later he married Lu-shih, but the happy occasion did not lift him out of the melancholy into which he had fallen. In the fifth month he returned to his post at Chenghsien with Lu-shih.

Not many days afterwards, as Yi and Lu-shih were lying in bed one night, he suddenly heard a noise outside the bed curtains and saw, when he looked, a handsome man of about twenty years of age standing concealed behind the curtains and beckoning to Lu-shih. Yi jumped out of bed and rushed at him but lost him after pursuing him a few times around the bed. After that Yi became very suspicious and jealous of his wife and their married life became quite intolerable. Then just as his friends and relations had convinced him of the groundlessness of his suspicions, another incident set him off again.

One day he came home and found Lu-shih playing the lute. Suddenly an inlaid box of rhinoceros horn was thrown in from the outside and fell in Lu-shih's lap. It was about an inch in diameter and was tied with a piece of ribbon in a "knot of one heart." Yi picked it up, opened it, and found inside two seeds of the love-one-another tree, a kowtow bug, an obscene instrument made from a young he-ass's member, and a small package of aphrodisiacs. In his passion Yi roared like a tiger and struck his wife with the lute and commanded her to confess her guilt. There was nothing she could do that would convince him of her innocence, and in the end she had to bring suit for divorce, unable to stand his abuse and beatings any longer.

After this Yi always became jealous and suspicious of the maids and concubines that he happened to have relations with, sometimes to the extent of killing them in his rage. Once he purchased a courtesan by the name of Ying Shih-yi-niang, renowned for her beauty. He was very fond of her but was all the more jealous and was always threatening her with the idea of keeping her faithful. He would tell her that he once secured such and such [3] a concubine from such and such a place, that she was caught in such

[3] Such perfunctory treatment of details is typical. Compare "The Dragon's Daughter," p. 36.

and such a situation and that he killed her with such and such a weapon. When he went out, he would put an overturned bath tub over her on the bed and seal it all around. On his return he would examine to see whether the seal had been broken before he let her out. He always carried with him a sharp sword which he was wont to brandish before his maids and concubines and say: "This sword is made of Kochi steel for the express purpose of cutting off the heads of faithless women."

For the rest of his life he never met any woman without becoming jealous of her. He married three times but each time the marriage ended in disaster.

Li Yahsien, a Loyal Courtesan

Po Hsing-chien
776-827

Li Yahsien, the Lady of Chienkuo, was once a courtesan in Changan, but because her loyalty was unique and her conduct noteworthy, I have undertaken to write her story.

During the T'ien Pao period (742-55) there was a certain governor of Changchou whose native place was Jungyang but whose name I shall omit. He was a man of great prestige and wealth. He was about fifty years of age and had a son close on twenty, whom I shall call by the personal name Yuanho. The latter was talented and skilled in literary composition and stood out among his fellows, and was in consequence greatly esteemed by the people of the time. His father was very fond of him and held great hopes for his future. "This," he used to say, "is the thousand-li colt of our family." When Yuanho was about to set out for the examinations, his father provided him with fine clothes and a richly decorated carriage and gave him a generous sum of money for his expenses at the capital, saying, "Judging from your talents, you ought to succeed on the first attempt. However, I am giving you more than enough for two years so that you will be sure to fulfill your aspirations." Yuanho, on his part, was confident and deemed it as simple a matter to pass the examinations as to turn his palm.

He began his journey at Piling and reached Changan a little more than a month later, and there he took up quarters in Pucheng Street. One day, returning from the East Market, he entered the city by the east gate of the Pingkang quarter and was on his way to visit a friend in the southwestern part of the town when, as he passed through Mingko Lane, he saw a house of which the gate was not particularly spacious but which was neat and attractive in itself and far removed from the street. One leaf of the door was open and at it stood a girl leaning on a young maid servant. She surpassed in beauty and charm anything the world has ever seen, and so impressed was Yuanho that he unconsciously reined in his horse and was for a long time unable to go on. He purposely dropped his whip on the ground and as he waited for his servant to pick it up he kept glancing at the girl. On her part, she returned his glances and seemed to be very well disposed toward him. However, he went on without daring to speak to her.

From that time on he acted like a man lost. Finally he confided the encounter to one of his friends who knew Changan well and asked him about her.

"The house you saw," his friend replied, "is occupied by a woman of ill-repute by the name of Li. The girl's name is Yahsien."

"Is the girl approachable?" Yuanho asked, and his friend answered, "The woman Li is quite well off, for she entertains only men of wealth and rank and is accustomed to receive large sums from them. She will hardly show any interest in you unless you are ready to spend millions of cash."

"My only worry is that she may not receive me," the young man said. "I care not if it does cost me a million."

The next day, dressed in his best clothes and accompanied by a large retinue of servants, he went to Li's house and knocked at the gate. Presently a maid servant came to open the door. "Whose house is this?" Yuanho asked. The maid did not answer but rushed inside shouting, "The young man who dropped his whip the other day is here!" Yahsien was delighted, for she said to the maid, "Make him wait a while. I shall come out after I have done my toilet and changed my clothes."

Yuanho congratulated himself on his good fortune as he followed the maid into the court. There he saw an old woman with gray hair and bent back, whom he took to be Yahsien's mother. He bowed low and spoke thus: "Is it true that you have a compound to spare? If so, I should like to rent it."

"I am afraid," she answered, "that it is entirely too dingy and small to merit the honor of your presence, even if we dared to offer it to you as a gift, so how dare I say anything about rent?"[1] She then invited Yuanho into the guest hall, which was a very handsome one, and sat down with him saying, "I have a daughter who is still young and immature and but poorly trained in the arts of music and singing. However, she likes to meet visitors and I should like to present her."

Thereupon she called to her daughter to come out. The girl's eyes were bright and her wrist white; her carriage was graceful and bewitching. Yuanho jumped to his feet and was so dazzled by her beauty that he did not dare to raise his eyes to look at her. As he exchanged salutations with her and made remarks about the weather, he observed that everything about her was such as he had never seen before in his life.

They sat down again. Tea was served and wine poured. The vessels used were very elegant. He lingered till the sun was set and the sound of drums heralding the twilight watch[2] rose from all sides. When the old woman asked Yuanho where he lived, he answered untruthfully, "Several li outside the Yenping gate," in the hope that she would ask him to stay because of the distance. But the old woman said, "The drums have sounded. You had better go right away so that you will not violate the curfew." "I have been so engrossed in the pleasure of your company," the young man said, "that I did not realize that the eve of day is upon us. The journey is long and far away and I have no friends in the city. What shall I do?"

Here the girl said, "Since you have shown a readiness to live here in spite of its dinginess, what harm is there if you stay for the night?" Yuanho looked to the mother for encouragement and when she repeated her daughter's invitation, he summoned one of his servants and commanded him to bring in two rolls of fine silk. These he presented to the woman Li for his food and lodging for

[1] This subterfuge is not only childish and unnecessary but quite improbable. It is as if the author had come across the sentences in a phrase book and had inserted them in here because he liked them so much.

[2] The night is divided into five watches beginning with the first watch at dusk and ending with the fifth at dawn.

the night. Yahsien, however, would not hear of it, saying, "That is not the way to treat a guest. Tonight you must allow us, poor as we are, to offer you what crude fare we have. You can do your part some other time." Yuanho tried to refuse, but she would not let him.

Presently they all moved into the west hall where the curtains and drapes and screens and couches dazzled the eye with their brightness and where the toilet boxes and the quilts and pillows were all of the most luxurious kind. Candles were lighted and supper served; the food was rich in variety and delicious in flavor.

After supper, the mother withdrew while Yuanho and Yahsien continued their eager conversation, laughing and joking and indulging in all sorts of pleasantries. "When I passed your house the other day," he said, "you happened to be standing at the door. After that I have thought of you all the time; you are always in my heart whether I am eating or sleeping."

"It has been the same with me," Yahsien answered.

"I have come," he went on, "not just to look for a place to live. What I really want is to fulfill the wish of a lifetime. I wonder what will be my fate?"

Before he had finished speaking, the mother came in and asked them what they were saying. When they told her, she said, laughing, "Is it not said that between man and woman there is a great passion? When the feeling is mutual, not even the command of their parents can stop them. However, my daughter is very uncultivated and quite unworthy to share your mat and pillow."

Thereupon Yuanho rose and bowing low to her, said, "I beg you to take me as your slave," and the old woman thereafter treated him as if he were a son-in-law. Then they parted after having drunk to their full.

The next morning Yuanho brought everything he had and settled in the Li household. Henceforward he covered his traces and hid his person and completely cut off his contacts with former friends and relatives. He consorted with such people as actors and courtesans entirely and indulged himself in a perpetual round of feasts and entertainments. When his purse became empty, he sold his horses and then his servants. In a year's time he had dissipated everything he had. In the meantime the old woman gradually cooled toward him, while Yahsien's love for him grew apace. One day she said to him, "Though it is a year since we have known each other, I am still without child. I have heard that the Spirit of the Bamboo Grove answers a woman's prayers as surely as an echo and should like to make an offering there. Would you go with me?"

Not suspecting a plot,[3] Yuanho was delighted with the proposal. He pawned some clothes in order to buy offerings of wine and meat and went to the temple with Yahsien to pray. They stayed one night at the temple and started back the next day, Yuanho riding behind Yahsien's carriage on a donkey. When they reached the north gate of the Pingkang quarter, Yahsien said to him, "In a narrow lane east of here is my aunt's house. Could we stop there and rest a while?" He consented and in about a hundred paces they came to a carriage gate leading into a spacious compound. "This is the place," said Yahsien's maid from the back of the carriage. As Yuanho descended, some one came out of the house and asked who was calling. "Li Yahsien," was the answer. She went in with the message and presently a woman about forty years old came out and greeted Yuanho, saying, "Is my niece here?" When Yahsien descended from the carriage, the aunt greeted her and asked why she had not been to see her for such a long time. Then the two women looked at each other and laughed. After Yuanho had been introduced, they all went into a compound near the west halberd gate.[4] It was a quiet and secluded place, with many bamboos and shade trees, and ponds and pavilions. "Is this your aunt's own house?" Yuanho asked Yahsien, but she only laughed and spoke of something else.

Presently tea and refreshments of rare quality were served but

[3] Note that a few lines back the girl's love is said to have grown apace. This inconsistency seems to have jarred even Chinese readers, for in later versions of this theme the writers always take pains to point out that the faithful courtesan is not party to the plot.

[4] In T'ang times officials of the third rank or higher were permitted to display halberds at the gate of their private residences.

before long a man bathed in sweat came galloping up on a horse and announced that Yahsien's mother had suddenly been taken ill and had practically lost her consciousness, and that they had better come back as quickly as possible.

"My heart is confused," Yahsien said to her aunt. "I shall ride on first and send the carriage back for you and my husband." Yuanho proposed to go with her but the aunt, after some whispered words with Yahsien's maid, stopped him, saying, "My sister will undoubtedly die soon. You should stay and advise me what to do about the funeral and other urgent matters instead of running off with my niece." He stayed, therefore, and figured the expenses for the funeral and the services. By the end of the day, the carriage had not yet come back.

"Why is it that no word has come from my niece?" the aunt said. "Why don't you go and see what has happened? I shall come soon myself."

Accordingly, Yuanho went. When he arrived at the Li house he was astonished to find it securely locked and sealed with clay. He inquired of a neighbor and received this reply: "The Lis had rented this house. The lease has recently expired and the owner has again taken possession. The Lis moved away yesterday." "Where have they moved to?" he asked, and the neighbor answered that he did not know.

Yuanho was about to hurry back to Hsuanyang and question the aunt, but he soon realized that the day was too far gone to undertake the journey. He pawned some of his clothes and bought himself supper and hired a bed. But he was so angry and outraged that he did not once close his eyes from dusk till dawn. As soon as day broke, he mounted his donkey and set out for the aunt's house. Arriving there, he knocked on the door repeatedly but for the space of a meal no one answered it. Then he shouted at the top of his voice several times and it was not until then that a servant came slowly out. "Is the aunt in?" Yuanho asked impatiently. "There is no such person here," was the answer. "But she was here yesterday," Yuanho said. "Why does she avoid me?" When he asked whose house it was, the man answered, "This is the house of President Tsui. Yesterday some people came and rented one of the compounds to entertain, so they said, a cousin arriving from some distant point. They went away before nightfall."

Yuanho was so perplexed that he almost went mad. Not knowing what else to do he went to his old quarters on Pucheng street, where his old landlord took compassion upon him and gave him food. But he was too upset to eat. For three days he touched nothing, and then fell seriously ill. After about ten days his condition became so critical that his landlord gave up hope for his recovery and, fearful of the complications that might arise from his death, moved him to a funeral establishment. There in a short time he won the sympathy of everyone, who took turns in feeding him. After a while he improved and was able to get up with the aid of a stick. The shop hired him to hold the funeral curtain and with his wages for this he was enabled to support himself.

After a month or two he regained his strength but whenever he heard mourners' songs, in which the living professed envy for the kinder lot of the dead, he would burst into sobs and tears in spite of himself. Then when he went home he would imitate their mournful songs. Being clever and quick to learn, he soon mastered all their tricks and became the best mourner in Changan.

Now there were two funeral shops that had been for a long time rivals. The shop to the east excelled in the quality of its hearses and biers but was somewhat inferior in the skill of its mourners. Having heard of the surpassing art of Yuanho, the owner of the shop offered him twenty thousand cash for his services, and had his veteran mourners each teach Yuanho his particular forte. Thus the young man learned many new songs, which he practiced to the accompaniment of his fellow mourners. This went on for more than a month without anyone knowing anything about it.

Then the owners of the two rival shops said to each other: "Let us hold an exhibition on the Street of Heaven's Gate of all the paraphernalia that we have for hire, so that we can determine who has the better equipment. The loser will forfeit fifty thousand cash to pay for wine and refreshments." An agreement was drawn up and signed by guarantors before the competition.

The crowd that gathered to watch the spectacle numbered tens of thousands. Even the governor of the Metropolitan District became aware of the proceedings, having heard about it from the chief of police, who had in turn got it from the constable of the quarter. People poured into the thoroughfare from all directions so that the streets of Changan became empty. From morning till noon each shop paraded in turn their coaches and hearses and other funereal trappings and in all these things the shop to the west came out the loser, much to the humiliation of its owner. Then he had a platform set up in the southern corner of the square. A man with a long beard now came forward carrying a handbell and attended by several assistants. As he mounted the platform he tilted up his chin, raised his eyebrows, and clasped his right wrist with his left hand by way of defiance. Then he cleared his throat and began to sing "The Dirge of the White Horse." Confident because of his former victories, he glared to his right and left as if to defy anyone that dared to dispute the supremacy of his art. He was applauded on all sides.

Then the owner of the shop to the east set up a platform to the north of the square and a young man in a black hat came forward, accompanied by five or six attendants and holding a hearse plume in his hand. It was Yuanho himself. As he adjusted his clothes and trilled a few preliminary notes he manifested an air of diffidence as if unequal to the task, but when he proceeded to sing "The Dew on the Garlic" his voice was pure and shrill and shook the forest trees, so that before the end of his song the entire audience was sobbing and wiping away their tears.

The owner of the shop to the west was now greeted with boos and taunts. His humiliation was so great that he quietly placed his forfeit before the other owner and then slipped away unseen. The spectators were amazed at the unexpected turn and could not imagine where the owner of the shop to the east had procured so remarkable a singer.

Now it happened that the Emperor had recently issued an edict commanding the provincial governors to come to the capital once a year to confer on government policy. Because of this, Yuanho's father was in Changan at the time. Hearing of the competition, he and some of his colleagues changed their official robes and went to see the proceedings. With him was an old servant, the husband of Yuanho's nurse. When he saw Yuanho's gestures and heard his voice, he recognized them to be those of his young master, but the circumstances made him doubt his own senses and he did not dare to accost the young man though he was several times on the point of doing so. However, he could not suppress the tears that this reminder of his young master had prompted, and Yuanho's father, seeing him weep, asked him what was the cause. "The singer," he said, "looks very much like your lost son." "How could that be," Yuanho's father answered, "since my son was murdered by robbers because he had too much money with him?" He too began to weep.

Afterwards the old servant went to the funeral shop and inquired among the members of the troupe. "Who was that singer?" he asked them. "How wonderful he is." They told him the young man's name, but it meant nothing to the old servant as Yuanho had changed it. The servant, however, was still not satisfied and decided to have a closer look at the young man. When Yuanho saw his old servant, he winced and turned away to hide himself among the crowd, but the old servant caught him by the sleeves and asked him if he was not his young master. Thereupon they embraced and wept, and then went back together to his father's lodging. There his father berated him, saying, "Your conduct has disgraced the family. How could you have the brazenness to show your face again?" Then he took him on foot to a secluded spot west of Chuchiang and east of the Apricot Gardens, and there he stripped him naked and thrashed him with his horsewhip till Yuanho, unable to stand the pain, apparently died. The father then left him and went away.

Fortunately Yuanho's singing master had told some of the young man's friends to follow him. When the scout returned and told the troupe what had happened, they were all greatly distressed and delegated two of their number to go back to the spot with a reed mat and bury the body. Arriving there, however, they found that he was still warm under the heart. They raised him and after a long while he began to breathe weakly. They carried him back and fed him liquid through a reed pipe. After a night he regained consciousness, but for more than a month he could not move his arms or legs. The cuts left by the whip festered and broke and made him a most revolting object. At last his friends could endure the distressing sight no longer and one night they carried him out and abandoned him by the side of the road. The passers-by all took pity on him and many gave their left-over food to him. Thus he was able to sustain himself until about three months later he was able to get about with a stick. Clad in a cloth coat patched in a hundred different places and tattered like a quail's tail, and carrying a broken bowl in his hand, he began to tramp the streets of Changan as a beggar.

Thus through the autumn and into the winter he crawled in caves and dung piles to sleep at night and frequented the market places by day. One day it snowed, but driven by hunger, Yuanho had to go out and brave the snow. His cries were so pitiful that none who heard him could remain unmoved. But the snow was heavy and few houses had their outer gates open. Finally near the east gate of the Anyi quarter, about seven or eight houses along the north side of the wall to the quarter, he came to a gate that was half open. It was, in fact, where Yahsien was now living but he did not know it and began to cry out his woes in an intolerably sad voice. When Yahsien heard it in her room, she said to her maid, "That must be Yuanho. I recognize his voice." She hastened out and there she saw her old lover standing at the door, so emaciated by hunger and disfigured by sores and scabs that he hardly seemed human. She was deeply moved and said to him, "Are you not Yuanho?" But he was so overcome with shame and anger that he collapsed and was, for a while, unable to speak. He only nodded.

Yahsien rushed up to him and threw her arms around his neck. Then, wrapping her embroidered jacket around him, she helped him into the western chamber. There she wailed, "It is my fault that you have come to this," and then swooned. Her mother was by her side when she regained consciousness. "What does this mean?" the old woman asked and when Yahsien pointed to Yuanho, she said, "You should have driven him away instead of bringing him in here."

Yahsien, however, looked at her steadily and said: "Not so! He is the son of a good family. He came to us in a splendid carriage carrying with him quantities of gold. When in a short time he had squandered everything, we plotted against him and abandoned him to his fate. It was hardly human. We are responsible for ruining his career and bringing upon him the contempt of his own kind. It was because of us that his father suppressed his natural feelings for him and abandoned him after almost beating him to death. Every one knows that it was because of me that he has come to this pass. He has influential connections at court. Should they one day learn all the circumstances, disaster will be upon us. Moreover, such conduct as ours is against the laws both of heaven and of men and will not be countenanced by the gods. Let us not bring further retribution upon ourselves.

"Now I have been your daughter for twenty years. During this time I must have made for you more than a thousand pieces of gold,[5] which is ample to provide for your remaining years. However, to buy my freedom I shall give you another sum of money, enough to cover what I might have cost you in food and clothing. I shall then find another place to live with this young man. We shall live not far away, so that we can call to pay our respects to you morning and evening."

From the way the girl spoke the old woman realized that she could not be shaken in her determination and agreed, therefore, to her proposal. After paying for her freedom, Yahsien still had a hundred pieces of gold left. She rented a house a few doors north. Here she had her lover bathed and put on him a new suit of clothes. First she fed him with soups to condition his stomach and then sour cream to purify his intestines. It was not until some days later that she began to set before him all the delicacies of land and sea. She also provided him with hats, shoes, and stockings of the

[5] Not to be taken literally.

finest quality. In a few months Yuanho had taken on some flesh; by the end of the year he had completely recovered.

One day Yahsien said to her lover: "Your body is now strong and your spirit firm. Now ponder well and see how much you can remember of your old literary studies." After he thought a while, he answered, "I can only remember two or three parts out of ten." Then she ordered her carriage and drove to a bookshop by the south side-gate near the Flag Tower followed by Yuanho on horseback. Here she had him pick out all the books he needed, costing a hundred pieces of gold. They put the books in the carriage and drove home. She made him banish all other thoughts from his mind and concentrate on his studies night and day. She would sit up with him and they never went to bed until far past midnight. When he was tired from his studies, she would have him compose verses for relaxation.

In two years he had mastered his subjects and read all the books then extant in the land. "Now I am ready to try the examinations!" he said to Yahsien, but the latter answered, "Not yet!" You must acquire even more proficiency before you enter the lists." Another year went by before Yahsien said to him, "Now you can try!"

And indeed he came out in the front rank at the first attempt. So great was his fame that he overshadowed all the other candidates, and when his compositions fell under the scrutiny of his seniors, even they were filled with admiration and respect and all sought his friendship.

Yahsien, however, would not let him relax in his efforts. "You must not," she said to him, "fall into the folly of young students of the time. The minute they pass their examinations, they begin to think that high court posts are within their grasp and world-wide reputations already established. Moreover, you cannot compare yourself to other candidates because of your disreputable past. You must, therefore, apply yourself even more diligently to your studies in order to prepare for the next ordeal. Only then can you hope to compete with the other scholars and establish your supremacy among them."

Because of this wise counsel, Yuanho became even more industrious and as a result enhanced his fame. It happened that the triennial examinations fell within that year and an imperial edict was issued summoning qualified candidates for the test. Yuanho entered the section for "straight advice and extreme remonstration." He came out the first on the roster of successful candidates, and was appointed military counselor to the governor of Chengtu. He numbered among his friends the highest officials at court, from the three chief ministers down.

When Yuanho was about to set out for his post, Yahsien said to him: "By helping you to restore yourself to your proper place in life, I have redeemed the wrong I have done you. I want now to spend the remaining years of my life taking care of my foster mother. For yourself, you must marry the daughter of a noble family, who will be worthy to prepare the sacrificial dishes. You must not burden yourself with an unworthy person like myself. Take good care of yourself! I must now leave you!"

"I shall kill myself if you leave me now," Yuanho said, but in spite of his threat she would not change her resolve. He continued to implore her to go with him, and to placate him, she said, "I shall cross the river and go with you as far as Chienmen. There you must let me go."

Yuanho agreed and in a little over a month they had reached Chienmen. There before he started out again, the report of promotions arrived and he found that his father had been, after an audience at the capital, appointed governor of Chengtu and concurrently intendant of Chiennan Circuit. The next morning his father arrived and Yuanho sent in his card and waited upon him at the posting station. His father did not recognize him at first but when he saw on his card the names of his father and grandfather, he was astonished. He bade his son mount the steps and putting his hand on his son's back he wept as he said, "From now on we are father and son as before." Then he asked his son how it had all happened and when he heard everything he was greatly impressed and asked where Yahsien was. "She has accompanied me here," his son answered, "but she is going back." At this the father said that they must not let her go.

The next day he ordered carriages and went to Chengtu with his son, after having set Yahsien up in suitable quarters at Chienmen. As soon as he had attended to his most pressing duties at his new post he sent a matchmaker to Chienmen with a formal proposal for uniting the two families through marriage ties. The wedding soon followed with all the appropriate rites.

In the years following the marriage, Yahsien showed herself a most dutiful daughter-in-law and was very capable in the management of the household. She was greatly beloved by her parents-in-law.

Some years later when Yuanho's parents died, he was so pious in his mourning observances that the sacred fungus grew on the roof of his mourning hut, each stem bearing three heads, and more than a score white swallows made their nests in the rafters. These auspicious omens were duly reported by the provincial authorities to the Emperor, who was greatly impressed and conferred upon Yuanho special favors and honors. After his mourning period was over, he was successively appointed to distinguished posts and in the course of ten years was governor of several provinces. Yahsien was given the title of Lady of Chienkuo. They had four sons, all of whom rose to high offices, even the lowest being the prefect of Taiyuan. The sons all married into great families so that Yuanho was without equal in the number of distinguished relations.

How remarkable that a woman of the courtesan class should manifest a degree of loyalty and constancy such as is rarely exceeded by the heroines of antiquity! How can such a story fail to provoke sighs of admiration!

My great-uncle was once governor of Chinchou, then a vice-president of the Board of Revenue and later a commissioner of grain transportation. In all these three posts he had Yuanho as his predecessor and was consequently familiar with the story of his past. In the Cheng Yuan period (785-804) I was one day talking with Kung-tso [6] of Lunghsi about women of notable virtue and told him the story of the Lady of Chienkuo. With his hands clasped, Kung-tso listened with rapt attention, and when I finished he asked

[6] Li Kung-tso, author of "Hsieh Hsiaowo."

me to write down her story. So I took up my brush and dipped it in ink and wrote this sketch of her life. This happened in the eighth month of the twelfth year of the cycle,[7] the narrator being Po Hsing-chien of Taiyuan.

[7] In this instance, A.D. 795. The sixty-year "cycle of Cathay" is supposed to have been instituted in 2637 B.C. See note on chronology.

The Story of Ying Ying

Yuan Chen

779-831

In the Cheng Yuan period (785-804) there lived a man by the name of Chang. He was gentle by nature and handsome in appearance, and he had a strong character which made it difficult for others to corrupt him with improprieties. When by chance he found himself in roistering company he was tolerant but aloof and would never take part in the revelries which others present were so eager for that they acted as if they should never again have the chance. Because of this he had not at twenty-three yet enjoyed the favors of a woman. When asked why he was so indifferent to the beauty of women, he answered: "Men like Master Teng T'u [1] are not true lovers of beauty; they are merely carnal. On the other hand, I truly love beauty and it is only because I have not encountered a woman whom I consider really beautiful that I appear indifferent to the charm of her sex. I know this to be true because in everything else I am very susceptible to beauty and my mind dwells on beautiful things that I happen to see. I know, therefore, that I am not a completely cold person." This answer did not, however, satisfy his questioners, who only sneered at him.

Not long afterwards Chang had occasion to visit Puchou, and took lodgings in the Pu Chiu Temple about ten li east of the city. It happened that the widow of a certain Tsui was returning to Changan. She passed through Puchou on the way and was staying at the same temple.

The widow of Tsui was born of the Cheng family and Chang's

[1] Famous rake of the fourth century B.C.

mother was also a Cheng. When they unraveled their relationship, it was found that Cheng was an "aunt" [2] to Chang.

In this year Hun Chen died at Puchou. One of his lieutenants—Ting Wenya by name—had mistreated his troops, and the soldiers now took advantage of Hun Chen's death to mutiny and plunder the district. Now the Tsui family was very wealthy and Cheng had with her many servants and a great many things of value. Finding herself away from home in the crisis, Cheng became greatly alarmed and did not know where to turn for help. Fortunately Chang had a friend among the officers of the garrison, and obtained from him a guard for the temple. Because of this the temple escaped the depredations of the soldiery. Some ten days later General Tu Ch'ueh assumed command of the troops by command of the Emperor and restored order.

Cheng was very grateful to Chang and prepared a feast to entertain him in the central hall. At the table she said to Chang, "In the recent disturbances I, a poor widow, could hardly have saved myself, to say nothing of the children that I have under my care. My small son and my young daugther, therefore, owe their lives to you. It is no ordinary favor that you have rendered them, and I now propose to have them meet you and acknowledge you their elder brother in token of their gratitude." She first summoned Huanlang, her son. He was about ten years old and a gentle and handsome boy. Next she called to her daughter, saying, "Come out and greet your elder brother who has saved your life." For a long time the girl would not come out and then sent word that she was not feeling well. Cheng grew angry and said, "Your brother Chang has saved your life. If it were not for him you would now be a prisoner. How can you, under the circumstances, allow ordinary considerations of propriety to stand in the way of your sense of gratitude?" [3]

After a long while she came in, dressed in everyday clothes and wearing no special jewels for the occasion. Her hair hung down in

[2] That is, the widow Tsui was of the same generation in the Cheng family tree as Chang's mother.

[3] Women are not introduced to male visitors except when they are immediate relations. Young women are seen hardly at all.

two coils and she had on no make-up except for a little black that joined her two eyebrows and a slight touch of rouge on her cheeks. But her features and complexion were extraordinarily beautiful and shone with dazzling brilliance. Chang was amazed. After salutations were over, she sat down by her mother with the injured air of one who has been forced to do something that she did not wish to do. She stared before her as if unable to endure the ordeal.

When Chang asked her age, Cheng answered, "She was born in the seventh month of the chia-tzu year [4] of the present cycle. As this is the keng-ch'en year,[5] she is now seventeen."

Chang tried to draw her into conversation, but she would not answer. Soon the banquet was over and Chang took his leave. From that time on Chang fell completely under her spell. He wanted very much to convey to her an expression of his love, but had no way of doing so.

Ying Ying [6] had a maid named Hungniang, whom Chang had encountered and greeted several times. One day he took advantage of one of these chance meetings and told her of what was in his heart. The maid was startled as he had expected, and ran away in panic. Chang repented his rashness, so that when he saw the maid the following day he apologized for his conduct and said no more of what he had in mind.

But the maid broached the subject herself, saying, "I dare not convey to my mistress what you told me yesterday, or even hint at it. But you know many relatives of the Tsui family; why don't you send a formal proposal for marriage? You stand an excellent chance of success because of the recent favor that you have done the family."

"I have been of a fastidious nature from childhood," Chang answered, "and have never allowed my glance to dwell on any women that I have met since my youth. I little thought that I

[4] The first year of the cycle.

[5] The seventeenth year. In China age is reckoned by the "calendar year," that is, one is "one year" old on the day of his birth and "two years" old on his first new year's day (though in reality he may be only two days old if he is born on the last day of the old year).

[6] In the original the name is not introduced until the last paragraph.

should at this time of my life suddenly encounter my fate. It was almost impossible for me to restrain myself the other day at the banquet; during the last few days I know not where I am going when I walk nor the taste of things when I eat. I fear that I shall not last many days if things go on like this. If I were to seek her hand through the matchmaker and go through the usual ceremonies, it would take several months. By that time you might as well look for me in the dried-fish shop.[7] Don't you have any better suggestion to make?"

"My mistress," the maid said, "is so chaste and proud that not even her elders dare to say anything improper in her presence, much less a mere servant like myself. However, she is skilled in composition and is often lost in sadness and admiration when she chants to herself her favorite verses. Why don't you try to provoke her with a love poem? I cannot think of anything better than this."

Chang was delighted and immediately composed two poems and gave them to the maid. That evening Hungniang returned and gave Chang a sheet of decorated paper, saying, "This is from my mistress." It bore the title "The Bright Moon of the Three Times Five Night," and the poem ran:

> I wait for the moon in the western chamber;
> I greet the wind with the door ajar.
> When against the wall the flower shadows stirred,
> I thought it was my lover coming.

Chang saw the significance of the message. It was then the evening of the fourth day after the first decade of the second month. East of the wall of Tsui's compound there was an apricot tree which he could climb and thereby get over the wall. On the night of the full moon Chang used the tree as a ladder and went over the wall. When he reached the western chamber the door was half open with Hungniang sleeping on the bed. He awakened her

[7] "For I shall be as dead and withered as the fish." A stock expression of great antiquity.

and she said, startled, "Why have you come here?" Chang replied, half truthfully: "Your mistress told me to come in her message. Go and tell her that I am here."

Presently Hungniang returned, saying, "She is coming! She is coming!" Happy and surprised, Chang told himself that success was surely at hand. But when Ying Ying came in, her dress was correct and her face serious and she began to berate Chang severely, saying, "By saving our lives you have done our family a great service. It was because of this that my beloved mother had entrusted to you her small son and her young daughter. How could you have sent me those improper poems through that unworthy maid? You acted nobly in protecting us from danger, but by taking advantage of your position to force your improper advances upon me you are only substituting one wrong for another. What difference is there between your conduct and that of the mutineering soldiery?

"I want very much to say nothing about your poems, but it does not seem right to connive at evil; I have thought of telling my mother about it but it does not seem right to treat a person one is obligated to in this manner. I have also thought of conveying my view of the matter through my maid, but I was afraid that she would not adequately represent me. Because none of these steps seemed satisfactory, I considered writing you a short letter to tell you what I felt, but I was afraid that you might not understand. Therefore I resorted to those trite and suggestive lines to make sure that you would come. It was not without a sense of shame that I took this step, but I was confident that we would be able to hold ourselves within the bounds of propriety and restrain ourselves from any wrong."

With these words she vanished. For a long while Chang stood abstractedly as if lost; then he climbed over the wall and went to his own room quite resigned to the hopelessness of his suit.

A few nights later, Chang was suddenly awakened out of his sleep by someone, and when he started and sat up, he found that it was Hungniang who had come with bedclothes under her arm and a pillow in her hand. "She is here! She is here!" she said, patting him gently. "Why sleep at a time like this?" Then she left him, after having put the pillow next to his and laid the bedclothes on top of his own. Chang rubbed his eyes and for a long while thought that he must be dreaming as he sat upright in wakeful waiting.

Presently Hungniang came back with her mistress leaning on her arm. Ying Ying was meek and coy, and so languid that she appeared as though she could not support her limbs. She had lost the severe and correct demeanor that she showed on their previous meeting.

That night was the eighth of the second decade. The slanting moon was bright and crystalline and the bed was bathed in its light and shadows. Chang felt as light and ethereal as if he had been lifted into the upper air of the immortals, for it did not seem possible that his visitor had come from the world of man.

Soon the temple bell sounded and the sky began to dawn. Hungniang returned to hasten her mistress's departure. For a while Ying Ying clung to her lover and uttered many a sweet moan, but at last she rose and went away leaning on Hungniang's arm as before. She had not spoken a word the whole night long.

Chang rose with the first light of day and wondered to himself if he had not been dreaming. But when the day grew brighter he could see Ying Ying's rouge still on his arm, and her perfume still lingered in the bedclothes. And then there were her tears still glistening on the mattress.

For more than ten days afterwards he saw and heard nothing from her. He began to compose a poem called "Meeting a Fairy" [8] in thirty couplets. He had not yet finished it when Hungniang happened to come and so he gave it to her to take to Ying Ying.

After this Ying Ying again let him see her and for almost a month the two lovers were happy together in the western chamber previously mentioned, Chang creeping out at dawn and in at dusk.

Once Chang asked her what her mother thought of him, and she answered, "She suspects things, but since nothing can be

[8] This story is known also by this title.

undone, she is inclined to say nothing and to hope that our union will be formalized by marriage."[9]

Not long after this Chang had to go to Changan. When he told her his intention, Ying Ying was meek and did not reproach him, but her face was a touching sight to behold, so full of sadness and distress it was. On the night before he set forth on his westward journey, he was not able to see her.

A few months later he returned to Puchou and for several months he again spent much of his time with Ying Ying. The latter was skilled with brush and paper and in literary composition, but she never showed her work to him in spite of his frequent requests. Chang tried to draw her out with his own compositions but she did not show much interest in them.

The fact was that Ying Ying excelled in everything she touched though she acted as if she knew nothing about it. She was quick and keen in speech, but she had a disinclination for superficial conversation. She was devoted to Chang but said nothing to show it. She was frequently subject to spells of sadness and melancholy, but acted as though she was stranger to them, and as to outer manifestations of pleasure and anger, there were rarely any at all.

Sometimes she would play the harp when she was alone at night. Her music was full of overtones of sadness and showed great depth of feeling. Chang had often listened to her playing from his own side of the wall, but when he asked her to play for him she always refused.

These elusive ways made Chang love her all the more.

The time soon approached when Chang must attend the examinations and it again became necessary for him to set out for the west. The evening before his departure he felt unequal to the task of expressing his regret over the necessity of their separation; seated by Ying Ying's side, he could only sigh in profound sadness.

Ying Ying had, on her part, a premonition that this meeting would be their last. She appeared resigned to her fate and her voice

[9] The text is obscure here, and the context justifies both my own interpretation and Mr. Waley's, which reads: "I know she would not oppose my will. So why should we not get married at once?"

was gentle when she spoke to him thus: "If you should abandon me after you have corrupted me, I shall not dare to complain, for that has ever been the way with men. But should you care to see this affair through to a happy ending, your kindness would indeed be great and our oath of faithfulness till death will not be in vain. Whatever the issue may be, little will be altered by this separation. So why should we mourn because you have to go away? However, since you feel sad, I shall do what I can to comfort you. You have praised my harp-playing, but I was bashful and would not play for you. Now that you are going away, I shall do my best."

Thereupon she had her harp brought and began to play the prelude to "Rainbow Skirts and Feather Jackets" but before she had played more than a few notes she broke off into such a plaintive and sorrowful dirge that one hardly recognized the tune for what it was. All those [10] present began to choke with sobbing. Suddenly Ying Ying stopped, pushed away her harp, and went away weeping to her mother's room.

She did not come back that night, and early the next morning Chang set forth on his journey.

In the examinations the following year Chang had no success and so tarried in the capital for another attempt. He wrote a letter to Ying Ying explaining the necessity for his continued absence. Here is, roughly, Ying Ying's reply:

"I have read your letter and my heart is filled with both sorrow and joy at your deep love and solicitude. You sent with your letter a box of ornaments and five sticks of paste so that I may brighten my hair and moisten my lips. I am grateful for your kindness, but for whom am I to make myself beautiful now? I am afraid that these things will only remind me of you and increase my sorrow and regret.

"You say that you are staying at the capital so that you may prosecute your studies; this is the way of advancement and it is as

[10] The reader may well ask where do "they" come from. The answer is that the Chinese writer is apt to ignore such factual details when he embarks on rhetorical flights.

it should be. My only complaint is that this bids to make permanent what started out only as a temporary separation. But it is my fate; there is no use talking about it.

"Since last autumn I have lived in a daze as if I have lost I know not what. In the clamor of the daytime I have sometimes forced myself to laugh and talk, but when alone at night I have done nothing but weep. Even in my dreams I am subject to sobbing fits and the sorrows of parting. Sometimes I dreamed that you came to me as you used to and made me happy by your love and tenderness, but before the consummation of our secret meeting something always startled my dream soul and recalled it to the realities of life. On waking, though half my bed seemed to hold the warmth of your body still, how well did I know that you were far, far away!

"The old year has vanished since we parted; it seems only yesterday. Changan is a city of pleasure and many are the things that claim one's fancy. How fortunate I am that you have not yet forgotten one so sequestered and insignificant as I, but have, on the contrary, shown a continuing interest in her! Though an uncultivated person like myself is quite unworthy of your notice, I can at least offer you unswerving fidelity to our oath of love.

"As cousins, we met at the banquet. Then through a maid servant I was tempted to see you in private. A girl's heart is not always strong in its own virtue, and so when you 'tempted me with the strains of your harp,'[11] I did not have enough strength of character to 'throw the shuttle.'[12] As we shared mat and pillow, profound was our abiding faith; and I in my simple and unsophisticated mind believed I had found a support for the rest of my life. Little did I think that the meeting with my Prince would fail to result in solemn wedlock, and that I would only incur the shame of self-surrender without winning the privilege of openly waiting upon you with your cap and kerchief. This regret that will torture me to

[11] As Ssu-ma Hsiang-ju tempted Cho Wen-chün, second century B.C.

[12] As the neighbor's daughter did to Hsieh Kun (A.D. fourth century), in order to repel his advances.

the end of my life, I can only sigh over in secret but may speak of to no one.

"If in the capaciousness of your kind heart you should deign to fulfill the secret hopes of this infinitesmal speck of life, I shall live forever, come when death may.[13] But even if you should choose to be like a man of the world, who scorns the voice of the heart and discards things he considers of no consequence for the sake of what he considers to be of real moment, and decide to look upon a former love merely as an accomplice in sin and to regard the most solemn vows as something to be lightly broken—even then my love shall endure as the cinnabar endures the fire and I shall, though my bones be consumed and my form dissipated, follow the dust of your carriage with the wind and dew.

"This is all I have to say, in life as in death. As I write I am shaken with sobs and I cannot tell you all that is in my heart. Ten thousand times take care of yourself; take care of yourself ten thousand times!

"I send you a jade ring which I have had since I was a child. I want you to wear it at your girdle, for jade symbolizes firmness and constancy, while the ring represents a beginning without end. I send you, too, a skein of unraveled silk and a tea grinder of mottled bamboo. None of these things are of any value. My thought in sending them is to remind you to be as true as jade and to assure you that my love is without end like the ring. When you see the mottled specks on the bamboo, think of my tears; when you regard the tangled mass of unraveled silk, know that my sorrow is just as hopeless. I send them only as a means of communicating my heart and in token of my eternal love.

"My heart is near you but my body far away, and there is no sure date of our next meeting. Yet where the yearning is strong, the soul will seek its mate despite a thousand li.

"Ten thousand times take care of yourself! The spring wind is often treacherous, so fortify yourself against it with plentiful

[13] I hope this makes as much sense as the original ("The day of my death will be as the years of my life") and that it sounds no less tragic.

nourishment. Be discreet in all things and guard yourself well; do not worry yourself too much about your uncultivated handmaid."

Chang showed the letter to his friends and so the story became generally known among people of the time. Yang Chü-yuan, one of his more intimate friends, wrote a quatrain about it and I myself wrote thirty couplets[14] after having read Chang's "Meeting a Fairy."

All of Chang's friends who heard the story were deeply moved, but Chang himself had decided in the meantime to break with Ying Ying. Being an especially close friend of Chang's, I asked him why he did so and this was his answer: "I have observed that in treating a woman of extraordinary beauty Heaven generally ordains that she shall bring disaster either upon herself or upon those with whom she is associated. If this daughter of the Tsui family should meet a man of wealth and rank and bring him completely under her spell, she would be transforming herself into cloud or rain,[15] into scaly or horned dragons, and I know not what else. In ancient times, Hsin of the Yin dynasty and Yu of Chou dynasty ruled over kingdoms of ten thousand chariots and their might was great. Yet a woman brought them to ruin, dissipating their hosts and causing them to die violent deaths, so that to this day they are the laughing stock of the world. I know that my virtue is not strong enough to avert the calamities that Heaven has ordained for such unnatural creatures, and because of this I have suppressed my passion." At these words all those present at the time sighed deeply.

A year or so later Ying Ying married some one else, and Chang also took a wife. Happening once to pass Ying Ying's house, he sent word to her through her husband, requesting to see her as her cousin. Her husband conveyed to her Chang's request, but she would not come out. Chang was so disappointed and hurt that he

[14] Omitted from this translation.

[15] As the Goddess of Kao T'ang did. (See "The Kao T'ang Fu," in Waley, *The Temple and Other Poems,* p. 65 ff.) However, the force of this and the following allusion to the dragons is not clear. In the ancient poem the transformations of the goddess suggest an elusive quality rather than anything reprehensible.

showed it in his face. When Ying Ying learned about it, she secretly sent him a poem, which read:

> Since I have wasted and lost my beauty,
> I have tossed and turned, too lazy to leave my bed.
> I am not ashamed to face others in my faded state
> But I dare not face him who brought it about.

But she did not come out to see him.

A few days later, when Chang was on the point of departure, she sent him another poem to say final farewell.

> I shall not speak of your heartless abandonment,
> But let us each devote our love to our proper mate,
> And give the love that we bore for each other
> To the spouse that has been decreed for us by fate.

After that they never heard of one another again.

The people of the time who knew the story all gave credit to Chang for his readiness to rectify his mistakes. I have myself spoken of this affair on many occasions so that those who hear it will not commit the same mistake and those who have already fallen into erroneous ways will emulate Chang and cast off the spell under which they find themselves.

In the ninth month of the Cheng Yuan reign [16] I told this story to Li Kung-ch'ui on the occasion of his visit to my house on Chingan street. He was greatly impressed and wrote "The Song of Ying Ying" to commemorate the event. He gave the song this title because Ying Ying was the girl's child name.

[16] Year not given.

Hsieh Hsiaowo, or A Monkey in the Carriage

Li Kung-tso
c. 770-850

Hsiaowo's unmarried name was Hsieh. She was a native of Yuchang and the daughter of a merchant. She lost her mother at the age of eight and was married to Tuan Chucheng, a native of Liyang and a man of generous impulses with a wide circle of friends. Her father was a man of great wealth who was content to pass his life in the obscurity of trade and, with his son-in-law, used to load ships with goods and travel back and forth on the lakes and rivers.

When Hsiaowo was fourteen both her father and her husband were murdered by pirates and robbed of all their money and goods. The brothers of her husband and her own cousins, who were aboard the boat, were all drowned, together with more than a score of servants and other menials. Hsiaowo, too, suffered injuries in the chest and broke her legs but she was rescued from the water by a passing boat and was revived after a night passed in unconsciousness. After recovering, she went begging from place to place until she came to the Shangyuan district where she found refuge under the roof of Changwu, a nun in the Miao Kuo Temple.

Now, just after the calamity Hsiaowo's father came to her in a dream and said to her: "If you would know my murderer, think of *a monkey in a carriage, and the grass east of the gate.*" A few days afterwards her husband likewise appeared to her in a dream and said, "If you would know my murderer, think *of a man who walks across the wheat,* and *a husband for one day.*" Unable to make anything of these words, Hsiaowo wrote them on a piece of paper and sought a solution to the conundrums from all she met who were likely to know, but for several years she met with no success.

In the spring of the eighth year of Yuan Ho (811), having been relieved of my post in Kiangsi, I sailed down the Yangtze and sojourned a while in Chienyeh (Nanking). While there I used to visit the Wu Kuan Temple and became acquainted with a monk by the name of Chiwu, a man fond of learning and wont to cultivate the friendship of men of like inclinations. One day he said to me: "There is a widow by the name of Hsiaowo who has been coming here and every time she comes she shows me two conundrums of six characters each. I have not been able to make anything of them." I asked Chiwu to write down the words for me and then, leaning over the railing, I began to concentrate my thoughts on them and to trace the characters in the air with my fingers. Before long I saw the significance of those words and immediately sent a boy for Hsiaowo. When she came and sobbed out her story, I said to her, "If that is your story, I think I have the solution. The man who killed your husband must be a man by the name of Shen Chun. For if you omit the top and bottom strokes from the word for carriage (車) you would have the character *shen* (申). Moreover, monkey is the symbol for the hour of *shen* (申).[1] If you add the character for gate (門) under the grass radical (艹) and the character for east (東) inside the gate, you would have the character *lan* (蘭). The first conundrum, therefore, indicates a man by the name of Shen Lan as your father's murderer. To *walk through the wheat* is walk across the field (田), and that also indicates the character *shen,* which is the character for field with the vertical stroke prolonged at both ends (申). As to *husband for one day,* you will have the character *chun* (春) if you add the character for one (一) on top of the character for husband (夫) and place the character for day (日) underneath

[1] Under the old Chinese system the day is divided into twelve hours, from 11 A.M. to 1 P.M., etc., each hour being given a special name and associated with a symbolic animal.

it (一 + 夫 + 日 = 春). It is obvious, therefore, that Shen Lan killed your father and Shen Chun killed your husband."

Hsiaowo burst out crying as she thanked me. Then she wrote the names Shen Lan and Shen Chun inside the lining of her coat and made an oath she would not rest until she had sought out the two murderers and avenged the death of her father and her husband. Before she went away, weeping, she asked me for my name, my official title, and my native place.

After this Hsiaowo disguised herself as a man and hired herself out as a servant in the region between the lake and the Yangtse. More than a year later she worked her way thus to the Poyang region and there she came to a house where on the bamboo gate was a poster with the words "Serving man wanted." She went inside to answer the advertisement and upon inquiring the name of the master of the house found it to be Shen Lan. Though gnawed at heart by hatred, she played the part of a faithful servant. Soon she won her master's complete confidence and was entrusted with the money and goods that came in and went out. More than two years went by without any one's discovering her true sex.

During this time Hsiaowo had many opportunities to convince herself that Shen Lan was her father's murderer, for she was always coming upon jewels and other articles of value in his house that had belonged to her family. They reminded her of the grievous deaths of her father and her husband and caused her to shed many a tear when she knew no one was looking.

Shen Lan and Shen Chun were cousins. At this time Chun lived at Tushupu, north of the Yangtze, and was a frequent visitor at Lan's house. Sometimes they would be gone together for a month at a time and on their return never failed to bring back quantities of money and valuables. During these absences Lan always left Hsiaowo and his wife in charge of the house. He provided Hsiaowo generously at all times with wine and meat and clothes.

One day Chun came to see Lan with wine and some carps. Hsiaowo said to herself with a sigh, "Everything in the dream has come true just as Mr. Li interpreted it in his ingenuity and prescience. Heaven must have inspired him so that I may have my revenge." That evening Lan and Chun feasted their men and they all drank heavily. After the other pirates left, Chun, who was completely drunk by now, went into the room to slump into bed, while Lan fell asleep in the yard. Hsiaowo quietly locked Chun inside and then drew her sword and cut off Lan's head. When the neighbors arrived at the outcry that she raised they found Chun locked securely within and Lan lying dead without. The loot recovered amounted to tens of millions. Moreover, the accomplices of Lan and Chun, numbering more than a score, were all arrested and executed with Chun, for Hsiaowo had taken care to make a list of their names. The governor of Hsunchou at the time was impressed by her resolution and heroic deed, and as a result of his intercession Hsiaowo was absolved of any guilt in her killing of Shen Lan. This happened in the summer of the twelfth year of Yuan Ho (817).

After avenging the death of her father and her husband, she returned to her native village. There she was much sought after in marriage by the principal families of the district, but Hsiaowo vowed that she would not marry again. Subsequently she cut off her hair and donned sackcloth and became a novice under the abbess Chianglu of the Ox Head Mountain. She was firm in her faith and untiring in her prayers; she pounded rice when it rained and cut wood when there was frost, and never spared her muscles and strength. In the fourth month of the thirteenth year she took orders in the K'ai Yuan Temple at Ssuchou and used Hsiaowo as her clerical name, thus manifesting her loyalty to her origin.

In the summer of the same year, on my way back to Changan I passed by the banks of the Ssu and went to call on Ta Te the abbess of Shan Yeh Temple. There on either side of the abbess were more than a score of newly consecrated nuns who had come to be presented to her. They made an impressive sight with their freshly shaven heads and new religious robes. One of the nuns asked the abbess: "Is this official not Judge Li of Hungchou, the twenty-third of his family?" "Yes," answered the abbess, whereupon the nun turned to me and said, weeping, "It was through your kindness, Judge, that I was able to avenge the death of my father and my husband." As I did not recognize her I asked her what she meant, and she answered: "My name is Hsiaowo, once a begging woman. Don't you remember that you once told me that Shen Lan was the name of my father's murderer and that Shen Chun was the name of my husband's?" "I did not remember you at first," I said, "but I do now." Hsiaowo then told me, weeping, how she had written down the names and how she had after many vicissitudes finally succeeded in her vengeance. "I hope," she concluded, "the day will come when I shall be in a position to repay you for what you have done for me."

Ah, the justice of the gods is indeed unerring! It was with their assistance that I was able to divine the names of the two murderers; and it was again they who made it possible for Hsiaowo to have her revenge.

Hsiaowo was kindly in manner and gentle in speech. She was quick of wit and meticulous in propriety. After she joined the orders she never wore any silk on her person or seasoned her food with salt and spice. She devoted herself to prayer and meditation and never opened her lips except to expound the mysteries of Dhyana.

A few days after our meeting she went back to Ox Head Mountain. She later sailed the Huai and traveled through the southern provinces.[2] I have never seen her since.

A princely man [3] says of her: "She never wavered in her resolve and eventually avenged the death of her father and her husband—that is loyalty; she mixed herself with menials and yet never betrayed her sex—that is chastity. And loyalty and chastity are the maximum virtues that can be expected of women. A woman like Hsiaowo serves to warn those who harbor murder and evil

[2] The sentence may be interpreted, with equally good reasons, as applying to the narrator. This is but one of the many instances wherein the translator must also act as editor.

[3] *Chüntzu,* sometimes translated as "gentleman," which is unsatisfactory because of its snobbish connotations. It is a formula used by ancient chroniclers to introduce his own comments (or sometimes perhaps actual consensus).

in their hearts and to set an example for those who cherish chastity and filial piety."

Since I am familiar with all the circumstances of the case and had a part in unraveling the conundrum, I have written this story of Hsiaowo to commemorate her virtue. In doing so I am only following the principle of praising good deeds laid down by the author of *Spring and Autumn Annals*.[4]

[4] Confucius.

The Kunlun Slave

P'ei Hsing

FL. LATE 9TH CENTURY

In the Ta Li period (766-799) there lived a man by the name of Tsui. His father was a high official and was on intimate terms with Ipin, one of the most powerful ministers of the time. He himself was then an officer in the imperial guard. He was young and as handsome as jade; he was of an independent and scrupulous nature, quiet and meticulous in his ways, and elegant and refined in speech.

Once his father sent him to inquire after Ipin's illness, and the latter summoned him into his chamber after he had commanded one of his dancing maids to roll up the screen. Tsui bowed and conveyed his father's compliments, and Ipin, having taken a fancy to the young man, asked him to sit down and talk with him.

There were three dancing maids and they were all of surpassing beauty. One of them was peeling peaches and putting them in a gold bowl. After she had finished, she poured on sweet cream and served some to Ipin, whereupon the latter turned to a dancer in red and told her to give a bowl to Tsui. Tsui was shy before the girls and refused, whereupon Ipin told the girl in red to feed it to him with a spoon, and there was nothing for Tsui to do but swallow what was fed to him, much to the amusement of the dancer herself.

When Tsui took his leave, Ipin said to him, "You must come to see me when you have time; do not neglect an old man." He commanded the dancer in red to escort Tsui out. In the court, when Tsui looked back, the girl in red raised three fingers, turned her palm three times with all the fingers outstretched, and then said, pointing to a mirror hanging from her breast, "Remember!" And that was all she said.

After reporting to his father his interview with Ipin, Tsui returned to his own quarters in a daze. He spoke to no one and could hardly bring himself to eat. He kept on humming to himself a quatrain in which he compared the dancing girl in red to a fairy goddess on the Isle of Penglai. None of his attendants guessed the cause of his abstraction.

Finally a Kunlun slave [1] of the family by the name of Molo asked him, saying, "What is in your heart that you look so distressed? Why not confide it to your old slave?"

"What good would it do to confide it to you?" Tsui asked.

"I shall relieve your distress if you will but tell," Molo said. "Whatever you desire, however far away the object of your desire may be, I shall enable you to accomplish it."

Impressed by his promise, Tsui told him everything.

"That is a small matter," Molo said after hearing his story. "Why didn't you tell me earlier instead of distressing yourself about it?"

When Tsui told him of the puzzle that the girl in red had posed, Molo said, "That is easy to understand. Ipin has ten dancing girls, each housed in a separate compound. She raised three fingers to indicate that she lived in the third compound. By turning her hand three times with her fingers outstretched, she meant to suggest the number fifteen, in this case the fifteenth of the month. She confirmed it by pointing to the mirror hanging from her breast, for on the fifteenth the moon is round like a mirror. What she tried to tell you, young master, was that you should go to her when the moon is full."

Tsui was overjoyed and asked his slave how he might get to his love.

"Day after tomorrow is the fifteenth," Molo said with a smile. Please give me two bolts of black silk so that I can have a special costume made for you. The dancers' quarters are guarded by dogs from the famed kennels of Meng Hai of Tsaochou. They are as

[1] It is generally agreed that this term indicates an African slave. By itself Kunlun is the name of the mountain range on China's westernmost frontier.

keen as supernatural beings and as fierce as tigers, and will devour any one who dares to intrude. I am the only man that can handle them. I shall kill them tonight."

Tsui gave Molo meat and wine. That night at the third watch Molo went to Ipin's mansion and returned in the space of a meal, saying, "I have killed the dogs. That obstacle is now removed."

On the night of the fifteenth, at the third watch, Molo dressed his young master in the black costume and went with him to Ipin's house. There, with Tsui on his back, he jumped over one wall after another until he reached the third compound. The door to the dancer's chamber was left ajar, and from it shone a dim light from a lamp of gold. The dancer was sitting up as if expecting some one and from time to time she would heave a long sigh. Then she intoned a quatrain in which she regretted that she had not heard from her lover.

The guards were all asleep and all round there was no sound. Tsui lifted the screen and went inside. It was some time before the dancer recognized him but when she did, she jumped off the couch and took his hands, saying, "I knew that you are clever and would understand the language of my hand. But I did not know that you have such magical power as to enable you to come to me." Thereupon Tsui told her about Molo. "Where is he now?" she asked. "Just outside the screen," he answered. She summoned Molo and gave him wine in a gold cup.

Then she said to Tsui: "I came from a wealthy family in the north and have been forced into servitude by my present master. It is only because I have no way to end my life that I am still living. Though my face is bright with powder and rouge, yet my heart is black with sorrow and regret. Though I eat with chopsticks made of jade and burn rare incense in an incenser of gold, though my gowns are made of the finest silks and my jewels of priceless gems and pearls, I feel as unhappy as a fettered bird. Since your 'claws and fangs' is so mighty in magic power, will you not have him deliver me from my prison cage? If I can get my freedom, I shall brave death without regret. I shall be your handmaid and wait upon you with gladness. What do you think of it, my beloved one?"

Tsui was saddened by the appeal because he did not know what to say. Molo said, "Since you have resolved to leave this place, it will be a simple matter to get you away." He first carried away the dancer's boxes and bags in three trips and then said, "We must make haste as daylight is beginning to break." So saying, he carried Tsui under one arm and the dancer under the other and jumped over the walls and so out of Ipin's mansion without any of the guards knowing.

It was not until the following morning that the disappearance of the dancer became known in Ipin's household. At the same time the bodies of the dogs were discovered. Ipin was greatly alarmed by these discoveries. "Our walls," he said, "have always been closely guarded and the doors securely locked. It looks as if some one had flown in and left without a trace. It must have been some swordsman [2] who carried the dancer away. Let us raise no alarm so as not to antagonize him further."

For two years the dancer in red hid herself in Tsui's house. Then, when spring returned, she went out to Chuchiang to see the flower festival. There she was seen by one of Ipin's servants, who reported what he had seen to his master. Ipin summoned Tsui and questioned him. Not daring to conceal the truth any longer, the latter told Ipin all the circumstances.

"It was wicked of the dancer to have done what she did," Ipin said, "but after she has been in your service for more than a year I shall not insist on punishing her guilt. However, I must rid the land of the menace of such a man as your slave Molo." He despatched fifty heavily armed men with instructions to surround Tsui's house and capture Molo.

But armed with a dagger, Molo flew over the walls and flashed through the air like an eagle. So quick was he that though the

[2] *Hsieh-shih, hsieh-k'o* or *chien-hsieh.* He is like a knight-errant except that he does not champion any lady; he is something of a Robin Hood except that he works as a lone wolf. In some legends (as in "Yinniang" immediately following) he is endowed with supernatural powers. See T. K. Chuan, "Some Hsieh Shih Episodes," *T'ien Hsia Monthly,* May, 1939.

arrows of Ipin's men filled the air like rain, not a single one touched him. In a moment, he had disappeared, much to the astonishment of Tsui's household.

Afterwards Ipin regretted his action and for more than a year he surrounded himself with armed men at night to guard against Molo's revenge.

Molo was not seen again until about ten years later when one of Tsui's servants encountered him in Loyang where he was selling medicine in the market place. He did not look any older for all those intervening years.

Yinniang the Swordswoman

P'ei Hsing

FL. LATE 9TH CENTURY

Yinniang was the daughter of Nieh Feng, a general under the viceroy of Weipo during the Cheng Yuan period (785-804). When she was ten years old a mendicant nun saw her and took such a liking to her that she asked Feng to let her take the child for a disciple. Feng was angered by her impudence and rudely refused.

"I shall take her even though you keep her in an iron box," the nun said. That night Yinniang indeed vanished from Feng's house, and was nowhere to be found in spite of all efforts to discover her. Her parents grieved for her loss but they could do nothing except weep.

Five years later the nun brought Yinniang back. "She has completed her training," she said to Feng. "You can have her back." With that she disappeared.

The family was filled with joy and asked Yinniang what she had learned. "I have been doing nothing but read the sutras and recite magic formulas," she answered. Feng did not believe that this was all she had learned and begged her to tell him the truth.

"You will not believe me if I tell you," Yinniang said, but again Feng insisted and she told her story as follows:

"When the nun carried me away that night, I had no idea how far we traveled. The next morning I found myself in a large cave under an inaccessible cliff. There were no human inhabitants near by, only monkeys and other wild beasts. The mountain side was covered with pines and creepers. There were two young girls in the cave already, both about ten years old. They were clever and beautiful and had no need of food. They could jump about the sheer cliffs like monkeys or could fly from tree to tree without ever falling.

"The nun gave me a pill and also a sword, which she told me to carry with me always. It was about two feet long and so sharp that you could cut a hair by blowing it against the blade. From the two girls I learned to climb the rocks and trees and soon my body grew as light as the breeze. After a year I was able to kill monkeys and tigers and leopards with little effort; after three years I could throw my sword and strike down eagles and hawks without fail. The sword had gradually shrunk to about five inches, and it flashed through the air so fast that the birds never knew what had struck them.

"In the fourth year of my stay, the nun left the two girls in charge of the cave and took me to a strange city. There in the market place she pointed out a man to me and enumerated all his crimes. Then she gave me a small dagger and said to me, 'Go and strike off his head. Have no fear, for it is no more difficult a feat than bringing down a bird on the wing!' And so in broad daylight I struck down the man's head without any one's seeing me. I put the head in a bag and returned with the nun to our lodgings, where she sprinkled some medicine on the head and caused it to turn into water.

"The next year she told me about a certain great official who had harmed many innocent people and commanded me to go to him in his own room and bring back his head. I went with my dagger and crawled through the crack in the door into his room. I hid myself in the rafters and returned that evening with his head. The nun was angry, saying, 'Why has it taken you so long?' I answered, 'He was playing with a child and I did not have the heart to kill him until afterwards.' 'When you find yourself in a similar situation again,' the nun commanded, 'take the child away and then execute the man.' I apologized and promised to abide by her command.

"Then the nun said to me, 'I shall cut open the back part of your head and conceal your dagger in there.[1] You will suffer no harm and you can take out the dagger whenever you need it.' After she had done this, she said, 'You have now mastered your art, and may go home. Twenty years from now, we shall meet again.' And so she brought me back."

After hearing this account Feng became very much in fear of his daughter. She would disappear at night and return at dawn, and Feng did not venture to question her, nor did he much care now for his extraordinary daughter.

One day a young mirror grinder happened to pass by the house. When Yinniang saw him, she said, "This man will be my husband." She told her father of her wish and as he did not dare to oppose her, she and the young man were married accordingly. Her husband had no other accomplishment than his skill in polishing mirrors. Her father supplied them with food and clothing and assigned them a compound to live in.

After her father's death a few years later, she and her husband were retained by the viceroy of Weipo, who had heard something about her accomplishments. Thus for the next few years she and her husband were in the service of the powerful war lord.

During the Yuanho period (806-820) the viceroy of Weipo had a disagreement with Liu Chang-yi, the viceroy of Chenhsü, and sent Yinniang to assassinate him. Yinniang took leave of her master and she and her husband set out for Hsüchou, the capital of Chenhsü.

It happened that Liu was an excellent diviner and foresaw their coming. He sent one of his lieutenants to wait for them north of the city. Finally they appeared, one riding a black and the other a white donkey. Near the city gate a magpie fluttered and chattered before them and the husband drew his bow and shot at it, but missed. The wife then took the bow and brought down the bird with one pellet.

Liu's emissary now went up to them and told them that he had come to welcome them on orders of the viceroy of Chenhsü.

[1] Some conceal their magic swords in their viscera and spit them out when the occasion demands.

"His Excellency," Yinniang and her husband said, "must indeed be endowed with supernatural powers, else how could he know of our coming beforehand."

Liu received them with great courtesy and when they apologized for intending to kill him, he said, "You need have no feeling of guilt, for you were but trying to serve your master. However, I am, like your master, His Majesty's servant and merit your service just as much as he."

"It is our desire to serve Your Excellency," Yinniang said, "for we can see that Your Excellency is the wiser and more just man."

When Liu asked them what they needed, they said that two hundred cash a day would suffice. Liu granted their request.

Then the donkeys on which they had come suddenly disappeared. Liu tried in vain to have them found. Then one day he searched a cloth bag that the couple had and found in it two donkeys cut out of paper, one black and one white.

After about a month Yinniang said to Liu, "The viceroy of Weipo knows nothing of our change of allegiance. I should like to cut a strand of my hair, tie it with red silk and leave it beside his pillow to show that we shall never come back." To this Liu assented.

She returned at the fourth watch, saying, "I have left my message. Tonight he will send Ching-ching-erh to kill me and take Your Excellency's head. However, there is nothing to fear as I shall be able to take care of her." [2]

Being a man of courage, Liu showed no signs of fear. The latter half of that night Liu observed in the bright candle light two pennants, one red and one white, fluttering in the air around his bed and dodging each other as if they were two persons engaged in battle. After a long while one fell to the ground with a thud and turned out to be a woman with her head severed from her body. At the same instant Yinniang too became visible, and, saying "Ching-ching-erh has been disposed of," she dragged the body out

[2] The context furnishes no clue as to the sex of Ching-ching-erh or Kung-kung-erh (*infra*). I have made them feminine because of the diminutive suffix "erh," though it is by no means conclusive evidence.

into the yard and with some powder turned it into water, including even the hair.

"Tomorrow night," Yinniang said, "the Viceroy of Weipo will send Kung-kung-erh of the Wonderful Hands. Her magic is such that no one can estimate its power and her movement is so quick that not even the spirits can keep up with her. She can span the heavens or descend into the nether world; she can conceal her form and eradicate even her shadow. She surpasses by far my own skill. The only thing we can do is to protect Your Excellency's neck with a piece of Khotan jade concealed inside your collar and trust the rest to Your Excellency's luck. I shall change myself into a tiny gnat and conceal myself in Your Excellency's viscera and there wait for developments. This is the only thing we can do to guard against Kung-kung-erh; there is no escape from her."

Liu did so and at the third watch, just as he was gradually dozing off, something struck his neck with a hard metallic sound. Simultaneously Yinniang jumped out through his mouth and congratulated him, saying, "Your Excellency has no more to fear, for this person is like a proud pigeon hawk that will not strike again once she misses, but will fly far, far away to hide from the shame of her failure. At this moment she is already more than a thousand li from here."

When the jade was examined it was found that it had been marked by a dagger to the extent of half an inch.

From that time on Liu treated Yinniang and her husband with even greater courtesy and kindness.

In the eighth year of Yuanho (813 A.D.), Liu had to go to the capital to have an audience with the Emperor. Yinniang expressed reluctance to go with him, saying, "From now on I should like to go into the mountains in search of men who have achieved immortality. I shall be grateful to you if you will see to it that my husband does not suffer from want." Liu promised that he would. After that he lost trace of Yinniang.

Later, when Liu died, Yinniang came to the capital on her donkey and mourned at his bier. In the K'ai Ch'eng period (836-840) Liu's son Tsung was appointed governor of Lingchou and encountered Yinniang on the mountain trails of Szechwan. She looked much as she used to and was riding on a white donkey as before. She appeared to be glad to see Tsung. "You, sir," she said to him, "face imminent danger and should not be in these parts." Then she took out a pill and made Tsung swallow it, saying, "You must resign next year and return to Loyang if you want to avoid this impending disaster. The pill I gave you will only protect you for one year."

Tsung did not give much credence to her warning. He offered Yinniang a present of fine silk, but Yinniang refused it and went away after drinking heartily with Tsung.

At the end of a year Tsung did not resign and so died at his post at Lingchou. After that no one saw Yinniang again.

Predestined Marriage

Li Fu-yen

FL. LATE 9TH CENTURY

Wei Ku of Tuling was an orphan from childhood. When he grew up he desired an early marriage but for a long time had difficulty in finding a suitable match. In the second year of Cheng Kuan (628) he had occasion to visit Chingho and on his way put up at an inn south of Sungcheng. One of the guests at the inn said that he knew of a retired official by the name of Pan Fang who had a daughter of marriage age; he said that if Ku was interested he should go to the Lung Hsing Temple west of the inn and there discuss the matter with Pan's middleman.

As Ku was eager for marriage, he went to the temple early the next morning when the slanting moon was still bright in the sky. There on the temple steps he found an old man sitting against a cloth bag and examining a book in the moonlight. Ku went up to him and looked at the book but could not read the writing.

"What kind of book are you reading, venerable sir?" Ku asked. "I have studied industriously from my youth and am familiar with all kinds of scripts, including the Sanskrit writing of the Western countries, but I have never seen anything like the writing in your book."

"Of course you have never seen anything like it," the old man said, smiling, "for it is not a book to be found in this world."

"What kind of a book is it then?" Ku asked, and the old man answered, "It is a book of the nether world."

"How does it happen that you, a man of the other world, have appeared in this one?"

"It is because you are abroad too early in the morning that you have encountered me, not that I have no business to be seen in these parts," the old man retorted. "For since it is the duty of officers of the nether world to govern the destinies of men, how can they avoid visiting their domain? As a matter of fact, the highways belong half to men and half to ghosts; only most men are not aware of it."

"What are your special duties?"

"The marriage bonds of the universe."

Ku was delighted on hearing this and said, "I was orphaned from childhood and it has been my desire to marry early so that I can rear a large family. But for more than ten years I have searched in vain for a suitable match. I am to meet some one here this morning to discuss a marital bond with the daughter of Pan Fang. Would you tell me, venerable sir, what are my chances of success?"

"You will have no success," the old man answered. "Your future wife is now only three years old and will not become your wife until she is seventeen."

Then Ku asked him what was in his bag, and he answered, "It contains red cords with which I tie together the feet of couples destined for each other. Once their feet are tied with these cords, they will eventually become husband and wife, even though their families are hereditary enemies or are separated by the gulf of varying fortunes or of remote distances. Your foot has been tied to that of the girl I allude to; there is no use in your looking elsewhere."

"Where is this future wife of mine and what does her family do?"

"She is the daughter of the vegetable woman who lives north of your inn."

"Can I see her?"

"Her mother always takes her to the market," the old man answered. "If you come with me I shall point her out to you."

When day came, Pan's emissary failed to appear. The old man closed his book, took his bag and walked away, with Ku following. When they came to the market, there was a woman with a three-year-old girl in her arms. She was repulsive in appearance, having only one eye; the child too, was quite unprepossessing. Pointing to the girl, the old man said, "There is your future wife!"

"I shall have her killed before I will marry her," Ku said angrily.

"It will be futile for you to try," the old man said. "She is destined to become a titled woman through the merit of her son." With this the old man vanished.

Ku sharpened up a knife and gave it to his servant, saying, "You are a very capable servant. If you will kill that girl for me, I shall give you ten thousand cash."

The servant took the knife and went to the vegetable woman's stall the next day. There without warning he struck the girl with his knife and then fled in the confusion.

"Did you kill her?" Ku asked his servant when he came back.

"I aimed at her heart," the latter answered, "but I struck her just above the eye."

For fourteen years more Ku tried in vain to find a suitable match. Then by virtue of his late father's meritorious service he was appointed an assistant to Wang Tai, the governor of Hsiangchou, and was charged with the administration of justice. He performed his duty so well that Wang Tai gave his daughter to him in marriage. She was about sixteen or seventeen and very beautiful. Ku was well pleased with the match, but was puzzled by a curious circumstance. His wife always wore a small piece of filigree over her eye which she never took off even when she bathed herself.

When after a year or so Ku asked her about it, she answered thus with an air of sadness: "I am the governor's niece, not his daughter. My father was the magistrate of Sungcheng at the time of his death. I was then only an infant. My mother and brother also died shortly afterwards. My nurse took compassion on me and took care of me. She was able to eke out an existence by growing vegetables on a piece of land that my father left and selling them in the market. When I was three years old I was struck by a murderous maniac and was left with a knife scar which I have to this day. That is why I wear this piece of filigree. Seven or eight years ago I was found by my uncle and so it happened that he married me to you as his daughter."

"Is your nurse blind in one eye?" Ku asked.

"Yes," she answered, "how did you know?"

Thereupon Ku told her the whole story. The couple thereafter treated each other with even greater respect and consideration. Later she gave birth to a son, whom they named Kun. He rose to be governor of Yenmen and by virtue of his position his mother was given the title Lady of Taiyuan.

One can see from this story that it is impossible to change one's destiny.

When the magistrate of Sungcheng heard this strange story, he conferred on the inn where Wei Ku had stayed the name "Inn of the Predestined Marriage" and inscribed those words on its sign board.

Tu Tzu-chun

Li Fu-yen

FL. LATE 9TH CENTURY

During the Chou-Sui [1] period there lived a man by the name of Tu Tzu-chun. He was improvident in his youth and soon squandered his family inheritance. When he sought help from his friends and relatives, he was forsaken by them, so that winter found him tramping the streets of Changan with an empty stomach and only a tattered coat to protect him from the cold. At the end of the day he was still without food and did not know where to turn for help. He came to the west gate of the East Market and there as he shivered in the cold and sighed to himself over his cruel fate, an old man carrying a staff approached him and asked him what was the cause of his distress. Tzu-chun poured out his heart to him and expressed great indignation at the treatment of his friends and relatives.

"How much would you need," the old man asked him. "Forty or fifty thousand cash will free me from want," Tzu-chun answered. "That's hardly enough," the old man said. "Name another figure." Tzu-chun mentioned a hundred thousand and then a million, but each time the old man said that it was hardly enough and it was not until he named three million that the old man said that that might do. The old man now took out from under his sleeve a string of cash and gave it to him, saying, "This will suffice you for your needs tonight. I shall wait for you at the Persian's house on West Market tomorrow at noon. Be sure to be prompt."

When Tzu-chun went to the Persian's at the appointed hour,

[1] A.D. 558-618.

the old man gave him three million cash as he promised without even telling him his name. Now that he was rich again, his extravagant nature reasserted itself. "I shall never again be poor," he said to himself, and proceeded to acquire for himself fine horses and gorgeous clothes and to squander his substance in carousing with worthless companions in the gay quarters of Changan. He forgot entirely the necessity of industry and thrift.

In less than two years he had spent his entire wealth and gradually had to dispose of his fine possessions for things of meaner quality. He gave up his horse for a donkey and was then reduced to walking on foot. In short, he was again as poor as when the old man first found him. Again he wandered cold and hungry in the market place, but this time he had barely begun to utter a self-pitying sigh when the old man again appeared before him out of nowhere.

"How extraordinary that you should be like this again," the old man said to him, taking his hand. "I shall help you again. How much do you need now?" Tzu-chun was ashamed and did not answer, and became only more embarrassed when the old man pressed him to state his needs. Finally the old man enjoined him to go to the Persian's the following day at noon and when Tzu-chun did so, swallowing his pride the best he could, he received ten million cash from his benefactor.

As he took the money, Tzu-chun resolved to mend his ways and make prudent use of his wealth, so that beside him even Shih Ch'ung[2] would seem like a pauper, but the money had hardly passed into his hands when his heart began to feel its corruption. His profligate ways returned and in two years he was reduced to a poverty worse than he had ever experienced before.

Again he met the old man at the familiar spot, but Tzu-chun was so ashamed and embarrassed that he covered up his face and tried to walk away. The old man caught him by the flap of his coat and said to him, "It was because I did not give you enough that you are again reduced to this." He gave him thirty millions

[2] Second century A.D., famous for his love of display, and so hardly a person for a repentant man to emulate.

this time, saying, "If this will not cure you, then the cause of your poverty is too deep seated for any remedy."

"None of my friends and relatives," Tzu-chun said to himself, "has showed the slightest interest in me when I am destitute. This old man alone has come to my help, not once but three times. How can I thank him enough?" Then he said to the old man, "With what you have just given me I shall be able to restore myself to the society of my friends and give assistance to needy widows and orphans. I am most grateful to you, venerable sir, for your kindness and shall place myself at your disposal as soon as I have attended to my worldly affairs."

"That is what I have been hoping for," said the old man. "Meet me next year on the first day of the middle decade of the first month under the two locust trees before the temple of Laotze."

At this time there were a great many widows and orphans south of the Huai. Accordingly Tzu-chun repaired himself to Yangchou and there bought ten thousand acres of fertile land and built hundreds of cottages along the main roads. He summoned all the widows and orphans to him and established them in the cottages. Then he arranged marriages for his nieces and nephews and otherwise gave assistance to his kin and relations. He repaid his debts of gratitude tenfold and avenged all his grievances and wrongs.

After he had attended to all these affairs, he went to the appointed place on the appointed day, and there he found the old man whistling under the locust trees.

Together they went into the Hua Mountains and ascended the Cloud Terrace Peak. After they had penetrated into the mountains for about forty li they came to a fine mansion that was unlike the abode of ordinary men. It was enveloped by bright colored clouds, and over it hovered cranes that had soared up at their approach. In the central hall there was a cauldron over nine feet in height, with purple flames shooting from beneath it and casting a weird light on the walls. It was surrounded by nine attendant fairies and guarded by a black dragon in front and a white tiger in the back.

It was then toward the end of the day. The old man (now no

longer dressed in lay costume but in the hat and robe of a Taoist priest) gave Tzu-chun three white pills and a cup of wine and enjoined him to take them at once. This done, he laid down a tiger skin under the west wall and made Tzu-chun sit on it facing east. "Do not utter a single word no matter what you see," the old man cautioned him. "You will see gods and demons, *yakshas* [3] and wild beasts, and the tortures of hell, and you will see your dear ones subjected to their threats and tortures. But remember that nothing that you see is true and that nothing will hurt you, as long as you remain immovable and silent. Remember well what I say and be not afraid."

With these words the Taoist went away, and as Tzu-chun followed him with his eyes, he noticed in the court a huge jar filled with water.

No sooner had the Taoist gone than the cliffs and valleys began to echo with the hoofs of a myriad horses and the earth to shake with the shouting and tumult of their riders. Then a man who styled himself the General came into the hall with a guard of several hundred men. Both he and his horse were covered with armors of gold, while all his men carried swords and bows and arrows.

"Who are you that you presume not to hide away from me, the General?" he shouted. His guards, too, came forward, brandishing their swords, and demanded to know his name and what he was doing there, but Tzu-chun would not answer. His interrogators became very angry, and the clanging of their swords and the twanging of their bow strings became like thunder. Still Tzu-chun refused to answer. The General then went away in a fury, followed by his men.

Presently the hall was invaded by waves of ferocious tigers and foul-smelling dragons, and vipers and scorpions. They roared round him and crawled over him and made as if they were about to devour him, but Tzu-chun held his peace and stirred not a muscle. After a while, they, too, went away.

Then a storm broke loose in the sky and thunder and lightning

[3] Demon of Hindoo mythology, Sinicized *yeh-ch'a.*

filled the air. Fireballs rolled to his right and left and lightning bolts crashed in front and behind him, so that he could not open his eyes. In another moment the water was over ten feet high in the court while the mountains and valleys rumbled with torrential floods. Soon the water had reached where Tzu-chun was sitting. But still he sat upright and gave no heed to what was happening.

Then the man who styled himself the General returned with a number of Oxheads [4] and other demons of strange aspects. They placed before him a huge cauldron filled with boiling oil, saying, "If you tell us your name, we shall let you go. If not, we shall fry you in the oil." Again Tzu-chun refused to answer.

Next his tormentors dragged in his wife and threatened to torture her, but still Tzu-chun did not answer. Thereupon they whipped her until she was covered with blood, and then subjected her to shooting and hacking, boiling and burning, and all kinds of unbearable torture.

"Homely and crude though I am," his wife cried to him, "Yet for more than ten years I have waited upon you with hat and comb. Now even as I am suffering unbearable pain in the hands of these honorable deities, I do not presume to hope that you would go on your knees and beg mercy for me. All you need to do to save me is to utter but one word. How can you be so cruel as to deny me even this?" Her tears came down like rain and she howled and cursed, but Tzu-chun did not once look at her.

"Do you think that I would not go so far as to kill your wife?" the General shouted to him, and then began to cut her up inch by inch from her feet upwards. His wife cried more piteously than ever, but to the end Tzu-chun maintained his peace.

"This rascal has already perfected his black magic," the General said. "We must not allow him to live in this world any longer." So saying, he commanded his attendants to cut off his head. This was done and Tzu-chun's ghost was taken to the court of King Yenlo. There he was sentenced to the torture chambers of hell: molten bronze was first poured down his throat and then he was

[4] Oxheads and Horsefaces, tormentors of hell.

beaten with an iron rod, ground through a mill, pounded in a mortar with a pestle, and then subjected to the fiery pit and boiling liquid, and made to walk through mountains of knives and forests of swords. There was, in short, no torture of hell that he did not go through.

However, he remembered the Taoist's admonition and went thorugh all without even a groan. After the tortures of hell had been exhausted, he was again taken before Yenlo, who said thus: "This man is too wicked to be reborn a man; he shall be born a woman."

Accordingly he was born as the daughter of Wang Chuan, an assistant magistrate of Shanfu. She was sickly as a child and hardly a day went by without her having to take medicine of all sorts or suffer the pain of cauterization. Once she fell off the bed and another time she fell into a fire, but through all these trials she never uttered a single sound.

She was extraordinarily beautiful when she grew up but was looked upon as a deaf-mute because she never said a word, no matter what the provocation. A graduate of the district heard about her beauty and sought to marry her. When her family told him that she was dumb, Lu said, "What does she need of speech so long as she is a good wife? She will set a good example for wives with long, wagging tongues." Her family, therefore, betrothed her to Lu and in due time the marriage ceremony took place.

For several years husband and wife lived in happiness. She gave birth to a son, who was now two years old and a very clever and adorable child. Lu, with the child in his arms, tried to make her talk by all kinds of devices, but in vain. Finally he grew very angry and said to her thus: "Once upon a time the wife of Chia refused to smile because she held her husband in contempt for his lack of breeding. But even she yielded when her husband showed his skill in shooting down a pheasant. Now I am not as crude as Chia, while my skill in literary composition is of a higher order than archery. Yet you would not speak to me. What use does a man have for his son as long as he is scorned by his wife?"

With these words he seized their child by its feet and dashed its head against a rock. The child's head broke under the impact and spattered blood to a distance of several paces.

Tzu-chun's heart was so overwhelmed by love that he forgot the Taoist's injunction and cried, "Oh! Oh!" The words had hardly been uttered when Tzu-chun found himself sitting as before in the hall under Cloud Terrace Peak with the Taoist standing beside him. The night was then in the fifth watch. The purple flames shot up and set the hall on fire.

"You have betrayed my trust!" the Taoist said with a sigh. He seized Tsu-chun by his hair and ducked him in the jar of water in the courtyard, for his clothes had caught fire. "You have, my friend," he said to Tzu-chun, "suppressed such human affections as joy and anger, sorrow and fear, and evil desire, but you have not been able to conquer love. If you had not cried 'Oh! Oh!' my magic elixir would have become complete and you would have been enabled to become immortal. Ah, how difficult it is to find a perfect collaborator in the quest for immortality. I can try again, but I cannot make use of you because you are, by failing to suppress love, still of this world."

He wished Tzu-chun luck and sent him on his way out of the mountains. Before he went, Tzu-chun ascended a height and looked down into the cauldron. It was cracked and in the center there was an iron rod the size of a man's arm, which the Taoist proceeded to cut up with a knife.

Tzu-chun was greatly distressed by his failure to assist his benefactor. After a while he decided to seek out the Taoist and offer his services again, but when he made his way to Cloud Terrace Peak, he found no trace of the Taoist and had to go away sighing with regret.

The Jade Kuanyin

Anonymous

12TH-13TH CENTURIES

I

Do you wonder why I, the story teller, have recited to you so many poems[1] about the passing of spring?

Now in the Shao Hsing period (1131-1162) there lived in the capital[2] a certain Prince of Hsienan, a native of Yenanfu, Yenchou province. One day becoming conscious of the passing of spring he took his family out to enjoy the delights of the season. That afternoon, as he passed by the Carriage Bridge inside the Chientang Gate on his way home, he heard some one in a picture-mounter's shop say to his daughter, "Come, my child, and look at the Prince!" The Prince saw the girl and said to one of his orderlies: "I have been wanting to engage a girl like the one there. Now see that the girl is brought to the palace tomorrow." The orderly obeyed and set out to find the girl.

What sort of person was it that the Prince saw?

> Just as the dust behind the carriage will settle down,
> So will hearts destined to unite eventually meet.

Under the Carriage Bridge the orderly saw a house with a sign on which was written: "The House of Chu, Mounters of Painting and Calligraphy." Inside the shop there was an old man with his daughter. And what was his daughter like? Listen:

[1] I have omitted eleven poems prefaced to the story.
[2] The capital of the southern Sung dynasty was at Hangchou.

Her hair was fashioned in a "cicada's wing,"
Her eyebrows like a mist over a mountain.
Her lips were like a red cherry,
Her white teeth like two rows of jade chips.
Her lily feet were curved like tiny bows,
Her voice was as clear as the oriole's.

Thus was the girl who had come to look at the Prince.

The orderly went to a tea house opposite and when the old woman in charge brought the tea he said to her, "Please go to the shop yonder and tell Master Chu that I would like to speak to him." She went and soon returned with the craftsman. "What do you have to command, captain?" the latter asked after the two had exchanged greetings. "Nothing in particular," the orderly answered. "I just want to have a chat with you. Is the girl who came out to watch the Prince pass by your daughter?" "That is right," answered the craftsman. "There are only three of us in the family." "What is the age of your daughter?" the orderly asked. "Eighteen," the craftsman answered. "May I ask whether you intend her to marry soon or to have her enter service?" asked the orderly. "We are poor," the craftsman answered, "and unable to provide a dowry. We shall have to give her in service." "What can the young lady do?" the orderly asked, and the father answered that she was a clever hand at embroidering.

"Just a while back the Prince saw from his sedan chair the embroidered vest that your daughter was wearing. It happens that we need an embroideress in the palace. Why don't you, venerable one, offer your daughter to the Prince?"

The craftsman went home and discussed the matter with his wife. The next day he had a petition drawn up and sent his daughter to the Prince. The latter paid him and gave the daughter the name of Hsiu Hsiu.

One day the Emperor bestowed on the Prince an embroidered warrior robe. Hsiu Hsiu was so clever with her needles that she made an exact copy of it. The Prince was greatly pleased, and said, "Since the Exalted One has given me this fine robe, what cunning object can I present to him?" He went to the storehouse and picked out a fine piece of translucent mutton-fat jade and then summoning the jade carvers attached to the palace he said to them: "What can this piece of jade be made into?" "It will make a fine set of wine cups," said one. "It would be too bad to use such an excellent bit of jade for wine cups," said the Prince. "It will make a fine *mohoulo* [3] since it is pointed at the top and round at the bottom," said another. "A *mohoulo* is only suitable for the Seven Seven festival," [4] the Prince said. "It is of no use for ordinary days."

Now among the jade carvers there was a young man about twenty-five years old by the name of Tsui Ning. He was a native of Chienkang, Shengchou province, and had been in the service of the Prince for several years. He stepped forward and said, "May it please Your Highness, the jade can be best made into a Kuanyin of the South Sea."

"That's exactly what I am thinking," said the Prince, and commanded Tsui Ning to proceed with the task.

In about two months' time the jade Kuanyin was completed and was presented to the Emperor. The Dragon Countenance was greatly pleased and Tsui Ning was rewarded handsomely.

The days went by and soon spring returned. Tsui Ning and a few of his friends were in a wine shop near the Chientang Gate after a spring outing. After a few cups they suddenly heard a commotion on the street, and on looking out of the balcony window they saw a throng talking excitedly about a fire in the direction of the Well Pavilion Bridge. They hurried out on the street themselves and this was what they saw:

At first it was like a firefly, then it was like lamp flames.
Soon it was brighter than a thousand candles and stronger
than ten thousand buckets could extinguish.

[3] A popular term for dolls of the Sung and Yuan times and frequently encountered in fiction and plays of the period. It is a transliteration of some Sanskrit word. As is evident from the text here, the doll is large at the bottom and tapers off at the top, so that it cannot be upset. This form of doll has survived to modern times and is known as *pu-tao-weng* or "old man who would not fall."

[4] Seventh of the seventh month, sometimes translated as All Souls Festival. Offerings to ghosts in general are made at this time so as to provide for homeless spirits that might otherwise go hungry.

It was as if the Liu Ting gods had emptied the Celestial furnaces and the Eight Mighty Ones had kindled the mountain-consuming fire.
Could it be that another King Yu had set off the beacon fires to make his consort laugh [5]
Or another Admiral Chou Yü had made a conflagration of the enemy fleet?

"It is not far from the palace," the craftsman cried and dashed off in the direction of the fire. When he arrived at the palace he found that it was lit up like day and quite deserted. Then as he walked along the verandah on the left side a woman came out from the inside and ran straight into him. It was no other than Hsiu Hsiu, the bondmaid. He stepped back and greeted her.

Now the Prince had one day promised Tsui Ning that he would give Hsiu Hsiu to him in marriage after she had served her time, and every one had remarked what a fine couple they would make. Tsui Ning was a bachelor and looked forward to the union; Hsiu Hsiu liked the young man and was filled with hopes.

And now on the day of the fire Hsiu Hsiu ran into Tsui Ning as she came out from the inside with gold and jewels tied in a kerchief, and she said to him, "Master Tsui, I have been slow in getting away. You will have to help me and take me to a place of safety."

Thereupon Tsui Ning and Hsiu Hsiu left the mansion and walked along the river till they came to the Rock Lime Bridge. "I can't go on any farther, Master Tsui," Hsiu Hsiu said. "My feet hurt." "It will take only a few more steps to reach my house over there," Tsui Ning said, pointing ahead. "Why don't you come in and rest a while?"

So they went to Tsui Ning's house and sat down. Then Hsiu Hsiu said, "I am hungry. Won't you go out and buy some refreshments for me, Master Tsui? I should like to have some wine to quiet me after the fright I have received."

[5] The same King Yu alluded to on p. 85. To make his consort laugh, he had the beacon fires (signal of invasion) lighted. She did laugh when his vassals rushed to the rescue, but later when the barbarians actually came, no one paid any attention to the beacon signals.

Tsui Ning got the wine and after two or three cups the wine began to work on them as the couplet says—

> After three cups of Bamboo Leaves pass through the lips,
> Two peach blossoms begin to mount the cheeks.

To say nothing of another couplet—

> Spring is the best tonic for flowers,
> Wine the matchmaker for men and women.

"Do you remember," Hsiu Hsiu said presently, "the night on the Moon Terrace when the Prince promised me to you in marriage? It was a moonlight night and you were so grateful to the Prince. Do you remember?" "Indeed I remember it," Tsui Ning answered. "Then," Hsiu Hsiu said, "why should we go on waiting? Why shouldn't we become man and wife tonight? What do you think?" "But I don't dare," Tsui Ning said. "If you won't do as I say," Hsiu Hsiu threatened, "I shall shout for help and ruin you. I shall go to the Prince tomorrow and say that you forced me to come to your house!" "I am perfectly willing," Tsui Ning said; "but there is one thing: we cannot continue to live in this city. We must take advantage of the present confusion and flee from here." "It is as you say, since you and I are going to be man and wife," Hsiu Hsiu said.

And so they became man and wife that night. After the fourth watch, they took what gold and silver and valuables they had and slipped out of the city, and they "ate when they were hungry and drank when they were athirst, and rested by night and traveled by day" as wayfarers do until they came to Chuchou.

"Where do we go from here?" Hsiu Hsiu said to Tsui Ning.

"Five main roads lead out from this town. I think we might go to Hsinchou, for I am a jade carver and have there several acquaintances among the trade who might be of use to me."

And so they went to Hsinchou. But after a few days Tsui Ning became uneasy. "This is not a very safe place," he said. "Here people come and go from all over the empire and some one we know might see us and tell the Prince, and the Prince is bound to send men to seize us. It is better that we leave Hsinchou and go elsewhere."

And so they set out again and headed for Tanchow, a far-off place. There they rented a house and put up a sign reading: "Master Tsui, Jade Carver from the Capital."

"It is over two thousand li here from the capital," Tsui Ning said to Hsiu Hsiu. "We ought to be safe. Let us put our minds at ease and be husband and wife always."

There were some retired officials at Tanchow and they all patronized Tsui Ning, seeing that he was a carver from the capital. Tsui Ning was thus seldom without occupation.

Tsui Ning sent some one to the capital to make inquiries and found that a bondmaid was found missing after the fire, that a reward had been posted for her but that the matter had been dropped after a few days when no trace of the bondmaid was found. They knew nothing about Tsui Ning and that he and Hsiu Hsiu were then living at Tanchow.

"Time passes like the flight of arrows and the sun and moon course through the sky like shuttles." More than a year soon passed. One day in the morning just after Tsui Ning had opened his shop front, two men dressed in the black costumes of official runners entered the shop and said to Tsui Ning: "We are runners from the Hsiangtan District. Our magistrate has heard of a Master Tsui, jade carver from the capital, and wishes to have some work done by him."

Thereupon Tsui Ning left his wife in charge of the shop and went to Hsiangtan with the runners. He was taken to the magistrate and given some pieces of jade to take home to work. On his journey home a carrier passed him on the road. Tsui Ning did not note who the man was, but the man saw Tsui Ning. He stared at him for a moment and then turned around and followed him.

> What naughty children have cast the stone
> That scattered the Mandarin ducks [6] hither and yon?

[6] Symbol of conjugal happiness.

II

Along the bamboos the morning glories climb,
Through the hedge-trees the moonlight peeps.
In the glass cups there is crude wine
And in the jade dish some salted beans.
  Regret not
  But be gay
For laughter is life's best pay;
Once you rode at the head of a hundred thousand men
While no one remembers who you are today.

This song was written to the tune of "Partridges across the Sky" by a certain General Liu of the Hsiungwu troops. After the battle of Shunchang he lived at Hsiangtan in very modest circumstances, for he was a general that cared nothing about money. He used to go to the country wine shops to drink, but no one remembered him and few paid him any respect. And so he composed this poem to express how he felt.

Now this poem was seen by certain important personages in the capital and they all felt sorry for the general. Among these were the Prince of Yangho and the Prince of Hsienan, Tsui Ning's erstwhile master, who both sent money and presents to General Liu. It was the messenger of the Prince of Hsienan that Tsui Ning passed on the Hsiangtan road. His name was Kuo Li, one of the Prince's bodyguards. He followed Tsui Ning to his house and surprised both Tsui Ning and Hsiu Hsiu, saying, "So you are here, Master Tsui! And Hsiu Hsiu here too!"

Tsui Ning and his wife were frightened to death and implored Kuo Li not to betray them. "Why should I betray you?" Kuo Li said. "The Prince knows nothing about you two and it is not for me to meddle in other people's affairs." Then he partook of the feast that Tsui Ning set out for him, thanked his hosts and went away.

After he had reported to the Prince he said, "Your Highness, I saw two persons at Tanchow that Your Highness would probably like to know about." "Who are they?" the Prince asked. "The bondmaid Hsiu Hsiu and Tsui Ning the jade carver," Kuo Li answered. "They invited me to a feast and begged me not to tell Your Highness about them."

Thereupon the Prince commanded the prefect of Linan to have Tsui Ning and Hsiu Hsiu arrested. The prefect obeyed and sent an official note to the prefect of Tanchow. In due time Tsui Ning and Hsiu Hsiu were returned to the Prince. Thereupon, the Prince went into his great hall to confront the fugitives. Now when the Prince was in the wars against the barbarians he carried in his right hand a sword called Great Blacky and in his left hand a sword called Little Blacky and many were the barbarians who had perished under those swords. The swords were now hanging on the wall. At the sight of Tsui Ning and Hsiu Hsiu the Prince became very angry. With his left hand he took Little Blacky down from the wall and with his right he unsheathed it. His eyes were opened wide as when he slaughtered the barbarians, and he gritted his teeth so that the grinding sound they made echoed in the great hall.

Luckily for Tsui Ning and Hsiu Hsiu, the Princess was at the moment standing behind the screen. "Your Highness," she said from behind the screen, "you mustn't kill them! For we are now living under the shadow of the Emperor's carriage, not on the frontier. The two should be sent to the prefect's yamen and punished according to law." "They deserve death for escaping together," the Prince said, "but since you intercede for them, let Hsiu Hsiu be taken to the garden in the back and Tsui Ning sent to the prefect's yamen."

At the trial Tsui Ning confessed the true circumstances, and when the Prince found that he had not been the instigator of their escape, he did not insist on the extreme punishment. Tsui Ning was sentenced to exile at Chienkangfu.

Tsui Ning and his guard had just gone out of the North Gate when they noticed a sedan chair following them. Then Tsui Ning heard the voice of Hsiu Hsiu calling to him, saying, "Master Tsui, wait a while for me!" He wondered what Hsiu Hsiu was up to but like "a bird that has had experience with the bow," he did not dare to get further involved and so went on without answering. But soon the sedan chair overtook him and out came Hsiu Hsiu, saying, "Master Tsui, what am I to do now that you are going to Chienkang?" "I don't know," Tsui Ning said. "Let me go with you," Hsiu Hsiu said. "The Prince had me given thirty strokes of bamboo and dismissed me from service." "In that case, you can come along with me," Tsui Ning said.

They hired a boat and soon reached Chienkang. The guard returned to the capital. Now if the guard had been a telltale, Tsui Ning and Hsiu Hsiu would have been in for more trouble, but he was a sensible man and decided to mind his own business, especially since he had no connection with the Prince's palace. Moreover, Tsui Ning had been very generous to him, providing him with food and wine all along the way, and he was inclined to say nothing of what he had seen.

To return to Tsui Ning. He had now nothing to fear as he had been tried and sentenced. As before, he opened a jade turner's shop. Then said his wife to him, "We are now happy together, but my parents have suffered many anxieties on account of us. Let us send for them and have them live with us." To this Tsui Ning said, "Excellent," and immediately sent a messenger to the capital to get his parents-in-law, giving him their address. Arriving at the capital, the messenger went to the street to which he had been directed and inquired of the neighbors for old Chu and his wife. He located their house but found the door locked from the outside. From the neighbors he learned that they had been in great distress when their daughter was captured and that they had not been seen since.

In the meantime, as Tsui Ning was sitting home one day he heard someone say outside, "This is where Master Tsui lives." He went out to see who it was and who should it be but Old Chu and his wife! "It took us a long time to find you here," they said. After that the four of them lived together at Chienkang.

Now one day the Emperor was looking over his curios in one of the palace rooms. He took up the jade Kuanyin that Tsui had made and noticed one of the bells broken off. "How can we have this repaired?" the Emperor asked. One of the attendants examined the Kuanyin and noticed the words "Made by Tsui Ning" carved at the bottom. "It is easy," the attendant said. "It is only necessary to summon the man who made this Kuanyin."

The Prince of Hsienan was commanded to produce Tsui Ning, and the latter was accordingly summoned to the capital. He was presented to the Emperor and given the Kuanyin to mend. He found a piece of jade of the exact color and texture as the Kuanyin and did such a clever job of repairing that no one who did not know would have noticed that it had been broken. Tsui Ning was handsomely rewarded and commanded to live in the capital.

"Since I have nothing to fear should any one run into me," Tsui Ning said, "I shall rent a house by the side of the Clear Lake River and open up another jade shop."

Coincidences would occur. Only two or three days after Tsui Ning opened his shop who should come in but Kuo Li! "So you are here, Master Tsui," he said. "Congratulations, Master Tsui," he said. But when he saw Hsiu Hsiu behind the counter, his countenance changed and he hastily withdrew. "Call that man back," Hsiu Hsiu said to her husband. "I want to ask him a few questions." Well says the couplet:

> If one does nothing to cause the arching of eyebrows,
> He will have no one to spit in his face.

Tsui Ning ran after Kuo Li and soon caught up with him.

"How strange, how strange!" Kuo Li was murmuring to himself. He went back to the shop with Tsui Ning and there Hsiu Hsiu said to him: "We have been good to you and invited you to drink wine with us, but you betrayed us to the Prince. We are now in the Emperor's favor and no longer afraid of what you might say." Kuo Li had nothing to say to this accusation; he made his apologies and went away.

He went back to the Palace and said to the Prince: "I have seen a ghost!" "What are you talking about?" said the Prince. "Please, Your Highness, I have seen a ghost," Kuo Li said. The Prince asked, "What ghost?" Kuo Li said, "I was walking along the Clear Lake River and passed by Tsui Ning's shop. I went inside and there behind the counter I saw the bondmaid Hsiu Hsiu." The Prince said impatiently, "What nonsense! Hsiu Hsiu was beaten to death and is buried in the garden. You saw it happen yourself. How could you have seen her? Are you trying to make fun of me?" Kuo Li answered, "How dare I jest with Your Highness? I did indeed see her, and she spoke to me. If Your Highness does not believe it I am ready to sign a 'martial order.'"[7] The Prince said, "Sign a martial order then and produce Hsiu Hsiu if you can."

The luckless Kuo Li signed the order and gave it to the Prince. The latter ordered a sedan chair to go with Kuo Li, saying, "Go and get the girl! If she is really where you say she is I shall put her to death with my sword; if you cannot produce her, I shall put you to death with the same sword."

Kuo Li was a foolish and impetuous man; he should have known that it was no light matter to sign a martial order.

He and the two sedan bearers went directly to Tsui Ning's shop and there said to Hsiu Hsiu, "I have the Prince's order to take you to him." Hsiu Hsiu said, "I shall come with you as soon as I get myself ready." She went inside, washed and changed her clothes, came out and got into the sedan chair. Soon they arrived at the palace and Kuo Li went inside first and reported to the Prince that he had brought Hsiu Hsiu. The Prince said, "Bring her in." Kuo Li went out to the sedan chair and said, "Hsiu Hsiu, the Prince wants you to come in." Receiving no answer he lifted the curtain and thereupon he felt as if a bucket of cold water had been poured on him, and his mouth dropped open. For there was no Hsiu Hsiu to be found in the sedan chair! He asked the sedan bearers but they said that they had not stirred from the place. Kuo Li rushed into the palace, shouting and mumbling excitedly, and said to the Prince, "May it please Your Highness, there is indeed a ghost!" The Prince said, "I have no patience with your jokes!"

[7] *Chün-ling-chuang,* a term frequently encountered in popular fiction. The failure to carry out the order means death.

Then to the attendant he said, "Seize this man. I have his order and shall put him to the sword."

Kuo Li was frightened and said, "I have told the truth as the sedan bearers will bear witness." The bearers were summoned and they said that they did see Hsiu Hsiu getting into the sedan chair but that she had then disappeared without a trace. Then Tsui Ning was summoned and he told the story over from beginning to end. The Prince said, "Let him go since he knows nothing about it." But he had Kuo Li given fifty strokes of the penal rod.

On his part Tsui Ning went home and confronted his parents-in-law with what he had just found out. The couple looked at one another and then walked out of the shop and *plop, plop* both jumped into the river one after the other. Tsui Ning summoned help but the bodies could not be found. The truth was that the old couple had committed suicide by drowning soon after they heard of their daughter's death and it was their ghosts that had been living with Tsui Ning.

After a fruitless search for the bodies, Tsui Ning went home and found Hsiu Hsiu sitting on the bed, Tsui Ning said, "Please, sister, spare my life!" Hsiu Hsiu said, "I died because of you, and my body was buried in the garden. I could not rest in peace because I wanted to take revenge on Kuo Li. Now that he has been punished and I am known for what I am, I can no longer stay here." After saying this she rose and laid her hands on Tsui Ning and then uttering a sharp cry she fell to the ground. When the neighbors arrived on the scene they found—

> Her pulse had sunken until it was quite still,
> And she herself well on the way to the Yellow Springs.

Tsui Ning, too, had been dragged away by her so that he could be her husband in the other world. Posterity summed up the incidents thus:

> The Prince of Hsienan could not suppress his fiery temper;
> Kuo Li could not hold his evil tongue.
> Hsiu Hsiu could not bear to leave her mate in life;
> Tsiu Ning could not shake off his wife in death.

The Judicial Murder of Tsui Ning

Anonymous

12TH-13TH CENTURIES

Cleverness and cunning are gifts of Heaven,
Ignorance and stupidity may be feigned.
Jealousy arises often from a narrow heart,
Disputes are set off by thoughtless jokes.
For the heart is more dangerous than the River with its nine bends
And there are evil faces that ten coats of mail cannot conceal.
Wine and women have often caused the downfall of states
But who has ever seen good men spoiled by books?

This poem tells about the difficulties that beset men. The road of life is a tortuous one and the heart of man is hard to fathom. The great Way has receded farther and farther from the world and the ways of men have become more and more multifarious. Every one bustles about for the sake of gain but in their ignorance they often reap nothing but calamities. One should ponder on these thoughts well if one wants to maintain one's life and protect one's family. It is because of this that the ancients used to say:

There is a season for frowning,
There is a season for laughing.
One must consider most carefully
Before frowning or laughing.

This time[1] I shall tell you about a man who brought death upon himself and several others and ruin to his family because

[1] *Hui,* the word by which the chapter of popular novels is designated, is actually a numerical classifier equivalent to the English word "time." It is a vestige of the oral origin of popular fiction.

of something he said in jest under the influence of wine. But first let me tell you another story as an introduction.

In the Yuan Feng period (1078-1085) of our dynasty there was a young graduate by the name of Wei Peng-chu, with the derived name Chung-hsiao. He was just eighteen years old and had a wife as pretty "as flower and jade." He had been married for barely a month when "the spring tests approached and the examination halls were thrown open,"[2] and Wei had to take leave of his wife, pack his baggage, and set off for the capital to attend the examinations. Said the wife to her husband: "Come back home as soon as you can, whether or not you pass your examinations. Do not leave me all alone."

"Have no fear," replied Wei. "I am going only because I have to think of my career."

Then he set off on his journey and soon reached the capital. There indeed he passed the examinations, the ninth place in the first group. He was appointed to a post in the capital which he assumed with a great deal of pomp and ceremony. Of course he wrote a letter to his wife and sent it by a trusted servant. Besides the usual inquiries after her health and the news of his success, he wrote also the following at the end of the letter: "Since I have no one to look after me in the capital, I have taken a concubine. I look forward to your coming soon, so that we can enjoy our good fortune together."

The servant took the letter and went directly to Wei's home. He congratulated his mistress and presented the letter. After tearing open the letter and reading what it had to say about this and that, she said to the servant: "What a faithless man your master is! Here he has just received his appointment, and yet he has already gotten himself a concubine!"

Whereupon the servant said: "It must be one of the master's jokes, for no such thing had happened when I left the capital. Please do not worry about it. Madame can see for herself when she arrives at the capital."

[2] A stock phrase which I have encountered more than a score of times in popular fiction.

"I'll give the matter no more thought, then, if that is the case," Madame Wei said, and, as she was not able to secure boats for the journey right away, she wrote a letter to her husband and sent it by some one who happened to be going to the capital. In the meantime she packed and got herself ready for the journey.

When the messenger reached the capital he inquired his way to Wei's house and delivered the letter. Needless to say, he was given food and wine for his trouble.

Now when Wei opened the letter and read it, he found only this: "As you have taken yourself a 'little wife,' I have also taken myself a 'little husband.' We shall set out for the capital together at the first opportunity." This did not disturb Wei at all, for he knew that his wife was only joking.

But it happened that before he had a chance to put the letter away, one of his fellow graduates came to call on him, and as he was one of his intimate friends and knew that Wei did not have his family with him, he went straight to his inner chamber. After a few minutes of conversation, Wei had to excuse himself and leave his friend alone in the room. While the latter was looking at the papers on Wei's desk, he came upon the wife's letter and was so amused by it that he began to read it aloud. Just then Wei came back into the room. He blushed and said, "It is a very stupid thing. She is only joking because I have joked with her." His fellow graduate guffawed and said, "It is hardly a matter to joke about." Then he went away.

Now this fellow was also young and "liked to talk and loved to gossip," and as a result what was said in the letter was soon all over the capital. What was worse was that some of the officials, jealous of Wei's youthful success, took the matter up and impeached Wei in a memorial to the throne, charging him with impropriety and branding him as unfit for the important post which he occupied. Wei was as a consequence demoted and banished to a provincial post. Regret was then useless. Wei's future was completely ruined and he never rose high in official position.

This is a case of a man who lost his opportunity for official advancement because of a joke. Now I shall tell you about another man who, because of a jest uttered under the influence of wine, threw away his own life and caused several people to lose theirs. How did this happen?

> The paths of this world are tortuous and sad
> And the jeering mouths of men open and shut without cause.
> The white clouds have no desire to darken the sky
> But the wild wind blows them hither without pause.

Now in the time of Kao Tsung, Hangchou, being the capital, was not inferior in wealth and glory to Kaifeng, the old capital. There lived at that time to the left of the Arrow Bridge a man by the name of Liu Kuei, with the derived name of Chun-chien. He came from an old and solid family but its fortunes had declined during his time. He studied for the examinations at first, but later on he found it impossible to continue his scholarly pursuits and had to change his profession and take up business. He was like a man who enters the priesthood after middle life. He knew nothing of business and as a consequence he lost his capital. He had to give up his large house for a small one and ended up by renting only a few rooms. He had a wife by the name of Wang-shih and a concubine whom he took because Wang-shih did not bear him any children. The latter's name was Chen, the daughter of Chen the pastry peddler, and she was called Erh Chieh.[3] He took her before he became quite destitute. The three of them lived together, without any one else in the family.

Liu Chun-chien was a very good-natured man and was beloved by his neighbors, who used to assure him that his poverty was due to his bad luck and not to any fault of his own and that better days would come when his luck turned. This was what his neighbors said, but his fortune did not grow any better and he lived at home depressed and helpless.

One day as he was sitting home doing nothing, his father-in-law's servant Lao Wang, about seventy years old, came to him and said: "It is the master's birthday and I have been commanded to come and escort the young mistress home for the occasion."

[3] "Sister Two," because she was the "second wife."

"How stupid of me to forget the Great Mountain's birthday," Liu said. He and his wife gathered together a few articles of clothing that they needed, tied them up in a bundle, and gave it to Lao Wang to carry. Liu instructed Erh Chieh to take care of the house, saying that they would not be able to come back that day, as it was getting late, but that they would surely be back the following evening, and then set out for his father-in-law's house, which was about twenty li from the city.

Arriving there, he greeted his father-in-law but did not have a chance to tell the latter about his troubles as there were many guests present. After the guests went away he was put up in the guest room for the night. It was not until the next morning that his father-in-law came to talk to him, saying: "Brother-in-law,[4] you can't go on like this. Remember the saying: 'He who does nothing will eat a mountain clean and the earth bare,' and the one to the effect that a man's gully is as bottomless as the sea and the days pass like the shuttle. You must look ahead. My daughter married you in the hope that you could provide her with food and clothing. Don't tell me that you want to go on like this!"

Liu sighed and said: "You are quite right, Great Mountain. But 'It is easier to go up the mountain and catch a tiger than to open your mouth to ask for help.' At a time like this there is nothing for me to do but sit and wait. To ask people for help is simply to court failure for one's pain. There are not many people who have my welfare at heart as you do, Great Mountain."

"I do not blame you for feeling the way you do," his father-in-law said. "However, I cannot stand by without doing something for you two. How would you like me to advance you some money for opening a provisions store?"

"That would be excellent," Liu said. "I shall always be grateful for your kindness."

After lunch, the father-in-law took out fifteen strings of cash and gave them to Liu, saying, "Take this money for outfitting the

[4] That is, "my son's brother-in-law." This is considered more polite because it elevates, so to speak, the person addressed one generation higher than he actually is in relation to the speaker.

store. I shall give you another ten *kuan* when you are ready to open up. As to your wife, I should like to keep her here for the present. On the day of the opening I shall take her to you myself and at the same time wish you luck. What do you think of it?"

Liu thanked his father-in-law again and again and went away carrying the money on his shoulder. It was getting late when he entered the city. As he passed by the house of an acquaintance who was also a tradesman he decided to call on him and seek his advice. So he knocked at the man's gate. The man came out and greeted him, and asked him what had brought him. When Liu told him about his plans, the man said: "I have nothing to do at present and shall be glad to come and help you whenever you need me." "That would be fine," Liu said.

And so they talked about business conditions over a few cups of wine. Liu's capacity for wine was not very large and he soon began to feel the effects of the liquor. He got up and took leave of his host, saying, "Thank you for your hospitality. Please come over to my house tomorrow and talk things over." The man escorted Liu to the head of the street and then went home.

Now if I, the story teller, and Liu "had been born in the same year and brought up side by side," and if I "could have put my arms around his waist and dragged him back by the hand,"[5] Liu would not have suffered the calamity that he did. But because I wasn't there to prevent him, Liu died a more grievous death than Li Ts'un-hsiao of the *Story of the Five Dynasties*[6] and P'eng Yueh of the *Book of Han*.

Now when Liu reached his house and knocked at the gate it was already lamplight time. As Erh Chieh was dozing under the lamp, after waiting for him all day, it was some time before she woke up and said, "I am coming," and then went and opened the gate. Liu went into the room and his concubine relieved him of the load of money and put it on the table, saying: "Where have you got this money from? What is it for?" Now Liu was

[5] A formula often introduced by story-tellers when their heroes are about to walk into disaster.

[6] Historical romance which rivaled the *Three Kingdoms* in popularity at this early period.

still under the influence of wine and then too he was annoyed because his concubine had been so slow in answering the gate. He thought he would try to scare her. So he said: "I am afraid you won't like it when I tell you, but you'll have to know sooner or later. I have mortgaged you to a merchant because I am in great need of money. I shall redeem you when things are better with me. That's why I have not mortgaged you for more. But if things should not get any better, I am afraid that I shall have to give you up entirely."

The concubine did not know whether to believe him or not, for she found it difficult not to believe it because of the money right in front of her and she found it difficult to believe that her husband would have the heart to dispose of her thus because both he and his wife had always been so kind to her. The only remark she could make was, "You should have told my parents about it."

Liu said, "Your parents would never have consented if I had told them. After you have gone to that man's house, I shall send some one to break the news to your parents. Perhaps they won't blame me under the circumstances."

The concubine again asked: "Where did you get your wine?" "I drank with the man to bind the contract," Liu answered. "Why hasn't Ta Chieh[7] come back with you?" the concubine asked. "Because she cannot bear to say goodby to you," Liu answered. "She will come back after you have left tomorrow. Please understand that I can't help it and that there is no backing out of it."

After saying this, Liu went to bed without undressing, hardly able to hide his amusement. He was soon sound asleep.

But the concubine could not fall asleep. "What sort of man has he sold me to?" she wondered to herself. "I must go to my parents' house and tell them about it. If he did sell me and the man comes for me tomorrow he can look for me at my parents'."

After thus turning the matter in her mind, she piled the money at his feet and taking advantage of his drunken sleep she gathered a few things together and slipped out of the house, pulling the door shut behind her. She went to the house of a neighbor by the

[7] Elder sister; that is, the first wife.

name of Chu San and asked Chu's wife to let her stay with them for the night, saying, "My husband has sold me for no good reason at all. I want to let my parents know about it. Please tell him to come to my parents' house if he wants me."

"That's the right thing to do," her neighbors said. "You can go on tomorrow and we shall let your husband know." The next day the concubine took leave of her host and went away.

> A fish that once frees itself from the hook
> Will swim away never to return.

Now to return to Liu Kuei. When he woke up at the third watch the lamp was still burning but there was no sight of his concubine. Thinking that she might be in the kitchen he called to her and asked her to bring him some tea. There was no answer and he fell asleep again after a half-hearted attempt to get up.

Now it happened that a bad man was out that night to steal, having lost at gambling that same day, and he came to Liu's house. He tried the door and it yielded readily as the concubine had only pulled it to after her. He tiptoed into Liu's room and soon discovered the pile of money by Liu's feet. He began to help himself to it but in doing so he woke up Liu, who got up and shouted: "You can't do that! I have borrowed the money in order to go into business to feed myself. What am I to do if you steal it from me?"

The robber did not answer but struck at Liu's face with his fist. The latter dodged and struck back. After battling thus for a while the robber, seeing that he could not get the better of Liu, retreated to the kitchen and there picked up an axe that happened to be handy and struck Liu in the face just as he was about to raise the alarm. As Liu fell, the robber struck him again and alas! Liu became as dead as can be and quite ready to receive the sacrificial offerings of his heirs.

"I had to make a thorough job of it once I began," the robber said, half to himself and half to the corpse before him. "I did not mean to kill you, really; it was you that forced me to it." So saying he turned back to Liu's room and took the rest of the money, wrapped it up securely and went off, pulling the door to after him.

The following morning when the neighbors found that Liu's door was still shut at a late hour, they shouted to him and receiving no answer, they went inside and there they found his body and his concubine gone. They raised the alarm.

Then Chu San, the neighbor at whose house Erh Chieh had stopped for the night, came forward and told the neighbors assembled that the concubine had stopped at his house and had gone early that morning to her parents' house. "We must send some one to find her and at the same time notify Liu's wife," he said, and his suggestion was carried out accordingly.

Now to return to the concubine. She had hardly gone a li or two after she left Chu San's house that morning when her feet began to hurt so that she could not go on but had to sit down by the road and rest herself. Presently a young man carrying a shoulder bag full of money appeared on the scene and stopped to look at her. She was not beautiful but her eyebrows were nicely arched and her teeth bright, and she was undeniably attractive.

> Wild flowers are especially pleasing to the eye
> And country wine goes more to the head.

The young man bowed to her and asked her where she was traveling alone by herself. She returned the bow and told him that she was going to her parents and had stopped to rest. "And where have you come from and where are you going?" she asked. The man, keeping a proper distance, answered: "I have just come from the city where I had gone to sell some silk and I am bound for Chuchiatang." "My parents do not live far from there," the concubine said. "May I go with you?" "Certainly," the man answered. "I shall be honored to escort you there."

The two went on together thus for about two or three li when they noticed two men running after them, running so fast that their feet hardly touched the ground, and they were sweating and panting and their coats were open at the front. They shouted, "Will the young lady please stop for a moment for we want to have a word with you?"

The concubine and the young man stopped and when the two pursuers caught up with them, each laid his hand on one, saying, "Come along with us, you two!"

The concubine was astonished. The men were her neighbors, one of them being Chu San who had given her shelter for the night. She said, "I told you last night where I was going. Why are you pursuing me?" Chu San said, "There has been a murder in your house; you have to come back with us." "I don't believe you," the concubine said. "I left my husband home last night safe and sound. I must go on to my parents. I cannot come with you." "It is not for you to say whether you'll come or not," Chu San said, and thereupon began to shout for help.

When the young man saw the gravity of the situation he said to Erh Chieh, "You had better go with them since things are as they say. I'll go on myself." "But you can't go," the two neighbors cried, "for since you are found in company with her you will have to explain yourself." "Why can't I?" the young man said. "I have only chanced to meet her on the road; it is not as if we had met by design. The road is a free thoroughfare."

But it was useless for Erh Chieh and the young man to explain themselves. By this time they were surrounded by spectators and they all said that the young man could not go away, especially since:

> He that has done nothing unlawful during the day
> Need have no fear of knocks at his door at night.

"If you don't come with us willingly," the two pursuers said, "it means that you have a guilty conscience and we shall have to force you."

There was nothing for the young man and Erh Chieh to do but go with the two neighbors. When the four of them arrived at Liu Kuei's house there was a curious crowd at the door. Erh Chieh went inside and there found Liu Kuei lying dead on the ground and the fifteen strings of money gone from the bed where she had left them. Her mouth dropped open and her tongue stuck out and thus she remained for a long time. The young man too was frightened, saying, "Oh luckless me! That I should be involved in such a calamity just because I walked a distance with the young lady!" The crowd talked excitedly among themselves.

Then Liu Kuei's wife and her father, old Mr. Wang, came running and stumbling on the scene and burst out crying at the sight of the body.

"Why have you killed your husband," Mr. Wang said to Erh Chieh, "and run away with the money? What have you to say for yourself now that by the justice of Heaven you have been caught?"

The concubine told them what had happened and that she knew nothing of her husband's death, but Liu Kuei's wife said, "It couldn't be! Why should he say that he got the fifteen *kuan* from selling you when my father had given it to him to start a business? It is evident that you have been unfaithful and have plotted the murder with your lover and run away with the money. Your stay at the neighbors' was only a ruse. There is no use denying it, for how can you explain that man found in your company?" Then turning to the young man she made a similar accusation.

"My name is Tsui Ning," the young man explained. "I had never seen the young lady before until I chanced to meet her on the road this morning. I asked her where she was going and we have traveled together only because we were going in the same direction. This is the truth; I know nothing of what happened before that."

But the crowd did not believe what he said. They searched his shoulder bag and found in it exactly fifteen *kuan* of cash. "'The net of Heaven catches everything though its mesh is wide,'" they cried. "You must have had a part in the murder. If you had made good your escape we would have had to answer for your crime."

Thereupon Liu Kuei's wife caught hold of Erh Chieh and Mr. Wang caught hold of Tsui Ning and they dragged the suspects to the prefect's yamen, with the neighbors following them for witnesses. When the prefect heard that a murder case had come up, he immediately entered the trial hall and summoned all the parties concerned and commanded them each to tell his story.

First old Mr. Wang told the circumstances of the case as he knew them and ended by appealing for justice against the culprits. The prefect then summoned the concubine and commanded her to confess. But Erh Chieh said, "Though I am only Liu Kuei's concubine, he has always been good to me and the mistress too has always been kind and considerate. So why should I want to do this terrible thing?" Then she went on and told exactly what happened after Liu Kuei's return the evening before.

The prefect was inclined to see things as the neighbors did and was eager to have the case closed, so he brushed aside the prisoners' protestations of innocence and had them mercilessly tortured until they confessed to the crime that they did not commit. The confession was duly signed, witnessed by the neighbors, and Erh Chieh and Tsui Ning were put into heavy cangues and shut up in the death prison. The documents of the case were presented to the throne through the usual channels, and in due course the concubine and Tsui Ning were both sentenced to death, the first by quartering and the second by decapitation. The sentences were duly carried out. Even if the two had had mouths all over their bodies they could not have explained away the evidence against them.

> He who is dumb cannot tell of his distress
> Though the gentian root tastes bitter in his mouth.

Now reflect on the circumstances of the case, reader. If Erh Chieh and the young man Tsui Ning had been really guilty of the murder, would they not have fled the scene during the night? Why should the concubine have gone to the neighbors to stay for the night and thus allow herself to be caught the next morning? If the trial official had thought about the matter carefully he would have seen the falsity of the accusation. But, in his eagerness to close the case, he did not think at all. What confession can you not force if you rely on torture alone? But one's deeds are marked in the book of another judge and one is bound to be punished in due time, punished oneself if the judgment is swift or punished through one's descendants if it is slow. The ghosts of these two who have been unjustly put to death will not rest until they have been revenged, of that you may be sure. For this reason alone—to say nothing of the fact that the dead cannot be called back to life and that which has been broken cannot be mended—those in official positions should not try cases carelessly and resort to torture but should try to establish justice by every means possible.

But to return to our story. After the trial, Liu Kuei's wife returned home, and set up a spirit tablet to her husband to observe the period of mourning. When her father suggested that she remarry, she said, "I must at least observe one year of mourning if not the required three." At the end of the year her father sent his old servant Lao Wang to fetch her, saying, "Tell the young mistress to get her things together and come back here. She can remarry now after her year of mourning." As there wasn't much else for her to do, Liu Kuei's wife decided to follow her father's suggestion. She tied her things up in a bundle and gave it to Lao Wang to carry. Then saying goodby to the neighbors, she set out for her father's house. On the way she was caught in the rain and went into the wood to seek shelter, and thereby she

> Drew nearer to death step by step,
> Like sheep and hogs that wander into a butcher's house.

In the wood they suddenly heard a voice shouting: "I am the King Pacifier of the Mountains. Halt, wayfarers, and pay me toll for the use of the road!" Then a man wielding a huge sword jumped out from behind the trees.

Well, Lao Wang's time must have been up, for instead of handing over what he was carrying to the robber, he rushed at him shouting defiance. The robber dodged and Lao Wang fell to the ground by the force of his own headlong rush. "How dare you defy me, little calf," the robber cried with anger, and brought down his sword on the prostrate figure. Blood squirted out and Lao Wang lived no more.

Realizing that it would be useless to try to run away from the robber, Liu Kuei's wife decided to resort to a ruse. She clapped her hands and said, "Well done, well done!" The man stared at her and said, "Who are you?" She answered, "I am an unfortunate woman who has recently lost her husband and was mated to this old man by a deceitful matchmaker. He was no good at all except to eat and eat. You have relieved me of a burden with your sword."

Pleased with her words and seeing that she was not bad looking, the robber said, "Would you be the mistress of my mountain domain?" Since there wasn't much else she could do, she said, "I shall most willingly serve you, great king."

On hearing this the man's anger changed to joy; he threw Lao Wang's body into a swamp, picked up his sword and led Liu Kuei's wife to an isolated house. He picked up a clump of earth and threw it on the roof, whereupon a man opened the door. Inside the robber ordered a sheep killed and wine brought and performed the wedding ceremony with Liu Kuei's wife.

> One knows well that it is not a proper match,
> But it is better than to lose one's life.

After the robber took Liu Kuei's wife, he made several good hauls in succession and became quite rich after about half a year's time. Being a sensible woman, she tried to persuade him to mend his ways. Thus she used to exhort him day and night: "It is said that the water jug will, sooner or later, break over the well platform and that a soldier will die on the battle ground. Just so you will come to a bad end if you keep on doing things against the laws of Heaven. Since we have now accumulated more than enough for the rest of our lives, why don't you give up your present profession and take up some kind of lawful business?"

Finally the robber gave way to her exhortations. He rented a house in the city and opened up a general store. When he could spare the time he would go to the temples to make offerings to atone for his crimes.

One day he said to Liu Kuei's wife: "Though I was a highwayman once, I know well the maxim that each act of injustice must be atoned for, just as a debt must be paid. In my career of evil in the past I have done nothing worse than thieving and robbing except in two cases. In each case I was responsible for killing a man and in one of them I was indirectly responsible for two other lives. These lives have weighed on my mind and I shall not be able to rest in peace until I have hired some priests to pray for their souls."

"How were you responsible for destroying two lives?" Liu Kuei's wife asked.

"One is, as you know, your husband, whom I killed in the forest when he rushed at me. He was an old man and had done nothing against me. His soul must be crying for revenge, especially since I have taken his wife."

"What is done cannot be undone," Liu Kuei's wife said. "Moreover, if you had not killed him we would not have become man and wife. Let us say no more about that. But who was the other man that you killed?"

"It was even a greater crime," the robber said, "for it caused two innocent persons to be put to death." Then he went on and told her about the murder of Liu Kuei, for he was in fact the man who stole into Liu Kuei's house on that fatal night and murdered him in order to make his escape. "These are the worst crimes in my life as a highwayman," he concluded. "I must do something for their souls."

"So this is the man who killed my husband and caused the unjust deaths of Erh Chieh and that young man," Liu Kuei's wife wailed to herself. "Since I was partly responsible for their deaths by my false testimony, their spirits must also hold me responsible." However, she said nothing of her thoughts to the robber but watched her opportunity. When it came she went to the prefect's yamen and shouted for justice.

There was then a new prefect for Linanfu, who had been in his post only half a month. Liu Kuei's wife was brought to him in the trial hall and there weeping and wailing she told her story. The robber was seized and under the prodding of instruments of torture, confessed everything. He was sentenced to death and the case was sent up to the throne for review. An edict was issued after the usual period of sixty days ordering the immediate execution of the robber. The original trial official was demoted for miscarriage of justice, and the authorities were charged to seek out the nearest kin of the concubine and Tsui Ning and to compensate them for the injustice done. Since Liu Kuei's wife had married the robber under duress and since she was instrumental in avenging her husband's death, she was given half of the robber's property, the other half being confiscated.

After watching the execution, Liu Kuei's wife took the robber's head and made offerings at the tomb of her husband and those of the concubine and Tsui Ning. She gave her share of the robber's estate to the temples and devoted the rest of her long life to praying for the dead.

Good and evil both end up in the grave
But a jest may bring about untimely death.
So pray remember always to tell the truth
For the tongue is ever at the bottom of calamity.

The Flower Lover and the Fairies

Anonymous

C. 14TH CENTURY

All night long the wind and rain beat upon the faggot gate,
Scattering the red petals and leaving only the willow leaves.
I hesitated as I set out to sweep the steps with my broom,
For all around me I found sad traces of broken blossoms.

This poem was written to promote love for flowers.

In the time of the Tang Dynasty there lived a man by the name of Tsui Hsüan-wei, who, being an aspirant to the Mystic way, remained unmarried and lived in retirement east of the river Lo. He built himself a little house in the midst of flowers and trees, which covered a wide expanse of ground protected by a wall of hedge, and lived in it alone. He provided quarters for his servants outside the garden and gave them instructions not to come in unless summoned. Thus he lived for over thirty years in his beloved retreat and seldom stepped outside its gate. In the spring when the flowers were in bloom he would wander among them morning and evening in solitary enjoyment.

One balmy and moonlight night as he was wandering among his flowers, he suddenly espied a maid in the moonlight. "Who could she be and how does she happen to be here at this hour of the night," Hsüan-wei said to himself in astonishment. The maid walked neither east nor west but came directly to Hsüan-wei and bowed herself low before him. "Who are you, young lady," Hsüan-wei said, returning the salutation, "and why have you come here at this late hour of the night?" The maid opened her vermillion lips and said, "I am a close neighbor of yours, sir. My mistress and her friends are on their way to Aunt Feng's house and they wonder if they could rest a while in your garden?"

Hsüan-wei was impressed by the way she had appeared from nowhere and readily gave his consent, whereupon the maid thanked him and went the same way she came. Presently she came back with a troop of girls, picking their way among the flowers and the willow trees. Every one of them was beautiful of feature and graceful of carriage, but they were dressed differently, some in dark and others in light colors. Hsüan-wei invited them to go into his house, and after they had seated themselves he asked them their names and who the aunt was that they were on their way to see. "I am Yang-shih," [1] said a girl in green, and pointing to a girl in white she said, "This is Li-shih," [2] and pointing to another in purple she said, "This is Tao-shih." [3] Thus she went on, introducing them all, and finally pointing to a girl in a deep red dress, she said, "This is Ah-tso, surnamed Shih.[4] Although we all have different surnames we are like sisters to one another. Our Aunt Feng [5] promised to come to see us but has not done so. Tonight, the moon being bright, we have decided to go to her and have stopped to pay our respects to you, sir, who have always been so kind to us."

Before Hsüan-wei could answer, one of the girls announced that Aunt Feng had come after all, and they all went out to meet her, while Hsüan-wei stepped aside and watched them at a discreet distance. "We were on our way to call on you, Aunt Eighteen," the girls said after saluting her, "but have been detained by our host here." "And where is your host?" Aunt Feng asked, whereupon Hsüan-wei stepped forward and was introduced. He noticed a certain air of aloofness about her and that her voice was cold and crisp, and as he drew nearer to her he felt a chill emanating from her that made his hair stand on end. Then they all entered the guest hall where attendants had already set the table with rare

[1] Willow.
[2] Plum.
[3] Chrysanthemum.
[4] Pomegranate.
[5] The Goddess of Wind.

fruits and delicacies and aromatic wine the like of which the mortal world had never seen. Aunt Feng was ushered to the seat of honor, the girls next sat down according to their age, with Hsüan-wei sitting at the lower end as host.

As the feast proceeded, the moon shone brighter and brighter until it was like day and the fragrance of flowers filled the entire room. After wine had been around a few times, the girl dressed in bright red poured out a large cup and presented it to Aunt Feng with a song in which she bemoaned the quick passage of flowering youth but said that she could only blame her own destiny and not the wind. She was followed by the girl in white with another offering of wine and a song on the same theme. Aunt Feng took offense at the songs. "Why should you two," she said, "sing such doleful songs in the midst of this joyful feast and on such a beauteous night as this? Moreover, I cannot fail to detect the ill-disguised personal affront to myself. This is no way to treat a guest. I propose, therefore, that each of you should drink a large goblet as a penalty and sing a song of a different tenor."

Whereupon she poured out two large goblets and passed them to the offending singers, but in doing so she upset one of the cups and caused it to spill on the bright red dress of Ah-tso, the youngest and proudest of the girls present. Now the accident would have been overlooked if the wine had been spilled on some one else, but Ah-tso, being young and beautiful and proud, and red being a color that spots most easily, said angrily, "My sisters may be afraid of you but I am not," [6] and so saying she rose abruptly and left the room. "How dare she speak so impudently to me?" Aunt Feng said, also rising angrily from the table. The other girls entreated her to stay, saying, "Ah-tso is young and ignorant. Pray forgive her and we shall bring her to Auntie tomorrow to offer her apologies." But their entreaties were in vain; Aunt Feng went off in a huff in an easterly direction, and the other girls, too, scattered and disappeared among the flowers. Hsüan-wei tried to follow them, but he slipped on the moss and fell, and when he re-

[6] Readers who know their flowers will recognize that this statement is not mere braggadocio on the part of Miss Pomegranate.

gained his feet they had vanished. "Could I have been dreaming?" he said to himself. "But then I have not been asleep. Could they be ghosts?" He wondered and marveled to himself on his extraordinary experience but was not afraid, as his visitors, be they human or supernatural, had appeared to be benign.

On the following evening the girls were already there among the flowers when Hsüan-wei went out for a stroll in his garden and they were trying to persuade Ah-tso to go to Aunt Feng to make her apologies. "But why should I go to that old woman," Ah-tso said angrily, "when we can ask our host here to help us." "You are right, sister," the others said, and then turning to Hsüan-wei they said, "We are all inhabitants of your garden and we have been the victims of unkind storms year after year. In the past we have sought protection from Auntie Eighteen, but since Ah-tso offended her last night we can no longer depend on her. If you, kind host, would give us your protection we shall try to repay you in some small way." "What can I do to help you?" Hsüan-wei asked. "All you have to do," Ah-tso answered, "is to prepare a red banner with the sun and moon and the Five Constellations painted on it and set it up to the east of the garden on the first of the year. That will protect us from all danger. But since the time has already passed this year, you can do so on the twenty-first of this month at the first sign of a breeze from the east." Hsüan-wei promised to carry out these instructions, whereupon the girls again vanished among the flowers.

Hsüan-wei had the banner made the very next day and on the twenty-first a wind began to blow briskly early in the morning. He immediately set the banner up to the east of the garden. Soon the wind waxed stronger and stronger until it caused the sand to fly and the rocks to roll and wrought destruction among the forests and gardens everywhere except in Hsüan-wei's garden, where not a single flower was disturbed. Then it came to him that the girls were no other than the spirits of the flowers, that the youngest of them was the spirit of the pomegranate, and that Aunt Feng was the Goddess of Wind.

That evening the flower fairies came to thank him. Each

brought him an armful of flower petals and told him that their gifts would stave off old age. Hsüan-wei ate the floral petals as directed and in time he became like a person of thirty years again. Eventually he became an immortal.[7]

Now, do not say, reader, that this story I have just told is incredible, for on the nine continents and the four seas there are all sorts of strange things that we have never seen or heard, things that are not recorded in the classics and histories, things of which even the *Book of Wonders* of Chang Hua contains only one or two parts and of which even Yü Shih-nan, the "walking library," knows but a very small part. Indeed, what I have told you is a matter of frequent occurrence, quite unworthy of your wonderment.

However, these are things that the Sage would not talk about,[8] so let us not press them. There should be no question, however, that one can bring blessings upon oneself by caring for the flowers and that one will shorten one's life by injuring them. If you are inclined to doubt this then listen to the story of "The Flower Lover and the Fairies" which I shall now tell to you. I hope that those who are already flower lovers will, after reading this story, love and care for them even more than heretofore, and that those who are not will heed my advice and begin to treat flowers with care. In any case I hope that this story, though it may fail to enable you to become immortals, will at least entertain you and dissipate your boredom.

In what dynasty and where did the events in this story take place? They happened during the reign of Jen Tsung (1023-1065) of the Great[9] Sung dynasty in a village known as Changlo,[10] about two li outside the east gate of Pingchiangfu in the region of

[7] This prologue is almost an exact paraphrase of a tale in the literary tradition included in the tenth-century anthology, *T'ai P'ing Kuang Chi*, Book 416.

[8] Confucius would not, among other things, talk about the supernatural. Hence a collection of ghost anecdotes by Yuan Mei (1716-1797) was entitled *Tzŭ Pu Yü* or *What the Master Would Not Talk About*.

[9] As the Chinese used to prefix the word "great" only to the dynasty under which they lived, some authorities take this as evidence that the story dates back to Sung times.

[10] "Long Happiness."

Kiangnan. There lived in the village an old man by the name of Chiu Hsien, who lived alone on a few ancestral acres, his wife having died a long time before without leaving him any children. He had been extremely fond of flowers from his youth and when he came into his modest inheritance, he gave up farming altogether and devoted his time to the cultivation of his garden. If he managed to obtain a rare specimen, he was happier than a man who had picked up a priceless treasure. If on a journey he encountered a garden in bloom, he would forget all about what he had set out to do and beg for permission to view the flowers. If the garden contained nothing remarkable or only flowers which were then in bloom in his own garden, he managed to drag himself away and return to his business, but should it contain flowers that he did not have or which had passed their season in his own garden, he would linger in it the whole day long, neglecting his own affairs entirely. For this reason people called him the "Flower Fool." If he met a flower seller with fine specimens, he always bought them even if he had no money and had to pawn his clothes in order to pay for them. Sometimes urchins in the region, knowing his weakness, would go out and cut sprigs of rare flowers, stick them in clumps of mud and pass them off as whole plants. The strange thing was that these sprigs never failed to take root after Chiu Hsien had planted them.

Thus Chiu Hsien gradually added to his garden until it became a very large one. It was surrounded by a wall woven of bamboos, covered with climbing roses and other flowering vines and backed up with hedgerows of all sorts of blossoming shrubs. Near the hedge he planted such common flowers as hollyhocks, balsams, cockscombs, and poppies, while farther away were cultivated rare specimens too numerous to mention. When the flowers were in bloom, the garden presented a sight as gorgeous as an embroidered screen; and he so planned it that there was always something in bloom whatever the season.

On the south side of the garden there was a gate in the fence, formed by two door leaves of woven faggots. Inside the gate a walk lined with bamboos led to a screen of cypress. Behind this was a thatched cottage, which was spacious and bright and airy though modest and covered only with grass. The front hall was simply furnished; there was a painting by an unknown artist on the wall, a wooden couch, a table, and a few stools. But everything was neat and clean and there was not a speck of dust on the ground. Back of the hall was his bedroom.

On rising in the morning Chiu Hsien would sweep up the fallen leaves and water the flowers one by one, which he did again in the evening. When he discovered a flower about to blossom forth, he would rejoice inordinately and, warming a pot of wine or making a pot of tea, would first pour a libation to the plant and then sit down to sip the wine or tea himself, gazing the while at the budding plant in admiration and enjoyment. Sometimes he would sing and whistle for joy or lie down to rest by the plant with his head pillowed upon a rock. He seldom left a flower unattended from the time it formed buds to the time it blossomed forth. If the sun should be strong, he would sprinkle the flowers with a palm brush, and on moonlight nights he seldom went to bed at all. In case of storm he would put on his rain coat made of rush and his broad brimmed hat and walk among the flowers to see whether there was a bent stem that needed propping. When a flower began to fade, he would grow melancholy and sigh all day long, sometimes even moved to tears. He would sweep up the fallen petals gently and put them on a plate and would cherish them and admire them until they withered; then he would put them in a jar and bury them with a touching offering of tea or wine. This he called "burying the flowers." If the petals should happen to be soiled with rain or mud, he would clean them with water and then scatter them in a near-by lake. This he called "bathing the flowers."

It used to provoke him more than anything else to see people cut and mutilate the flowers. "For," reasoned he, "a flower blossoms but once a year. Of the four seasons there is but one which it can call its own, and of this season there is but a period of a few days when it blossoms forth in all its glory, a brief period that comes only after three long seasons of cruel use by the unfriendly elements and of careless inattention by the general lot of men. As it dances in the wind and smiles at the appreciative faces, it is exactly like a man at the height of his fortune. What a pity it would be to destroy it and thus deny it these few days of happiness. How very hard it is for the flowers to come to these days and how easy is it to pluck them! If they could but speak would they not sigh and moan? Moreover, even without the cruel treatment of men, flowers in bloom are subject to the tickling of the butterflies and the scratching of the bees, the pecking of the birds and the boring of the worms, or the scorching of the sun and the beating of the wind, and the plaguing of the mist and the pounding of the rain. It is man's duty, rather, to protect them from these plagues; so how can we bear, on the contrary, to harm them ourselves?

Because of these views that he was wont to propound, he never in all his life broke off one single sprig or injured a single bud. He would linger all day around a favorite flower in other people's gardens but would not suffer his host to break off a stem and thrust it upon him. If he should see someone about to pluck some flowers, he would exhort him to stop, even to the extent of kneeling and kowtowing before the man if it was necessary to do so to make him spare the flowers. If he came upon children about to gather flowers to sell for money, he would pay them what they might make from the sale of the flowers in order to buy them off. If, in spite of all these attempts to protect the flowers, he should come upon broken branches and stems, he would take some wet soil and seal up the injured part. This he called "doctoring the flowers."

As acts of vandalism would occur in spite of his vigilance, he rarely allowed people to visit his own garden. When it was impossible to refuse his friends and relatives, he would, before he let them in, extract from them the promise that they would not touch the flowers. Moreover, he only permitted them to view the flowers at a distance so that their foul human odor would not contaminate the plants. Ordinarily the mildest and gentlest of men, he became quite ferocious if he caught one of his visitors breaking his promise. He would berate him fiercely and send him scurrying off with the injunction never to come back.

Now where there are trees there are always birds of all kinds, especially when the trees bear flowers and fruits. It matters little if they only peck at the fruits, but often they wantonly destroy the buds and flowers. To prevent this Chiu Hsien placed grains here and there in his garden with a prayer to the birds to spare the flowers. The birds seemed to respond to his prayers and would, after feeding themselves on the grain, fly and dance and sing among the flowers without harming a single petal or pecking a single fruit. Because of this, Chiu Hsien's garden produced better and larger crops of fruits than any other garden in the region. When the fruits ripened, he always made an offering of them first to the flower gods before he tasted them himself. Next he would make presents of them to his neighbors. Only then would he think of selling the fruits in the market. In spite of his generosity, however, he always managed to make something from his garden.

And because he so thoroughly enjoyed his garden and his flowers, his fifty years left no trace at all, but he seemed on the contrary to grow stronger as the years went by. He dressed plainly and ate simple food, but he was happy and serene. Whatever he had left after his own simple needs were satisfied, he gave away to the poor in the village. He was, therefore, respected by all the villagers and was addressed by them as Chiu Kung.[11] He, however, preferred to call himself, "Old man who waters the garden."[12]

Now we must digress and tell of a young bully by the name of Chang Wei in the capital of the district. He was the kind of man who oppressed the meek and helpless and who never failed to plot and scheme against those who happened to stand in his way until he brought about their ruin. He had a pack of servants as ferocious as tigers and wolves and was abetted in his depredations by other young bullies like himself. Innumerable were the people who had suffered harm at his hands. But at last he encountered some one even more powerful than he, the result being that he suffered a

[11] Chiu, the Venerable one. Sometimes the suffixing *Kung* means no more than "Mr."

[12] *Kuan yüan sou.*

severe beating and had to retire to his country estate, which happened to be just outside the village of Changlo, to hide his disgrace.

One day as he was strolling around the village with his cohorts after breakfast, they came to Mr. Chiu's gate and when they saw the bright flowers over the hedge and the inviting shade of the trees, they all said together, "What a nice place this is! Who lives here?"

"It is the garden of Mr. Chiu, known as the 'Flower Fool,'" one of the servants answered.

"I have heard about this old fellow and his way with flowers," Chang Wei said. "So this is where he lives. Let us go in and have a look around."

"He is an odd sort of man," said the servant. "He won't let people into his garden."

"He may not let others in," Chang Wei said, "but surely he won't refuse me. Go and knock!"

The peonies [13] were then in full bloom and Mr. Chiu, having finished watering them, was sitting by the flowers with a pot of wine and drinking in solitary enjoyment. Before he had drunk more than two or three cups, he suddenly heard an insistent knocking at his gate. When he went to the gate and opened it, he recognized the men standing before him to be idle curiosity seekers, and so he blocked the gate passage and demanded what they wanted.

"Don't you know who I am, you old gaffer?" Chang Wei said. "I am Chang Ya-nei [14] from the city. I have heard that you have nice flowers in your garden and have come to take a look."

"Please, Ya-nei," Mr. Chiu answered, "I haven't any nice flowers. Such common varieties as peaches and plums are all I have and these have all faded."

"What a disagreeable old fool!" Chang Wei said, glaring ferociously. "What harm can there be in just taking a look, and yet

[13] *Paeonia moutan* is here indicated, not the common peony. The *mutan* or *moutan* is traditionally regarded as the queen of flowers and has been in recent years proposed as China's "national flower." It is a shrub and is commonly regarded by the Chinese as of a different genus from the common peony.

[14] Title used in Sung and Yuan times for sons of noble families.

you lie to me and say that you haven't any. Do you think that I'd eat them up?"

"I am not lying," Mr. Chiu said. "There really isn't any worth looking at."

But Chang Wei would not take no for an answer. He brushed Mr. Chiu aside so violently that he almost knocked him over and there was nothing for the garden lover to do but to let them in and close the gate after them.

The garden was full of flowers of all kinds but the peonies were then especially in evidence. And Mr. Chiu's peonies were not of the common variety, such as the "Spring on the Jade Terrace," but of the five rarest breeds. They were: the Yellow Terrace, Green Butterflies, Watermelon Red, Dancing Blue Lion, and Red Lion Head.

Now the peony is the queen of all flowers and flourishes especially well in Loyang. There are such rare specimens as the Yellow of Yao and the Purple of Wei which cost five thousand cash a plant. Do you know why it flourishes especially well at Loyang? It all came as the result of a whim of the Empress Wu, the Heavenly One. One winter she conceived a desire to visit the imperial gardens and wrote on the spur of the moment a decree in four lines:

> On the morrow we shall visit the Shang Yuan gardens,
> So let it be known to Spring without delay
> That all the flowers must blossom out during the night
> Nor wait for the accelerating breeze of dawn.

It was a ridiculous decree but it happened that the Empress had been destined to rule in her own name as the Sovereign of all-under-heaven, and the flowers dared not disobey her command. So in one night they formed buds and put forth flowers. Only the peony, the proud queen of flowers, failed to obey; she alone stood her ground and refused to deck herself out to gratify the irresponsible whims of an earthly ruler and her fawning courtiers. When morning came and the Empress found that all had obeyed except the peony she became very angry and banished it to Loyang.

Because of this the peonies of Loyang surpassed varieties found any where else.[15]

Mr. Chiu's peonies were planted in front of his hut. They were surrounded with a wall of rocks and protected from the sun by a cloth canopy stretched across a wooden frame. The shrubs were about ten feet high; even the lowest were not less than six or seven feet. The flowers were as big as plates and were of all shades of colors. At the sight all the intruders exclaimed in admiration and Chang Wei stepped on the wall so as to smell the fragrance. This was one of the things that Mr. Chiu could not endure and so he said, "Ya-nei, please look at them from a distance and do not stand too close to them."

"Do you realize to whom you are talking?" Chang Wei shouted. He was still sullen because of Mr. Chiu's initial rebuff and had been waiting for a chance to vent his spleen. "Have you never heard of the power of Chang Ya-nei? You lied to me but I let it pass. Now you are again wagging your rude tongue. Do you think I'd ruin them by smelling them?" And so saying, he bent one flower after another to him and sniffed at them with his nose pressed against them.

Mr. Chiu was speechless with anger and only hoped that they would go away soon. But Chang Wei seemed bent on torturing him, for the bully now said to his friends, "It would be a pity to leave the flowers when they are at their best. Let us send for wine and have a party here." In vain Mr. Chiu remonstrated. Wine and meat were brought and a rug spread on the ground, and the garden soon resounded with the noise and laughter of the vulgar intruders, while Mr. Chiu sat by and watched helplessly with pouted lips.

But the worst was yet to come, for as the beauty of the garden impressed itself upon Chang Wei he grew covetous and began to devise means of robbing the rightful owner of it. "To look at you one would never think that you'd be such an excellent gardener," he said with a look of condescension. "Here is a cup of wine for you."

[15] This legend is used as the background for the novel *Flowers in the Mirror* by Li Ju-chen, b.c.1760, d.1830.

"I do not drink," the old man answered drily.

"Would you sell your garden?" Chang Wei said next, much to Mr. Chiu's consternation.

"Of course not," he said, "for it is all I have. It is my life."

"You had better sell it to me, life or no life," Chang Wei said. "If you have nothing else to turn to, you can enter my service and take care of the garden for me as you have been doing. I won't require you to perform other tasks." The others joined in, saying, "It is lucky for you, old fellow, to have Ya-nei take a fancy to you. Come and render him your thanks."

Mr. Chiu was so overcome with grievance that his limbs grew numb and he said not a word.

"What an impudent old fool," Chang Wei said. "Why don't you answer whether or not you accept my offer?"

"I have already said that I won't sell," Mr. Chiu answered.

"Nonsense!" Chang Wei said. "If you say that again I shall have you thrown into prison!"

In his rising anger Mr. Chiu was inclined to retort with some stinging remark, but thought better of it. "For," he said to himself, "he has influence and is moreover drunk. I must not come down to his low level. It is better that I put him off for the present." Then aloud: "You must give me time to think the matter over, for the transfer of property is not a matter to be settled on the spur of the moment."

"The old fellow is right," the others said. "Let us come back tomorrow."

By this time the merry makers were all completely intoxicated and rose to take their departure. Afraid that they might pluck his beloved flowers, Mr. Chiu hastened to stand on guard at the flower bed. This was indeed Chang Wei's intention, but just as he stepped on the rock wall and reached out for the flowers, Mr. Chiu stopped him, saying, "Ya-nei, though these plants are but insignificant things of nature, yet it has not been easy for them to bear these few flowers. It would be a great pity to cut short their lives. Moreover, they will soon fade after they are plucked. So why commit such a sin?"

"Nonsense," Chang Wei cried. "What sin is there in this? Besides, the garden will be mine after tomorrow; so what concern is it of yours even if I break off all the flowers?"

He tried to push Mr. Chiu away, but the latter held on to him and would not let go, saying, "You can kill me if you like, but you must not pluck these flowers."

"What a troublesome old fool!" the rest of the men said. "What is there to a few flowers that you make such a great fuss? Do you think that we would be afraid of you and refrain from plucking them?" So saying, they all began to reach out for the flowers and to pluck them at random.

The poor old man was frantic; he let go of Chang Wei and ran from one to the other in a vain effort to prevent them from their work of destruction. Then he lost all control over himself. "Robbers and bandits," he cursed, "you have come unprovoked to work destruction in my garden. What is the use of my living after this!" He rushed over to Chang Wei and dashed himself against him with such violence that the latter, being unsteady anyway from too much wine, staggered and fell. With a shout, "He has hurt Ya-nei!" the other men made a rush for Mr. Chiu and might have done him serious harm if a more prudent and kindly man among their own number had not stopped them for fear that Mr. Chiu might not, because of his advanced age, survive their rough treatment. They contented themselves by venting their ill nature on the flowers. They tore down every last bud and scattered them all over the ground and, still not satisfied, they began to destroy the plants and to trample everything under their feet. What a calamity it was for the innocent flowers!

> Cruel fists and violent hands fell in every direction,
> Green leaves and tender flowers were scattered all around.
> It was like a visitation of a malign fit of wind and rain
> That leaves in its wake havoc and desolation.

Mr. Chiu was so overcome with grief and compassion that he rolled on the ground and cried to Heaven and Earth. The commotion soon brought the neighbors running into the garden, and they finally managed to stay the wrath of Chang Wei and his men, and persuade them to leave the garden. At the gate Chang Wei said to them, "Tell the old bandit that all will be well if he quietly hands over the garden to me. If not, let him beware!"

The peacemakers did not take the threat seriously at the time, for they thought that he had spoken thus only out of the anger and the boastfulness of a drunken man. They returned to Mr. Chiu and stayed with him until they quieted him, and then took their leave. As they walked toward the gate, some of them who had taken offense at Mr. Chiu because he had refused them admittance into the garden said that in a way it served him right.

"He has brought this upon himself," argued they, "by his exacting ways. This incident ought to teach him a lesson."

But one with a better sense of justice reproved them, saying, "Do not say such unjust things. The proverb says well, 'A year of care, ten days of enjoyment.' A man who knows nothing about flowers will dismiss the most gorgeous flowers with a 'How pretty,' little dreaming of the difficulties involved in their culture. You can't blame the old man for being so particular about his pet flowers if you stop to think how much trouble he takes in tending them."

To return to Mr. Chiu. As he looked over the scene of ruin and desolation his heart became filled with grief and his tears began to flow. Picking up some broken and mud-soiled blossoms and examining them with tender care, he said weeping, "O Flowers! I have cherished and protected you all my life and have never injured a single petal or leaf. To think that you would suffer such a calamity today!"

Just as he was thus weeping to himself he suddenly heard a voice speaking behind him: "Why are you, sir, weeping like this?" When he turned to look, he beheld a beautiful girl of about twice eight, lovely of feature and dressed in simple elegance. He had never seen her before and knew not who she might be.

"Who are you, young lady, and what has brought you here?" he asked, wiping his tears.

"I am a neighbor of yours," the girl answered. "I have heard that the peonies in your garden are in full bloom and have come to see them, but it appears that they have faded already." At the mention of his peonies, Mr. Chiu burst into tears anew.

"Tell me," the girl said, "what sorrow you have that you cry like this." When Mr. Chiu told her how Chang Wei had ruined his flowers, the girl said, "If that is the cause of your grief, perhaps you would like to see the flowers restored to their stems."

"Do not jest with a poor old man, young lady," Mr. Chiu said, "for how could it be possible for fallen flowers to be returned to their stems?"

Said the girl, "But we have a magic formula just for this purpose which has been handed from one generation to another in our family and which has never been known to fail."

"Do you really have such a formula?" Mr. Chiu asked, turning from sorrow to joy.

"Of course I do," the girl replied, and thereupon Mr. Chiu fell on his knees before her, saying, "If you save my flowers, young lady, I have nothing with which to repay you, but I shall invite you to my garden to enjoy the flowers as each variety comes to bloom."

"Please rise," the girl said, "and fetch me a cup of water."

As Mr. Chiu rose to fetch the water, he thought to himself, "How could there be such a wonderful formula. She is probably making sport of me, seeing me in my grief. But how could she, a total stranger, indulge in jest with me? It must be true after all." Hastily he dipped out a cup of water, but when he looked up the girl had gone and the fallen flowers were restored to their stems. Moreover, whereas before each plant had only flowers of one shade of color, there were now on each plant flowers of all colors and shades, so that they were more gorgeous than ever. The following poem has been composed to celebrate this miracle:

> Hsiang Tzu had once dyed flowers with many hues,
> Now fallen flowers are returned to their original stems.
> Indeed extreme faith will move even insentient things,
> Though fools will continue to mock the Mr. Chius.

"So the young lady has indeed a magic formula!" Mr. Chiu exclaimed in joy and surprise, and thinking that she might be still somewhere about among the shrubbery, he put down the water and began to look for her so as to express his gratitude, but he found no trace of her. Then he went to the gate and there he found that it was shut as before. Outside he found two old neighbors, one called Yu Kung and the other Shan Kung, watching the fishermen drying their nets. When they saw Mr. Chiu they rose and saluted him, saying, "We heard about Chang Ya-nei's horrible behavior, but we were in the fields and have not had a chance to come and express our concern."

"What a nightmare it was!" Mr. Chiu said. "I have never seen such heartless people. But fortunately a young lady came and restored the flowers through some secret process. She came out before I had a chance to thank her. Did you notice in which direction she went?"

The two old men were amazed when they heard this. "How could ruined flowers be saved? And how long has the young lady been gone?"

"She came out just now," said Mr. Chiu.

"We have been sitting here for quite a long while," the two men said, "and we have seen no one come out of your garden."

"Then the young lady must be a fairy that has come down to perform a miracle," Mr. Chiu said with sudden comprehension.

"Tell us just how she saved the flowers," his neighbors begged, and Mr. Chiu told them everything that had happened and took them into the garden to see the miracle for themselves. "It must be the work of a fairy!" they exclaimed when they saw with their own eyes the restored flowers. "No mortal could have done this."

After Mr. Chiu had lighted the finest incense he had and rendered thanks to Heaven, they suggested that he should shame Chang Wei by inviting him to come and see the miracle the following day, but "No," he answered, "for his kind should be avoided like mad dogs, let alone inviting them into one's house."

Mr. Chiu was now in high spirits. He warmed up the bottle

of wine that he had been drinking when he was interrupted by Chang Wei's intrusion and invited his neighbors to join him. They drank and chatted under the flowers until it was dark, when Yu Kung and Shan Kung took their leave. Through them the news was soon spread all over the village and every one hoped that they would have an opportunity to see the miracle for themselves though they all had misgivings that Mr. Chiu would give them his permission.

When morning came, however, and some of the villagers went to Mr. Chiu's garden gate, they found it thrown wide open, for he had, after a night spent in meditation, come to realize the error of his former ways and had made haste to mend them. "I have brought this misfortune upon myself by my lack of generosity," he said to himself. "If my bosom had been, like that of the immortals, as capacious as the ocean, this would never have happened to me." Therefore, he opened the gate of his garden to anyone that cared to visit it and only cautioned his visitors not to pluck the flowers.

In the meantime Chang Wei was saying to his henchmen: "Let us now go to see the old bandit. I cannot let him off so easily after his impudence yesterday. If he won't hand over the garden, we shall lay it low for him."

"He will have to sell it to you," some one said; "but it is too bad that we did so much damage yesterday since it will soon be yours."

"The flowers will bloom again next year," Chang Wei said. "Let us make haste, for we must not give him time to take precautions against us."

On their way they encountered some of the villagers returning from Mr. Chiu's garden and heard them talking about the miracle they had seen. Chang Wei would not believe it but took it to be Mr. Chiu's invention for the purpose of deterring him from his evil intention. But when they reached the garden and wound their way to the court before the hut they found that the flowers had indeed been restored to their stems as they had heard. Chang Wei was amazed but he did not change his mind about the robbery that he had resolved upon. Then as he was looking at the flowers an evil plot suddenly occurred to him.

"Let us go now," he said to his men and when they followed him out he continued, "I have a scheme that will enable me to acquire the garden without consulting the old man at all."

"What scheme do you have, Ya-nei?" the men asked, and he answered: "Wang Tse of Peichou is in rebellion against the dynasty and derives his strength from black magic. The government has issued orders to the provincial authorities to suppress all practices of magic and witchcraft and to arrest all known evil doers of this kind. There is a reward of three thousand *kuan* posted for information against them. I shall use the restoration of the flowers as evidence and send my man Chang Pa to the prefect's yamen to accuse the old bandit of witchcraft. Unable to stand the torture, he will surely confess to the charge. Then his garden will be confiscated and publicly sold. As it is known that I want this garden, no one will dare bid against me and I shall thus come into possession of it. And I'll get the reward money besides!"

"It is a wonderful scheme," they all said and urged him to carry it out without delay.

The complaint was lodged as planned and the prefect, who had been on the lookout for such persons, immediately had Mr. Chiu seized. He brushed aside Mr. Chiu's side of the story and said, laughing, "Many men worthier than you have aspired to meet the immortal beings but have failed. How could it be possible that a fairy came to you just because you cried? Moreover, if an immortal had indeed come to you, surely she would have left her name for the world to know. This story that you have made up deceives no one. You must be an evil magician. Put his legs in the press!" he shouted, turning to the black gang. But just as the jailers rushed up to Mr. Chiu and were about to put him in the press the prefect was suddenly seized with such a violent spell of feeling faint that he almost fell off his chair. Try as he would, he could not summon up enough strength to continue the trial and so he had to adjourn the court and commit Mr. Chiu to prison.

On his way to the prison under guard, Mr. Chiu encountered Chang Wei. "Chang Ya-nei," he cried out to him, "What have I done to you that you now do me this foul deed?" Chang Wei turned away from him without replying. Then Mr. Chiu was joined by his neighbors Yu Kung and Shan Kung, who had come to console him and to assure him that they would get the entire village to testify to his innocence.

That night as Mr. Chiu was bemoaning his fate and praying for his deliverance, the fairy of his previous encounter suddenly appeared before him and with a wave of her hand caused his cangue and fetters to fall from him.

"I am the Flower Maid of the Queen Mother of the Jasper Pond,"[16] she said to him. "I have caused the flowers to be restored to their stems because of your sincere love for flowerkind, little thinking that this act would give wicked people an opportunity to play you foul. However, it is in your destiny to suffer this misfortune for a day. Tomorrow you will be delivered. As to Chang Wei, the Deity in charge of flowers has lodged a complaint against him before Shang Ti and it has been decreed that his natural span of life is to be cut short. Punishments have also been meted out to his accomplices, each according to his desert. As to yourself, I enjoin you to hold fast to your good resolve and cultivate the ways of the immortals. A few years hence I shall appear again and deliver you from this mortal world."

Mr. Chiu prostrated himself before the goddess and asked how he could best cultivate the ways of the immortals.

"There are many ways to cultivate immortality," she answered, "and each man must choose one according to his natural bent. Since you have achieved merit through your love of flowers you will achieve immortality by the same means. If you will nourish yourself with flowers you will grow light in body and in time ascend to the upper heavens." And she gave him the formula for preparing flowers to eat.

Mr. Chiu kowtowed again to thank the goddess, but when he

[16] The consort of the Emperor of Heaven in popular mythology of comparatively modern times.

looked up she was no longer before him but was standing on the prison wall instead. She beckoned to him and said, "Come up and follow me out." Chiu Hsien tried to scale the wall but found it hard going, and finally just as he was about to reach the top. he heard the alarm of gongs and the shout, "The prisoner has escaped!" He became paralyzed with terror, his limbs grew numb, and he fell to the ground, whereupon he woke up with a start. He remembered his dream so well that he was sure that the goddess had appeared to him and that all would soon be well. Therefore he began to feel at ease in his heart.

In the meantime Chang Wei, flushed with the success of his foul scheme, returned to Mr. Chiu's garden to celebrate with his evil companions. But in the garden they found that the peonies had again disappeared from the stems and were scattered over the ground just as they had been after their wanton destruction. "How extraordinary!" they exclaimed.

"The old bandit must indeed be a black magician," Chang Wei said, "else how could this have happened? The flower god could not have done this."

"He must have done this to embarrass you, Ya-nei," one of his companions said.

"We'll foil him by having our party here just the same," Chang Wei said, and with that remark he ordered his attendants to spread a rug on the ground and bring forth wine. He gave Chang Pa, the servant who had made the formal complaint, a few bottles of wine so that he might celebrate with his fellow servants. Thus they drank and made merry until by sunset time they were all somewhat intoxicated, when suddenly a strong wind began to blow. A terrible wind it was—

> It piled up the leaves in the courtyard,
> It scattered the duckweeds in the pond.
> It smelled as if it harbingered a host of tigers,
> It whistled like ten thousand pine trees in an uproar.

The gust of wind stirred up the flowers scattered on the ground, each of which became in the twinkling of an eye a little female figure about a foot in height. "How strange," the men exclaimed and before they had finished speaking the figures had with the next gust of wind become the size of ordinary human beings. They were all very beautiful and gorgeously dressed. The men were stupefied and stared at them. Then a girl dressed in red began to speak.

"We have lived here for more than twenty years under the loving care of Mr. Chiu," she said. "But now these wicked men have suddenly forced on us their malodorous fumes and laid on us their vile hands. They have moreover wrought harm to Mr. Chiu and plotted to rob him of this garden. Since they are now right before us, let us unite our strength and attack them, so that we can repay our benefactor on the one hand and have revenge for ourselves on the other. What do you think of this, sisters?"

"You speak rightly," the other girls answered. "Let us waste no time." So saying, they rushed at the men, waving their long sleeves in the air like banners and causing a wind that chilled the marrows.

"Ghosts!" the men shouted and each began to run in a different direction. Some of them stumbled over rocks, others were caught and scratched by tree branches. They fell and climbed to their feet and fell again. For a long while utter confusion reigned in the garden, but finally the wind stopped and the frightened men reassembled before the hut. All were accounted for except Chang Wei and Chang Pa. Torches were lit and a search was made. After a while they heard a groan in a corner of the garden and on approaching it found Chang Pa sprawled over the exposed root of a plum tree, his skull fractured. Two attendants were detached to carry him back, while the rest continued their search. They were over the garden four or five times but could not find a trace of Chang Wei. Could he have been blown away by the wind, they wondered, or swallowed up by the female ghosts? As they were about to give up the search and go home for the night, one of them suddenly shouted that he had found their master. When they rushed up to him, he pointed to a tree, saying, "Is that not the master's hat?" "He can't be far from here," the others said and they began to look very carefully along the wall. Suddenly there came a cry from those in front, for there in a manure pond before them they found the body of their master. He had fallen head foremost into the deep filth and was entirely buried except for his feet sticking up in the air. But they recognized him by his shoes and socks. They fished him out and after washing him off in a nearby lake the best they could, they carried him home. That same night, Chang Pa also died from his head wound. Thus these two evil doers provided an instance of quick superhuman punishment.

> As two wicked men depart from this world,
> A pair of sorry ghosts arrive in the other realm.

The following day the prefect again held court but before he could give orders to have Mr. Chiu brought in for questioning, one of the attendants told him what had happened. He was greatly surprised and incredulous but soon the inhabitants of the village came in a body to petition him for the release of Mr. Chiu and their testimony left no further room for doubt. Moreover, the sudden fainting spell of the day before had given him food for thought. Now he became convinced of Mr. Chiu's innocence and was glad that the latter had not been tortured to get his confession. He had Mr. Chiu brought in and had him unfettered and freed before all in the judgment hall. Furthermore, he issued an order prohibiting unauthorized persons to enter the garden and had it posted at the gate.

Chiu and his neighbors all thanked the prefect and then returned to the village. There they found that his peonies had again been restored to their stems, a sight which never failed to make them sigh in wonderment. The neighbors prepared feasts to congratulate Mr. Chiu's vindication and he in turn invited them. Thus the days immediately after his return were passed in feasting.

To conclude: after this Mr. Chiu began to substitute flowers for food and soon he became accustomed to them and stopped eating "things of fire and smoke" altogether. And he gave away all the money that he got from the sale of his fruits. In a few years' time his white hair turned black again and his complexion became like that of a young boy.

Then one day (it happened on the fifteenth of the eighth month, the Festival of the Harvest moon) as Mr. Chiu was sitting in meditation under a balmy and cloudless sky, there suddenly came up a gentle breeze and a patch of colored cloud. The air became filled with the sound of sweet music and the fragrance of rare perfumes. As the cloud drew near, the presence of the Flower Maid was revealed standing in the middle of it. In front of her a blue phoenix and a white crane fluttered and danced in the air, while on either side there were fairy maidens carrying and playing all kinds of musical instruments. At this wonderous sight, Mr. Chiu fell to his knees.

"Chiu Hsien," the Flower Maid said, "you have now completed your work of self-cultivation, and have been appointed by Shang Ti, upon my recommendation, the Protector of Flowers. You will have charge of all flowerkind found on earth and you are empowered to confer blessings upon those who love and care for flowers and to inflict disaster upon those who harm and destroy them. You are hereby given the privilege of joining the ranks of the deities and taking your possessions with you."

Thereupon Mr. Chiu kowtowed to render thanks to Heaven and rose up into the clouds together with the grass hut and all the plants in the garden and disappeared in a southerly direction. The miracle was seen by Yu Kung and Shan Kung and all the inhabitants of the village. Moreover, as they prostrated themselves, they saw Mr. Chiu raise his hands in token of farewell.

After this the village changed its name to Shenghsienli; [17] it is also called the village of a Hundred Flowers.

[17] "Village where a man rose to be an immortal."

The Oil Peddler and the Queen of Flowers

Anonymous

C. 14TH CENTURY

Young men like to speak of "breeze and moonlight"
And of their victories over waves and storms.
Money without beauty will not promote genuine feeling,
Beauty without money will also end in failure.
And even if you have both money and beauty,
You must above all practice solicitude,
For he who can read his fair lady's thoughts
Only he is without peer in the arena of love.

This poem is written to the tune known as "Moon over the West River" and expresses a most profound truth in matters concerning "breeze and moonlight." "The courtesan loves a handsome face, but Madame loves gold," goes the saying, and accordingly he who has the beauty of P'an An and the wealth of Teng T'ung will find no trouble in making himself generally welcome and in being lord in the castle of fair bandits. However, this is only true to a certain extent, for even more important than money and beauty is the lesson contained in the words *pang ch'en*. As a compound the expression simply means "to assist," but the root meanings of the individual words are more suggestive, for *pang* means the upper part of the shoe, and *ch'en* means the lining of a garment, both indispensable parts that make up two harmonious wholes. With proper "assistance" a lady with one part loveliness will appear like one with ten, while by the same token proper "assistance" will conceal what defects she may have. That is what is meant by *pang ch'en,* that and such little things as maintaining an attitude of humility toward the fair one, fanning her in summer and shielding her from cold in winter, and generally doing things that please her and avoiding things that do not. He who knows how to practice the art of *pang ch'en* is most likely to succeed in the arena of love. It endows the homely with beauty and the poor with health.

Cheng Yuanho [1] of the T'ang Dynasty was, for instance, empty of purse and sore-ridden in appearance when Li Yahsien encountered him cold and starved in the snow, yet she took compassion upon him and took him home with her, wrapped him up in silken covers and fed him with fine delicacies. It could not have been because she coveted his money, of which he had none, or because she admired his appearance, for he was emaciated and covered with sores. It was, rather, because Cheng Yuanho was attentive and knew well how to practice the art of *pang ch'en* when he had money to spend that Yahsien could not now bear to abandon him. If you but recall the incident in which Cheng Yuanho killed his favorite horse [2] in order to gratify Yahsien's wish for horse-tripe soup, you'll understand why she rescued him from his poverty. Later on Cheng Yuanho's luck turned; he became "optimus" in the imperial examinations, and Li Yahsien was given the title of Lady of Chienkuo. Truly it is as the couplet says:

When luck flees even gold loses its luster;
When luck returns even iron shines bright.

Now during the reigns of the first seven emperors of the Sung Dynasty (960-1280) the country enjoyed peace and prosperity. The warlike arts were neglected, while literature flourished. But when Hui Tsung ascended the throne as the eighth emperor he fell under the evil influence of such infamous ministers as Ts'ai Ching and Kao Ch'iu, and by his indulgence in wanton pleasures and ruinous extravagances he brought the empire to a very low state and caused disaffection among the people. The Kin Tartars took

[1] See "Li Yahsien" in this collection.
[2] Detail embroidered into later versions of the story.

advantage of the situation and invaded the northern provinces. The once prosperous and happy land was thrown into great turmoil, and the Emperors Hui Tsung and Ch'in Tsung (to whom the former had abdicated) were captured by the invaders. It was not until the miraculous escape of the Prince K'ang on a horse of clay and his ascension to the throne at Hangchow (which was renamed Linan or Temporary Security) and the division of the empire into the North and South dynasties that a measure of peace was restored. During the years of war and confusion, the people suffered untold hardships.

Among these unfortunate victims of war there was a man by the name of Hsin Shan who lived in a village outside the capital Pienliang.[3] He had a provisions store and was well off in a modest way. His wife Juanshih bore him an only daughter named Yaochin, a very beautiful and clever girl. Her parents sent her to the village school when she was seven, and by the time she was ten she was able to read poems and compose verses. At the age of twelve she was accomplished in playing the harp and at chess and also in painting and calligraphy. As for her skill with the needle, it was even more to be marveled at. Because he had no son of his own, Hsin Shan wished to get himself a son-in-law who would live with him and comfort him in his old age, but as his daughter was much sought after because of her beauty and accomplishments, he was not able to make up his mind which suitor to choose.

It was then that the Kin Tartars invaded the land and laid siege to Pienliang. There were many armies in various parts of the empire that were ready to rally to the protection of the Emperor, but as the prime minister was for treating with the invaders, they were not allowed to oppose the barbarians. As a result, the Tartar hordes became more insatiable than ever in their lust for conquest; they invested the capital and kidnapped both Hui Tsung and Ch'in Tsung. The people in the region all abandoned their homes and fled in terror before the barbarian hordes. Among them were Hsin Shan and his wife Juanshih and their daughter Yaochin. They dodged in and out of the road like

[3] Modern K'aifeng; capital of Northern Sung.

homeless dogs and scuttled hither and yon like fish escaped from the nets; they knew not whither they were going, their only thought being to escape the Tartars. Well says the proverb:

> Rather be a dog in time of peace
> Than a man in an age of war and separation.

The refugees did not encounter any Tartars but they did meet with a band of defeated imperial troops. When the demoralized soldiers saw the helpless refugees and the worldly possessions that they were carrying with them, they raised a false cry, "There come the Tartars!" and then proceeded to rob the refugees as they scattered in confusion. Those who refused to yield up their possessions were murdered. Indeed, it was confusion heaped upon confusion and bitterness added to bitterness.

Yaochin was knocked down in the confusion. When she got back to her feet, she had lost sight of her parents. Not daring to shout for help, she hid among the tombs by the road and there spent the night. When day came she found herself quite alone, with nothing in sight except dust in the sky and corpses lying about the road. She trudged on in the southerly direction that she had been following, weeping and crying as she went. After having gone about two li she began to feel tired and hungry. She was heartened by the sight of a hut in the distance, thinking that she might find there food and drink, but when she came to it she found it abandoned. She sat leaning against the wall and cried bitterly.

"There can be no story without coincidence," goes the ancient saying. Now it happened that one of her neighbors went by just at this moment. This man was named Pu Chiao,[4] an idler and a worthless fellow who lived by his wits. He too had been separated from the group of refugees by the imperial troops and was traveling by himself. At the sight of a neighbor Yaochin felt as if she had encountered one of her own kin. She stopped crying and asked, "Uncle Pu, have you seen my parents?"

[4] Homophone for "Unfortunately." Except in the case of historical romances, Chinese fiction writers have a weakness for such allegorical names.

"What luck!" Pu Chiao said to himself. "I have been robbed of everything by the soldiers but now Heaven has sent me this nice article for my use." But aloud he lied to Yaochin thus: "Yes, indeed. They are now a distance ahead. They asked me to take you to them if I should find you."

Though Yaochin was a clever girl, she suspected nothing in her joy at seeing someone that she knew. Gladly she went with him.

Pu Chiao gave her some of the food that he carried with him and said to her, "Your parents did not stop during the night and it may be that we shall not catch up with them until we reach Chienkang on the other side of the Yangtze. Let me call you daughter and you call me father, for otherwise we might arouse suspicion."

Yaochin consented and thereafter they traveled together by land and river under the guise of father and daughter. At Chienkang they heard that Prince Wuchu of the Kin Tartars was about to cross the Yangtze to attack that city, so they continued their journey southward and headed for Hangchou, where Prince K'ang had assumed the throne as Emperor Kao Tsung.

By the time they reached Hangchou, which was now known as Linan, Pu Chiao had spent what little money he had, and it became necessary for him to dispose of Yaochin. He made inquiries among the brothel keepers on West Lake and found that a certain Wang Chiu-ma was looking for a girl. He took the woman to the inn to look at Yaochin so that they could agree on a price. Chiu-ma was impressed with Yaochin's beauty and agreed to pay fifty ounces of silver for her. After the silver had changed hands, Pu Chiao took Yaochin to Chiu-ma's house.

Pu Chiao was a clever man. Before Chiu-ma he represented himself as Yaochin's real father and to cover up his deception he solicitously enjoined Chiu-ma to take good care of Yaochin and to be patient with her. To Yaochin he said that Chiu-ma was a close relation of his and that he would come back for her as soon as he had found her parents. The unfortunate girl was completely taken in and went gladly to Chiu-ma's house.

Chiu-ma gave Yaochin a complete change of clothes and housed her in the best room in her establishment. She served her the best of food and drink and comforted her with kind words. When after a few days Yaochin heard nothing from Pu Chiao, she said to Chiu-ma with tears in her eyes, "Why is it that Uncle Pu has not come to see me?" "What Uncle Pu?" Chiu-ma asked. "The man who brought me here," Yaochin said. "But he said that he was your father," Chiu-ma said. Then Yaochin told her how she had become separated from her parents, how Pu Chiao had found her and traveled with her to Linan. "I might as well tell you the truth," Chiu-ma said after she heard Yaochin's story. "That man Pu sold you to me for fifty taels of silver. As you are more beautiful than any of the girls that I have, I shall treat you as my own daughter and see that you have the best of food and clothing the rest of your life."

Yaochin cried bitterly on learning that she had been deceived by Pu Chiao, and it was a long time before Chiu-ma was able to quiet her. After this Chiu-ma changed her name to Meiniang and taught her singing and dancing until she excelled in those arts. By the time she was fourteen she had become a maiden of extraordinary beauty, much sought after by the rich and noble gallants of Linan. They came with generous offerings, some seeking to enjoy her beauty, others to get scraps of her accomplished verses and calligraphy. Soon she became one of the most famous courtesans of the empire, and was nicknamed the "Queen of Flowers."

Because of her fame she began to receive offers "to comb her hair," though she was but fourteen. She was, naturally, unwilling to have her chastity violated and Chiu-ma did not dare to force her because she brought in so much gold.

Another year went by and Meiniang became fifteen. Now among people of Chiu-ma's calling there were certain well-established conventions governing the "combing of the hair." When it was done at the age of thirteen, it was known as "testing the flower," a very unsatisfactory proceeding because of the extreme youth of the girl. It is seldom resorted to except by avaricious keepers who care nothing for the welfare of their charges. When it is done at the age of fourteen it is known as "emblossoming the flower." This is considered the best time, since it marks the beginning of reciprocity. At the age of fifteen, it is known as "plucking the flower" and is considered rather overdue, though in ordinary families fifteen is considered an immature age. When at the age of fifteen Meiniang's hair was not yet combed, the gallants who frequented the West Lake houses began to make jibes about a certain wood quince that was beautiful to look at but quite unfit to eat.

Chiu-ma was distressed by these jibes and tried to persuade her to receive patrons, but Meiniang refused, saying that she would never do so unless her own parents were there to command her. Although Chiu-ma was displeased with her scruples, she did not have the heart to discipline her. Then one day a certain rich man by the name of Chin came and offered Chiu-ma three hundred taels for the coveted privilege. Unable to resist the princely sum, Chiu-ma entered into a plot with Chin. They made Meiniang drunk and then forced the unwelcome ceremony upon her. . . .

When she woke up and realized what had happened, Meiniang rose from the bed of her undoing, got dressed, and then laid herself down on a bamboo couch, turned her face toward the wall and began to weep silently. Chin went to her and tried to comfort her, but he only got scratched in the face for his pains. He was naturally much put out and left the house precipitately at dawn.

Now it was the usual custom for a client who had just "combed the hair" of his favorite courtesan to stay a month or two or at least ten or twenty days in her establishment. Chin's behavior was unprecedented. Chiu-ma went up to Meiniang's room and found her lying on her couch weeping. She tried to console her but Meiniang only wept and said nothing.

After that Meiniang refused to leave her own room and would not receive any visitors at all. Chiu-ma became impatient but she did not dare to discipline her for fear of driving her to more desperate action. Yet she could not let things go on as they were; Meiniang was her money tree only so long as she received patrons. One day Chiu-ma suddenly thought of Liu Ssu-ma, one of her sworn sisters, a woman with a very clever tongue and Meiniang's confidante. "Why don't I get her to come and see what she could do to persuade Meiniang?" she said to herself. She sent Pao-erh, one of the servants, for Ssu-ma and when she came told her everything.

"I am a female Sui Ho and a woman Lu Chia,"[5] Ssu-ma said. I can make a Lohan[6] fall in love and persuade the Goddess of the Moon to consider marriage. You can depend on me."

"I shall kowtow to you in gratitude," Chiu-ma said. "But have some tea so that you won't find yourself handicapped by a dry throat."

"Don't worry," Ssu-ma said, "I can talk till tomorrow morning without the need of moistening my throat."

Meiniang's door was shut but she opened it when she recognized Ssu-ma's voice. On her desk was spread out a piece of silk on which she had sketched the outline of a woman's figure but had not yet filled in the colors. "What a fine picture!" Ssu-ma said, "and how clever you are! Indeed, Sister Chiu is lucky to have such a clever girl as you, so beautiful and accomplished in so many things. She couldn't find another one like you even if she searched the length and breadth of Linan with a cartload of gold."

"Don't make fun of me," Meiniang said. "What wind has brought you here, aunt?"

"I have been wanting to come to see you, but have not had the time," Ssu-ma said. "I heard about your 'hair combing' and have come to congratulate you and Sister Chiu."

Meiniang blushed at the mention of her shame. Ssu-ma drew her chair closer to her and taking Meiniang's hands in hers said, "My child, a courtesan cannot afford to be as tender skinned as a soft-shelled egg. You'll never accumulate any great amount of silver by being so shy."

"What need do I have of silver?" Meiniang said.

"But, my child," said Ssu-ma, "your mother expects you to bring in silver for her even if you don't care about it yourself. Remember

[5] First part of second century B.C.; famed for their eloquence.
[6] Buddhist saint.

the saying that he who lives near the mountain eats by the mountain and he who lives near the water eats by the water. Of the powdered faces that Sister Chiu has, is there one who can touch you? In her orchard you are the only melon that she can depend upon to supply her with seeds. You are an intelligent child and should know why it is that she has treated you better than any one else in the house. I have been told that you have refused to receive any client since your 'hair-combing.' What does this mean? If every one behaved the way you do how would your mother buy mulberry leaves to feed her hungry silkworms? Since she has been so kind to you, you should try to deserve her kindness. Otherwise the rest of the girls, always jealous, will criticize you."

"Let them criticize me!" Meiniang said. "I am not afraid of them."

"But that is nothing compared to what might happen to you if you persist in your stubbornness," Ssu-ma said. "We who are in the business depend upon our 'daughters' for everything. If by luck we get a promising girl, it is just as if a rich family had acquired a piece of fertile land. We nourish her and care for her till she is ready for her 'hair-combing,' which is to us as the harvest is to the farmers. After that we expect to get returns for our investment, we expect her to receive new clients at the front door after she has sent away the old from the back door, with Mr. Chang bringing rice and Mr. Li sending firewood."

"I can't bring myself to do that," Meiniang said.

"You talk as if you were your own mistress," Ssu-ma said, laughing. "It is for your mother to command. If you do not obey she can whip you until you are neither dead nor alive. Sister Chiu has never subjected you to such humiliation only because you are clever and beautiful. She has just complained to me about your behavior, saying that you are very obstinate and that you do not seem to appreciate such obvious things as the fact that a goose feather is lighter than a millstone, and she asked me to persuade you to change your ways. If you persist in your stubbornness, you may provoke her beyond endurance and make her scold you or even beat you. What would you do then? And once she gets started there will be no end to it; and in end you will have to yield to her wishes. Your reputation will be ruined and your position lowered in the eyes of your sister courtesans. In my opinion the best thing for you to do is to throw yourself in your mother's bosom and enjoy her favors while you can."

"I am from a self-respecting family," Meiniang said, "and have fallen into this life of shame through the treachery of someone else. If you, aunt, should make it possible for me to abandon this life and 'follow the path of virtue' [7] you would be doing a greater good deed than building a nine-storied pagoda; but if it is your intention to make me submit to this life of shame, I would rather die than do what you say."

"It is a worthy ambition to 'follow the path of virtue,'" Ssu-ma said, "but even if such is your wish, you have to begin by receiving patrons. In the first place, your mother will never let you go until she has made a thousand taels or more through you. Then surely you will want to marry some one worthy of your beauty and accomplishments, not any common, vulgar fellow that comes along. But how are you to know whom to marry if you see no one? If you persist in your refusal, your mother will probably sell you as a concubine to anyone willing to pay the price. You'll be committed for life then, whether the man be old or ugly or as ignorant as an ox. I think you should do what your mother wishes. With your beauty and talents you don't have to entertain any except noble and rich patrons. Thus you will be able to enjoy yourself while you are still young, enable your mother to make a fortune and save some money for yourself. After five or six years your mother will be willing to let you go. When the right man does come along, then I shall myself be your matchmaker."

Meiniang said nothing after hearing this, but by the smile on her face, Ssu-ma knew that she was beginning to weaken in her resolution. "Everything I have said is for your good," she said, getting up. "You will be grateful to me one of these days for the advice."

Meiniang escorted her to the door and there she saw Chiu-ma,

[7] Through marriage.

who had been listening outside. She blushed and withdrew, while Chiu-ma and Ssu-ma went to the front hall.

"Niece was as stubborn as iron," Ssu-ma said, "but I talked and talked to her until she melted completely and is now ready to receive guests."

Chiu-ma thanked her and asked her to stay for dinner, and did not let her go until she had eaten and drunk to repletion.

Meiniang's fame grew after she began to receive visitors again; the door of Chiu-ma's house became like a market place. Even at a fee of ten taels a visit people fought for her favors. Chiu-ma rejoiced at the money that she made, but Meiniang only looked forward to the time when she might meet someone to whom she could give herself in marriage; as the saying goes:

> It is easier to acquire a priceless treasure
> Than to find the man you love.

Now we must take up a different thread in the story. There was inside the Clear Wave Gate of Linan an oil shop belonging to a man by the name of Chu Shih-lao. A few years back he had adopted a refugee boy from Pienliang by the name of Chin Chung. The boy's mother died in his infancy and he was thirteen when his father sold him and entered the Upper Tienchu Temple as a lay attendant. Since Chu Shih-lao was recently widowed and without children, he looked upon Chin Chung as his own son. He changed the boy's name to Chu Chung and taught him his own business. Father and son managed very well until Shih-lao was forced by the infirmities of age to hire an assistant named Hsing Chuan.

"Time passes like an arrow." Soon Chu Chung grew up into a handsome young man of seventeen. Now Shih-lao had a bondmaid by the name of Orchid. She was already past twenty. She became interested in Chu Chung and time and again "set out hooks to catch him." But Chu Chung was a good and honest youth. Moreover, he found the maid distasteful because she was homely and untidy. And so "though the fallen flower was full of pity for itself, the flowing stream speeds it on without regret."

Failing to catch the younger Chu Chung, Orchid turned to Hsing Chuan. As he was a man over forty and unmarried, she succeeded without any difficulty. Then she and Hsin Chuan plotted to get rid of Chu Chung for fear that he might surprise them in their secret meetings. Orchid went to Shih-lao and accused Chu Chung of having made advances to her. As she had been more than a bondmaid to Shih-lao, the charge made the old man jealous. Then Hsing Chuan trumped up a false charge of his own against the young man, saying that he had been gambling and losing money and that he had stolen from the shop to pay his debts. At first Shih-lao did not believe them, but their repeated accusations finally swayed him. He called Chu Chung to him and gave him a severe scolding.

Though Chu Chung was innocent, he was wise enough not to try to expose the bondmaid and her lover, for his foster father might not believe him and the guilty couple would hate him the more for it in any case. He said to Shih-lao as a plan came to his mind, "Business has been light and there is no need for two men in the shop. Master Hsing can take care of the shop while I go out and peddle oil in the streets. That would increase the volume of our business."

Shih-lao was about to give his consent to this arrangement, but again he was misled by Hsing Chuan, who said to him, "That is only a pretext on his part. He has accumulated some money and wants to get married and set up a house of his own."

Thereupon Shih-lao said with a sigh, "I have treated him like a son but he has paid me ill. Well, there is nothing to do but let him go. He is, after all, not my own flesh and blood." So he sent Chu Chung away, giving him only three taels and permitting him to take only his clothes and bedding with him.

After leaving Shih-lao's house, Chu Chung found a room, deposited his belongings in it, and then set out to inquire for his father, who had not, it might be added, told his son where he was going. Chu Chung's search was fruitless and after a few days he had to give it up. As he had been scrupulously honest during the four years with Shih-lao, the three taels that he received as a parting present was the only money he had. It was hardly enough to start a business with. So after thinking things over he decided to become an oil peddler, since he knew something of the business and was acquainted with the millowners. He bought himself the necessary outfit and deposited the rest of his money with one of the mills.

Now the millowner knew Chu Chung to be an honest man and he knew the circumstances that had led to his disgrace. He was sympathetic and decided to do what he could to help the young peddler. He gave him the best quality oil at the lowest price and measured it out in a manner to give him the advantage. This in turn made it possible for Chu Chung to treat his customers in like manner, so that he had no difficulty in disposing of his load with a nice profit at the end of the day. As he lived frugally and practiced thrift in everything, he was able to save something and buy himself some clothes and necessary household articles. The only thing that preoccupied his mind was that he had not been able to find his father. "I must change my name back to Chin Chung," he said to himself, "so as to make it possible for my father to find me."

Now when a man of position wants to resume his original name, he has to present a petition to the Board of Rites and other appropriate authorities so that his action becomes a matter of public record. How was a humble oil peddler to let the world know that he had changed his name? Well, Chu Chung solved this problem in a very simple manner. He simply wrote on one side of his oil barrel the word "Chin" and on the other side the word "Pienliang," so that people would know at a glance who he was. And indeed the fact that he had resumed his own name soon became known over Linan and people began to refer to him as Chin the oil peddler.

It was the second month, when the weather was neither too cold nor too warm at Hangchou. Hearing that the monks at the Chao Ching Temple were about to hold a nine-day service and concluding that they must need more oil than usual, Chin Chung went thither with his barrels. The monks had heard of him as a peddler whose price was reasonable and whose oil was of the finest quality; they all patronized him and for those nine days he carried on his business at the temple.

> Sharp trade does not always bring profits;
> Honesty may not necessarily cause loss of capital.

On the ninth day Chin Chung left the temple after having sold all his oil. "The day was clear and bright, and pleasure seekers were out like ants." Carrying his empty barrels on a pole over his shoulder, Chin Chung walked along the bank of the lake and took in all the sights of that famous resort. When he began to feel a little tired, he went back to an open space to the right of the temple and sat down on a rock to rest. Presently he noticed several gentlemen in fine clothes emerging from a house not far from him, followed by a young lady. At the door she stopped and bade them good-by and then went back into the house.

In the meantime Chin Chung had been feasting his eyes on the young woman, for in beauty of feature and gracefulness of carriage he had never seen her equal. He became quite intoxicated with her beauty. However, he was an innocent youth and did not know what to make of what he had seen. As he was thus wondering to himself a middle-aged woman came out of the house with a young maid. When the woman saw Chin Chung's oil barrels she said to the maid, "We were just about to send out for oil. Since there is a peddler here, let us get it from him." The maid went inside and returned with a jug. But all this time Chin Chung was thinking about the young beauty he had just seen so that he did not come to himself until the maid approached him and called, "Peddler." Then he answered, "I have no more oil today, but I shall come back tomorrow if you want it."

The maid could read a little and, noting the characters written on the barrels, she said to the older woman, "The peddler's name is Chin." Now the woman had also heard about the reliability of Chin the oil peddler. So she said to him, "We need oil every day. If you are willing to call here I shall be glad to patronize you."

"Thank you, madam," Chin Chung said. "I shall come every

day without fail." Then he said to himself as the woman and the maid went in, "What is she to the young lady I have just seen? If I come to deliver oil to her every day I shall at least see the young lady, whether or not I make any money."

Just as he was about to pick up his load and go on, he saw two carriers stop at the house with a sedan, accompanied by two young servants. The latter went into the house. Presently two maids came out, one carrying a red cushion and another a woven bamboo box, which they gave to the carriers to put under the chair. Then the young lady whom he had seen came out followed by the two servants carrying a lute case, some scrolls, and a flute. She got into the sedan and went off, followed by the maids and servants on foot.

This made Chin Chung wonder even more than before. As he went slowly on his way, he passed a tavern by the lake. As a rule he was not given to extravagances, but on this occasion he decided to celebrate. He put down his load, went into the tavern and sat down at a small table.

"Are you expecting friends, sir, or are you going to drink alone?" the waiter asked.

"Alone," Chin Chung said. "Bring me your best wine and some plain relishes without meat." When the waiter poured his wine, Chin Chung asked, pointing to the house where he had seen the beautiful lady, "Who lives in that house over there?"

"It is Chi Ya-nei's [8] villa," the waiter answered, "but it is now occupied by a woman called Wang Chiu-ma."

"Who was the young lady that went off in a sedan chair a little while back?"

"She is the famous courtesan Wang Meiniang, known as the Queen of Flowers. She is a native of Pienliang and was stranded here as a refugee. She is not only skilled in singing and dancing and playing several instruments but is also accomplished in the game of chess and in painting and calligraphy. All her clients are rich men and pay ten taels of the bright metal for passing the night

[8] Ya-nei was a form of address applied to the sons of rich or noble families during Sung and Yuan times.

with her. She used to live outside the Yungchin Gate, but Chi Ya-nei, one of her intimates, lent this house to her."

When Chin Chung learned that the girl was a native of Pienliang, he felt even more drawn towards her. After finishing his wine, he paid the waiter and left the tavern, and as he walked on he thought thus to himself: "What a pity that such a beautiful girl should fall into a prostitute's house." Then he laughed to himself, saying, "But how could I, a poor oil peddler, have caught a glimpse of her if she had not fallen into such a house?" Then his thoughts grew bolder. "'A man has but one life to live and a plant sees but one autumn.' If I could have a beautiful woman like her in my arms for one night, I should die without regret." Then laughing at himself, he said, "I make but a few cash a day in selling oil. How could I think of such impossible things. Like the toad that longs after the flesh of the swan, I shall never have my wish. She would not receive me even if I had the money, since she is accustomed to dealing only with rich and noble people." But another thought occurred to him: "I have been told that brothel keepers care only for money and are ready to receive a beggar if he can pay the price. So she ought to be willing to receive me who carry on a respectable trade. Surely I need not fear that she would reject me if I had the fee. But where would I get so much silver?" And so he thought to himself as he wended his way home.

There was never such a silly man as he, a man who had only three taels of silver for his capital and yet entertained the idea of paying ten taels for a night with a famous courtesan. But "he who has the will will accomplish his purpose" and in the end he figured out a way. "From tomorrow on," he said to himself, "I shall put something aside toward making up my capital and save the rest for fulfilling my desire. If I save one fen a day I shall have three taels and six chien a year. In three years I shall have accumulated enough money. If I save two fen a day, it will only take a year and a half and if I can save more than that it will take only about one year." As he thus thought to himself he reached his room before he realized it. He unlocked the door, and went inside. Everything in the room was much as before, but because of the thoughts that had occupied his mind on his way home, he found it lonely and desolate. So without even eating his supper, he climbed into bed and there he tossed all night long, thinking about the beautiful lady he had met.

The next morning he got up at dawn, prepared and ate his breakfast, filled his oil barrels, and set out straight for Wang Chiu-ma's house. "You are indeed a man of your word," Chiu-ma said when she saw him. She bought a jug full of oil weighing about five pounds, and being pleased with the price, she said to him: "This will suffice us for only two days. If you will come every other day I shall buy from you entirely and patronize no one else." The peddler promised that he would and went away. He only regretted that he did not get a glimpse of the Queen of Flowers but he was a patient man and told himself that if he kept on coming he would see her sooner or later. There was one thing, however, to overcome: Chiu-ma's house was out of his way and it would not be profitable for him to come so far just to sell a jug of oil to her. "I must see," he said to himself, "what I can do at the Chao Ching Temple. The services are over now, but the monks probably need oil on ordinary days, too. If I can obtain their trade, I shall be able to sell all the oil along this route."

It was as Chin Chung had expected when he inquired at the temple. He made arrangements with the monks to come on even-numbered days, which coincided with his call at Chiu-ma's. So thereafter he covered the Chientang Gate section on even-numbered days and the rest of the city on odd-numbered days. On his calls at Chiu-ma's house he sometimes caught a glimpse of the Queen of Flowers and sometimes he did not. If he did not, he was unhappy and dejected; but when he did see her it only increased his longing and desire.

> Heaven and earth may one day come to an end,
> But this love and passion will never cease.

Time flashed by, and soon more than a year had passed. In the meantime not a day went by but Chin Chung put aside some small pieces of silver, sometimes as much as three fen, and sometimes two, but never less than one, so that now he had quite a large package of it, not knowing himself exactly how much. So on the first rainy day that happened to be odd numbered he decided to take it to the silversmith and have his hoard weighed. He took an umbrella of oiled cloth and went to the silversmith's shop opposite him and told the man that he would like to have the use of the scales. "How much silver can an oil peddler have that he wants to use the scales," thought the silversmith, and so instead of uncovering his scales, he brought out a small steelyard with a maximum capacity of five ounces, thinking that even with that he probably would not have to use the first knot. When Chin Chung opened his package, however, the silversmith was impressed with the pile of small silver that it contained—for it is a fact that the same amount of silver looks more in smaller pieces than when it comes in one lump—and being addicted to fawning upon those who have money, as silversmiths are apt to be, he smiled ingratiatingly now and made haste to uncover his scales, saying to himself, "Indeed, 'a man cannot be judged by his appearance, just as the sea cannot be measured with bushel barrels.'"

Chin Chung's silver came to exactly sixteen ounces, more than enough to pay for the favors of the Queen of Flowers even after deducting his capital of three taels. Then it occurred to him that it would not look very well to pay in small pieces of silver and that he should, since he was in the silversmith's shop, have them melted into larger pieces. Therefore he had the silversmith make for him one ten-tael piece and another piece of one and eight-tenth taels. From the remaining pieces he took some to pay the silversmith and bought for himself a new hat and new shoes and stockings. Then he returned home and laundered and starched his clothes and perfumed them with incense. On the first fine day, he dressed himself up, put his silver in his sleeve, locked his door and went directly to Wang Chiu-ma's house in high spirits.

But arriving at the courtesan's door, he began to grow diffident. "I have always come with my oil barrels," he said to himself. "How am I to broach the subject now that I come as a patron?" Just then Chiu-ma happened to come out and seeing him neatly dressed and without his peddler's outfit she said, "Master Chin, why aren't you carrying on your trade today? What is the occasion for your dressing up like this?"

It was now too late to retreat. Chin Chung steeled himself and said, bowing to Chiu-ma, "I have only come to pay my respects to you." Being an experienced woman, Madame immediately guessed Chin Chung's intention. "He must have taken a fancy to one of the girls," thought she, "and has come to pay a visit or even spend one night. Though he is not the kind of patron that I am used to receive, yet his silver is just as good as the next man's." Then she smiled and said, "Thank you, Master Chin, but I suppose there must be something that you want to see me about?" "Indeed there is," Chin Chung answered, "but I am too embarrassed to know how to begin." "Have no fear," Chiu-ma said. "Come inside and let us talk it over at leisure."

Though Chin Chung had been to Chiu-ma's house well over a hundred times, it was not until now that he had the honor of being invited into her reception hall. Presently a maid brought tea but when she saw who the visitor was she could not help feeling a little puzzled and she giggled under her breath. "What's so funny?" Chiu-ma reprimanded her. "How dare you be so impolite before a guest?" Then after the maid had left the room she again asked Chin Chung, "What is it that you wish to speak to me about, Master Chin?" "I should like to invite one of the girls in the house to a drink of wine," Chin Chung answered. "Surely not just to drink," Chiu-ma said. "You have always been such a steady young man, Master Chin. Since when have you become such a gallant?" "I have entertained this wish for a long time," Chin Chung said truthfully. "You know all my girls," Chiu-ma said. "Which of them have you taken a fancy to?" "I care for no one else," Chin Chung said. "I wish to spend a night with the Queen of Flowers."

Chiu-ma's countenance changed upon hearing this. "What are you saying?" she said testily. "Are you trying to make fun of me?" "I am a straight-forward man," Chin Chung said, "and have only spoken the truth." "But even a manure barrel has two ears:[9] have you not heard of the fee that I charge for my Meiniang? It is more than you could pay for half a night even if you sold your entire business. I would advise you to pick some one else." "I never imagined that the fee would be so enormous," Chin Chung said with a grimace of mock terror. "May I ask how many thousand taels it is?"

This remark convinced Chiu-ma that Chin Chung was only jesting, so her face softened as she said, "Not anywhere near that much. Her price is only ten taels, with wine and other incidentals extra." "If that is all," Chin Chung said, "it is not beyond my resources." Thereupon he took out his ingots and passed them to Chiu-ma saying, "The large piece is exactly ten taels. The small piece is about two taels which I hope will suffice for wine and other incidentals. I shall be forever grateful if you will be kind enough to help me accomplish my desire."

Chiu-ma was overwhelmed at the sight of the fine sycee and could not bear to see them leave her hand, but being afraid that Chin Chung might have his regrets later on when he needed his silver to carry on his trade, she said, in an attempt to clear her own conscience, "It is not an easy thing for a man in your position to accumulate so much silver. You should not be rash but should reflect well what it means to you." "Thank you for your thoughtfulness," Chin Chung said, "but I have made up my mind." "There is yet another difficulty," Chiu-ma said. "Our Meiniang is accustomed to associate only with the best of society and may therefore be unwilling to receive you who are only a humble tradesman." "Surely you must have a way to bring her around," Chin Chung pleaded. "I shall never forget your kindness if you would help me to accomplish my purpose."

Seeing that he was quite determined, Chiu-ma said with a smile, "In truth I have a scheme to help you but it depends on your destiny whether you succeed or not. Meiniang is not home now; she is helping to entertain at a lake party which Huang Ya-nei is giving today; tomorrow she is assisting at a versifying

[9] Handles.

party given by Chang Shan-jen; day after tomorrow the son of President Han is giving a party here, having made arrangements several days ago. So you will have to come and try your luck the day after that. Now another thing: get yourself a silk robe and wear it instead of your cotton garment so that you will not look too out of place here and will thus make it easier for me to pass you off as some one else."

Chin Chung promised to do everything that Chiu-ma suggested. For three days he did not go out to sell, but dressed in a half-new silk gown which he bought in a pawn shop, he strolled along the streets of Linan trying to feel and act like a fine gentleman. On the fourth day he went to Chiu-ma's house bright and early, but found her gate still closed. He left there for a stroll, avoiding the Chao Ching Temple for fear that the monks might see him and laugh at him. On his return to Chiu-ma's house, the gate was open with a sedan chair and horses in front of it and several servants sitting just inside. He discreetly asked one of the grooms and on learning that they were from the Han mansion, he concluded that the young gallant had not yet departed. He betook himself to a restaurant, lingered as long as he could over his food and again returned to Chiu-ma's house. There he found that the young Mr. Han had gone but when he went in, Chiu-ma thus apologized to him; "I am sorry that Meiniang won't be free today, for the young Mr. Han has taken her to his villa to look at the plums in bloom. He is a steady patron and I could not say no. Then Chi Ya-nei has been asking for an appointment two or three times, and I cannot refuse him either since he has loaned us this house. He is apt to stay here four or five days at a time, sometimes even longer. So if you want to see Meiniang you will have to wait, but if you don't want to wait, I still have your generous present untouched and shall return it to you." "My only worry is that you may not want to help me," Chin Chung said. "As long as there is hope, I am willing to wait even though it be for ten thousand years." "If that is the case, I am sure that I shall be able to help you."

As Chin Chung was about to take his leave, Chiu-ma said,

"There is another thing I want to tell you, Master Chin. When you come again, do not come so early, but come at twilight. By that time I shall know for certain whether she will be free or not that evening and can tell you accordingly. Do what I say and depend on me."

Thereafter Chin Chung went to Chiu-ma's house every day after his day's selling was over but for more than a month he had no luck.

Then on the fifteenth of the twelfth month his luck came. It had snowed and it was cold as the west wind began to blow. The ground was happily dry because of the cold. After spending the greater part of the day in carrying on his trade, Chin Chung dressed himself up as usual and went to Chiu-ma's house. She met him with a smile on her face, saying, "Luck is with you today, you are ninety-nine parts toward success." "What is the part that is lacking," Chin Chung asked. "It is that Meiniang is not yet home. But she ought to be back soon. She is at a snow party given by Yu Tai-wei. He is a man over seventy and no longer interested in matters pertaining to 'breeze and moonlight.' He said he would send Meiniang back before dusk. So go to the bridal chamber and drink a cup of wine against the cold while you wait for her to return."

With Chiu-ma leading the way, Chin Chung passed through several courts and made many turns before he came to Meiniang's quarters. It was only a one-story structure, but very bright and airy. To the left was a room for maids while to the right was Meiniang's own room, locked from the outside. There were also two side chambers attached to the main building. In the center was the reception room. A large painting by a well-known artist hung on the wall, and all manner of curios were on the tables. There were also many poems pasted on the walls. These Chin Chung passed over hurriedly, regretting that he could not lay claim to being a scholar. He marveled at the elegance displayed in the room and wondered to himself how much more elegant and luxurious Meiniang's own room must be and decided it was well worth spending ten taels to enjoy such luxury and elegance for one night.

Soon a table was spread with all kinds of unfamiliar delicacies and aromatic wine, and Chin Chung was urged to eat and drink while he waited for Meiniang's return. Chiu-ma kept him company, apologizing for the fact that all her girls were engaged.

It is said that waiting makes for an impatient heart. So it was with Chin Chung. He drank and ate but little and allowed Chiu-ma to monopolize the conversation, his mind being all the time on the object of his love. Thus time dragged on until after the second watch when a bustle of footsteps and voices in the front quarter told them that Meiniang had finally returned, and they both rose to meet her. The Queen of the Flowers was in a state of great intoxication and was leaning upon a maid. When she saw her room lighted and the remains of a feast on the table, she stopped and asked who it was that was being entertained there. "It is the Mr. Chin that I have been telling you about," Chiu-ma said. "He has been an admirer of yours for a long time and has been waiting for a chance to see you for over a month." "I have never heard anyone speak of a Mr. Chin," Meiniang said. "I don't want to see him." So saying she turned to go away, but Chiu-ma stopped her, saying, "He is an honest and trustworthy man. I am telling you the truth." There was nothing for the courtesan to do but turn back. When she came into the room and saw Chin Chung she was sure that she had seen him before but could not for the moment recall his name. "Mother," she said, "I think I know him. He is no one of any consequence. I shall ruin my reputation if I receive him." Chiu-ma said, "He has a silk shop inside the Yungchin Gate where we used to live. You must have seen him then. I could not refuse him because of his sincere admiration for you, and since I have promised him you must help me to keep my promise. Please entertain him for the night; I shall apologize to you and promise not to make engagements for you without consulting you." As she spoke, she pushed Meiniang gently toward Chin Chung and thus the girl could do nothing but go into the room and meet him.

Chin Chung heard every word that was said but pretended to have heard nothing. Meiniang kept looking at him and the more she looked the more she wondered where she had seen him. She had hot wine brought and poured out a large cup, which she drank herself at a gulp, instead of offering it to Chin Chung as Chiu-ma had expected. "Don't drink so much, my child," Chiu-ma warned. "You are drunk already." But Meiniang kept on drinking cup after cup, protesting that she was not drunk, until, unable to stand on her feet any longer, she had her room unlocked and slumped into bed.

"She is very spoiled," said Chiu-ma apologetically to Chin Chung. "She must have something on her mind, for I know it is not anything that you have done that makes her behave like this. Please forgive her." Then taking him into Meiniang's room, she whispered to him to make allowances for Meiniang's state and be gentle with her. She tried to wake up Meiniang and make her undress for bed, but in vain. She left, followed by the maids after they had cleared the table and brought a pot of hot tea at Chin Chung's request.

When Chin Chung turned to look at Meiniang, she was sound asleep with her face toward the wall and lying on top of her brocaded quilt. Afraid that she might be cold and loath to disturb her, he took another quilt folded across the bed rail and put it gently over her and then lay down by her side, nursing the pot of tea with his left hand and gently enfolding Meiniang with his right. He did not once close his eyes for fear that she might wake and want something.

Though he has not flown with the cloud or danced with the rain,
Yet he did inhale fragrance and fondle jade.

After midnight Meiniang woke up feeling sick and miserable. She sat up in bed with her head between her hands and kept on retching. Chin Chung sat up too and tried to ease her by stroking her back. Presently nausea overcame her and as there was no time to lose Chin Chung held his sleeve up to her so that she would not soil her bed. Then she demanded tea and Chin Chung poured for her the tea that he had so thoughtfully kept warm.

After drinking two cups she felt better but she was still tired and weak and fell back and went to sleep again.

Meiniang did not wake up again until daybreak. When she saw Chin Chung lying beside her, she asked him who he was and on being told began to recall vaguely the previous evening. "I must have been very drunk," she said. "No, not very," Chin Chung answered. "Did I vomit?" she asked. "No, you didn't," Chin Chung answered. "That's better," Meiniang said with relief, but after a while she said, "but I remember having vomited and drinking some tea. Could I have dreamed it?" Only then did Chin Chung tell her the truth. "What a thoughtful man!" Meiniang said to herself. She began to feel kindly toward Chin Chung.

Then as she looked at him more attentively, she suddenly was reminded of the peddler and asked him who in truth he was. Thereupon Chin Chung told her who he was, how he had admired her ever since he first laid eyes on her, how he had saved for a whole year in order to have his supreme pleasure, and how happy he was for having had a chance to be near her that night. Meiniang was more moved than ever after hearing this recital. "But don't you regret," she said, "that I wasn't able to entertain you last night and that you have spent your hard-earned money for nothing?" "How could that be possible?" said Chin Chung. "You are a goddess in exile and I consider myself fortunate that you do not take me to task for not having served you better." "You should have saved your money for supporting your family instead of squandering it here," Meiniang said, to which Chin Chung answered that he had no wife and children. "Are you going to come again?" Meiniang asked after a brief silence, to which Chin Chung answered, "The happiness I had last night will sustain me the rest of my life. How dare I hope for more?"

"Where can one find such a good man?" Meiniang thought to herself. "So honest and straightforward, and above all so thoughtful. You can't find one like him in ten thousand. It is a pity that he is a mere peddler, otherwise I should not hesitate to marry myself to him."

As she was thus thinking to herself, a maid brought in water for their morning toilet and two bowls of ginger water. Chin Chung washed his face, took a few sips of the ginger water and then begged leave to go. "Stay a while longer," Meiniang said. "I have a few words to say to you." "Nothing would make me happier to stay as long as I can," Chin Chung said, "but one must know one's place. It was enough impudence on my part to come here last night, for it will surely detract from your reputation when it is known that you have entertained a visitor such as I. It is best that I go as soon as possible."

Meiniang nodded and then sending the maid out, she opened a box and took out twenty taels of silver and gave it to Chin Chung, saying, "Please take this for all your trouble last night, but do not tell any one." Chin Chung refused the gift at first but Meiniang thrust it in his sleeve and pushed him away.

Now let us leave Chin Chung and Meiniang for a while and return to Chu Shih-lao's household, where the maid Orchid and the shop assistant Hsing Chuan had been carrying on their affair openly since Shih-lao was lying sick and helpless in bed. After a few reprimands from Shih-lao they decided to flee together and did so one night, taking with them all the money that was in the shop. Shih-lao then realized that he had been deceived by Hsing Chuan and wished to take Chin Chung back. He sent one of his neighbors to Chin Chung, begging him to remember only the good and forget the unpleasant things of the past. In response Chin Chung went immediately to Shih-lao, who turned over everything to him and put him in charge of the shop. Chin Chung also added his twenty taels to the capital, and changed his name to Chu again since he was again living with Shih-lao.

A month or so afterwards, Shih-lao's illness took a turn for the worse and soon, alas and alack! he died. Chu Chung mourned for him as if he were his real father and buried him with appropriate rites, so that all the people in the neighborhood praised him for his faithfulness. After the funeral he reopened his shop and soon restored it to the prosperity that it had enjoyed before Hsing Chuan ruined it with his dishonesty and sharp practices. It became necessary to hire an assistant and one day the middleman brought him a man over fifty years of age who was looking for a situation. He was no other than Hsin Shan, the father of Meiniang, who had recently come to Linan in the hope of finding his daughter and had been stranded there without means of subsistence. When Chu Chung heard that he was a fellow countryman from Pienliang, he was moved and said, "Since you have no friends to turn to, please come and live with me. I shall treat you as a relative." He gave Hsin Shan money to pay for his lodgings. The latter brought his wife and thenceforward they lived with Chu Chung and assisted him faithfully in tending the shop.

"Time passes like an arrow," and soon more than a year had gone by. As Chu Chung's business prospered and his reputation for honesty grew, he was approached from all quarters with proposals of marriage, but the beauty of the Queen of Flowers had spoiled him for plain, ordinary faces and made him unwilling to accept such offers.

> You cannot talk of water to him who has seen the sea,
> Nor of clouds to him who has viewed the mist over Mount Wu.

In the meantime Meiniang's reputation grew also, and her calendar was full from morning till night. Truly her mouth was satiated with meat and sweets and her body tired of silk and brocade. But her lot was not always an easy one; sometimes a drunken patron would give her annoyance, or a jealous one would make unreasonable demands; sometimes waking up in the middle of the night feeling sick and dejected, she found no one to comfort her. On these occasions she could not help thinking of the peddler and his thoughtfulness, and long for another chance to meet him. Then at the end of about a year, her luck turned and a misfortune befell her.

Now there was at the time a certain young Mr. Wu, the son of the governor of Foochow. He had recently returned from Foochow with a great deal of gold and silver and had been squandering it in gay pursuit of pleasure. He had heard of Meiniang but had not had a chance to see her, for the latter had heard of his ill temper and had refused to receive him. One day during the Clear Bright Festival when every family made offerings at their ancestral tombs and all went out to the countryside to enjoy the spring, Meiniang locked herself in her own room. She was tired from numerous outings and had some painting and calligraphy debts to pay. She lighted some fine incense and got ready the four treasures of the study, but just as she was about to lift her brush she suddenly heard a commotion outside. It was young Mr. Wu with half a dozen insolent servants. He had come to get Meiniang for a boat party, and when Chiu-ma made excuses for Meiniang, he had become angry and proceeded to vent his displeasure by breaking up furniture and household utensils. He was not deceived when he saw Meiniang's room locked from the outside, for being experienced in such matters he knew that it was only a trick to fool innocent customers. He had his servants break the padlock and then kicking the door open, burst into the room. Before Meiniang had time to hide she was seized by two of the servants and forcibly dragged out and through the streets to Mr. Wu's boat. Never before had Meiniang suffered such humiliation and rough handling; she refused to take part in the entertainment and sat in a corner and cried. Her tormentor berated her for her slight and threatened to have her beaten if she did not stop crying. But Meiniang had no fear; she only cried louder and attempted to throw herself into the lake. Finally in exasperation, the young tyrant took her to a deserted spot outside the Clear Wave Gate and there put her ashore after stripping her of her shoes and footbindings, saying to her, "Cheap whore, since you don't want to stay with us, you can go on home yourself."

Helpless in her barefooted condition, Meiniang sat on the ground and abandoned herself to weeping and lamentations over her cruel fate. Then by coincidence Chu Chung, returning home from Shihlao's tomb, passed that way and immediately recognized the Queen of Flowers though her hair was disheveled and her face distorted with grief. "What has happened?" he said in astonishment. Meiniang poured out her heart to him and told him everything. Chu Chung's heart ached for her and his eyes were filled with tears.

He took out a silk handkerchief and splitting it in two bound up her feet with the strips. Then he wiped her tears for her and did up her black silken tresses, and telling her to wait there, he went and hired a sedan and escorted her back to Chiu-ma's place.

In the meantime Chiu-ma was in a state of great agitation because she did not know what had become of Meiniang, so that when Chu Chung brought the girl back her joy was exactly as if she had recovered a priceless pearl. Moreover, she had heard about Chu Chung's inheritance of Chu Shih-lao's shop and was inclined to receive him with a new deference even if he had not done her such a great favor. She overwhelmed Chu Chung with her gratitude and had a feast prepared for him. After a few cups of wine Chu Chung rose to take his leave, but of course Meiniang would not let him go. "I have been thinking of you," she said, "but have not had the opportunity of seeing you. Since destiny has brought us together, you must stay tonight." Chiu-ma, too, added the weight of her invitation.

That evening Meiniang sang and danced for Chu Chung as she had never sung and danced before in her life, and on his part Chu Chung was as happy as a man being entertained by a fairy goddess. Needless to say, his happiness was even more ineffable when, after feasting far into the night, they both retired to their conjugal bed hand in hand . . .

Afterwards, Meiniang said to Chu Chung: "I have a request to make of you which you must not refuse." Chu Chung answered, "If there is anything I can do for you, I should not hesitate to go through fire and boiling water. So how can I refuse you anything?" Meiniang said, "I want you to marry me." Chu Chung said, smiling, "Do not jest with me, my lady, for even if you were to marry ten thousand men, it would never come to my turn." "I speak from the heart," Meiniang said. "For ever since I was tricked into losing my chastity at the age of fourteen I have wanted to follow the virtuous path but have not been able to carry out this wish because I have not met the right man. Though I have met many men in my time, they are all of them seekers of pleasure who have not the slightest consideration for my welfare. Among all I have seen, you are the only sincere one. Moreover, I understand that you are not yet married. If you do not despise me because of my past, I shall be most happy to marry you and serve you until death. If you refuse, I shall take three feet of plain silk and strangle myself before your eyes to prove to you the earnestness of my heart. It would be better than to perish in the hands of some vulgar men as I almost did yesterday." She began to cry after she finished speaking.

"Do not grieve," Chu Chung said. "The undeserved honor that you have conferred upon me is something I had not dared to dream of, to say nothing of refusing it. But my lady, you are a person of great fame, while I am poor and without influence. How could I then manage this thing, however willing I am myself?" "Your lack of means need not be an obstacle," Meiniang answered, "for I started long ago to put valuables aside for this very purpose." Then Chu Chung said, "Even if you are in a position to buy your freedom, I am afraid that you, who have been accustomed to luxuries, will find life in my poor house unendurable." "I am ready to wear cotton and eat coarse food without ever regretting it," Meiniang assured him. Chu Chung said, "But Chiu-ma will probably not consent to it." "I shall be able to take care of her," Meiniang said and then outlined to him her plan. Thus the two talked on until daybreak.

Meiniang had, in fact, stored away many boxes and trunks of jewels and other valuables with her clients. Now on the pretext that she needed them she gradually took them back to her own place and then had Chu Chung take them to his house. When she had everything safely put away, she went to Liu Ssu-ma and told her about her plan to follow the virtuous path. "We have discussed this matter before in some detail," Ssu-ma said. "But you are yet young and I don't know whom you have in mind to marry." "Do not mind who it is," Meiniang said. "Be assured that I have heeded your advice and that it is some one well qualified according to your specifications. I am sure that Mama will not object if Auntie is willing to speak for me. I have little to offer to Auntie to express my regard, but here is ten ounces of gold for Auntie to make some jewelry with." When Ssu-ma saw the gold, she smiled until her eyes were entirely closed. "It is a praiseworthy thing that you propose to do," she said. "I should not be taking this gold from you. However, I'll keep it for you and you may leave everything to me. But since your mother looks upon you as her money tree, she will not let you go unless she has an offer of a thousand taels. Is your party ready to put up this sum? Why don't you let me meet him and talk the things over with him?" "Please do not mind who it is," Meiniang said. "Just consider it that I am buying my own freedom." "Does your mother know that you have come to see me?" "No," Meiniang answered. "Then stay here and have something to refresh yourself," Ssu-ma said. "I shall go to speak to your mother and let you know the outcome."

Ssu-ma then hired a sedan and went to Chiu-ma's house. She asked the latter about Meiniang's recent misfortune and then said, "For us who are engaged in the business it is better to have girls of ordinary beauty, for they will be able to make money for us and cause us no trouble. But because Meiniang is over-famous she is like a piece of fish that has been dropped on the ground which even ants will not leave alone. This may appear like good business but actually it has its disadvantages. Even the vaunted fee of ten taels is only an empty name, for you have to entertain the guests and servants that the clients bring so that they will not make trouble for you or deliberately ruin your furniture or porcelain. Moreover, there are the poor painters and calligraphers and the poetry clubs and chess societies that are continually making demands on you and whom you must wait upon free several times in a month. Then finally, your rich clients are always fighting over Meiniang, and if you promise her to Li you have to refuse Chang, thus pleasing one but offending the other. This incident of Mr. Wu is but a sample of what might happen in the future. You were lucky that nothing worse happened, bad as it was, for you might have lost Meiniang and your capital investment. You know you can't sue those people. I have heard that Mr. Wu is not yet satisfied but is hatching a new plot against you. As long as Meiniang is as particular as she is, you will always be open to trouble."

"She has given me enough worries," Chiu-ma agreed. "Take Mr. Wu, for instance. He is by no means a nobody but a person of some consequence. Yet the girl simply would have nothing to do with him and thus brought this incident upon herself. She used to listen to me a little, but since she became famous, she has been acting terribly spoiled and insists on having her own way. When a guest calls she will receive him if it so pleases her, but if she is unwilling you can't budge her with a team of nine oxen."

"Girls are all like that the minute they enjoy a reputation," Ssu-ma said.

"I wish you would keep your ears open," Chiu-ma said. "If you hear of some one willing to pay a good price, let me know. It is better that I sell her and put an end to my worries."

"That's an excellent idea," Ssu-ma said. "With what you get for her you can buy five or six girls. With luck you might get ten or more. One would be a fool not to seize such a bargain."

"I have thought the matter over well," Chiu-ma said. "As a rule those who have power and influence always try to take advantage of their position and are not willing to pay a fair price. When some one willing to pay something turns up, Meiniang always finds fault with him. Please take care of this matter for me. If the girl should refuse after you have found a suitable match, you will have to talk to her, for she listens to you more than she does to me."

"I have, to tell the truth, come expressly to propose a match for Meiniang," Ssu-ma said, laughing. "How much silver must you have before you let her go?"

"You know how things are, sister," Chiu-ma said. "We in the business always try to buy cheap and sell high. Moreover, Meiniang is renowned all over Linan as the Queen of Flowers. We can't let her go for a mere matter of three or four hundred taels. I must have a thousand for her."

"I'll go and find out," Ssu-ma said. "If the party is willing to pay your price, I'll come back to report. If not, I'll not bother to come back." Then she asked as she was taking her leave, "Where is Meiniang today?"

"She has rarely been home since the Wu incident," Chiu-ma said. "She has been going the rounds of the houses of her clients, complaining to them of her grievance. She went to the Chis day before yesterday; yesterday she went to the Huangs. I don't know where she is today."

Ssu-ma said, "As long as you have made up your mind, Meiniang will have to give in. But in case she should refuse, you can depend on me to bring her around. But there is one thing: you must not change your mind and raise objections yourself."

"I have given my word," Chiu-ma said.

Liu Ssu-ma then went home and told Meiniang of what had passed between her and Chiu-ma. "She has given her consent," she concluded. "As soon as the silver passes hands the matter will be concluded." "The silver is ready," Meiniang said. "Please come to our house tomorrow and supervise the conclusion of this matter. Do not let the matter get cold so that we have to start all over again." "I shall come," Ssu-ma promised. Then Meiniang took her leave and returned to her house, without saying a word to Chiu-ma about her part in the matter.

The next day around noon, Liu Ssu-ma came to Chiu-ma's house as agreed. "How did it go?" Chiu-ma asked. "It's complete nine parts out of ten," Ssu-ma said; "we have now to talk to Meiniang." Thereupon she went to Meiniang's room and greetings over, she asked, "Have you seen your party? Where is the silver?" "It is there in those leather trunks," Meiniang said, pointing to the end of the bed. Then she opened the trunks one by one and took out thirteen or fourteen packages of silver of fifty taels each and enough jewels and precious stones to make up the remainder of the agreed amount.[10] Liu Ssu-ma was so surprised at this display of wealth that her eyes "gave out sparks and her mouth watered." For a long while she was speechless but wondered and marveled to herself how a young girl like Meiniang could have so much foresight and how she could manage to save up so much. Thinking that her silence meant that she was not satisfied with what she had given

[10] Note that it was said previously that Chin Chung had taken the valuables away for safekeeping.

her, Meiniang brought out four bolts of fine silk and some jewels and put them on the table, saying, "Please accept these things for the trouble you have taken on my account." Ssu-ma was overjoyed and went to Chiu-ma and said, "It is Meiniang herself who wants to buy her own freedom. It is even better than if some man had wanted her, for she will pay the entire sum agreed upon and there will be no need to go to the expense of feasting the idlers who would no doubt claim credit for the transaction."

Chiu-ma's countenance reflected displeasure when she heard of Meiniang's riches, for one must remember that there is no one in the world to surpass Madame Bustard in greediness and that she is never content unless she gets into her own hands everything that her girls acquire. If a courtesan accumulates a few things of her own, Madame never fails to ransack her room at the first opportunity and appropriate everything of value for herself. But Chiu-ma had not dared to do this to Meiniang because she was such a money maker for her and had many influential clients ready to defend her rights, and so she had no idea that Meiniang had managed to accumulate so much wealth.

Noting the change of color in Chiu-ma's face, Ssu-ma guessed what was in her mind and hastened to say: "Sister Chiu, be not 'of three hearts and two minds.' Niece has saved these things from her own proper share. If she had been inclined toward spending, she would have spent everything or even given it to her poorer lovers without your knowing. Moreover, if she had nothing of her own, you would have to buy her some new clothes and jewels; you know you could not send her away naked. Now, since Meiniang has money of her own, it means that you'll have to lay out nothing but can keep every ounce of the thousand taels for yourself."

This little speech made Chiu-ma feel better and she agreed to carry out the bargain she had struck. Ssu-ma then went to Meiniang's room and brought out the packages of silver and handed them to Chiu-ma, together with the jewels, which she appraised piece by piece, saying that if Chiu-ma sold them she was sure to get more money. The turtle—that is, Chiu-ma's husband—was summoned and he wrote a certificate of release and handed it to Meiniang.

"Since Auntie is here," Meiniang said, "I should like to take leave of 'father and mother' now and stay with Auntie until the wedding day. Would you let me do that, Auntie?" To this Ssu-ma readily consented, for since she had received so many valuable presents from Meiniang she was eager to get Meiniang out of Chiu-ma's house so that there would be no possibility for her to withdraw from the bargain.

Thereupon Meiniang packed her own things and took leave of her master and mistress and the other girls in the establishment. Ssu-ma put her in a nice, quiet room, and soon an auspicious day was selected and in due time the wedding took place. Boundless was the happiness of the conjugal chamber, for though theirs was an old love, the joys of marital consummation were not thereby diminished.

The day following the wedding, Hsin Shan and his wife—who, it will be remembered, were helping Chu Chung with the shop—asked to see the bride, and thereupon followed the recognition and reunion of daughter and parents. To celebrate this double happiness, Chu Chung feasted his friends and neighbors, and Meiniang sent presents to all her former friends who had helped her.

After the "Full Month" had passed, Meiniang opened up all her trunks and boxes and exhibited gold and silver and fine silks to a total worth of over three thousand taels. She turned the keys over to her husband, who made prudent and gradual use of the wealth in acquiring land and houses and in enlarging his business. In less than a year's time his house became quite impressive with fine furnishings and many servants. To show his gratitude to the gods for his blessings, Chu Chung made a vow to make offerings of candles and incense at all the temples in the region, together with a three-month supply of oil for the "eternal lights" of each. In the course of these pilgrimages he came to the Upper Tien Chu Temple where his father was serving as an incense lighter. Although his father did not recognize him (for both the years and his good fortune had tended to alter Chu Chung's mien), the writing on the oil barrels (for they were the same barrels on which he had written his name and his native city) attracted his father's attention, and a series of questions soon established their true relationship. His father did not wish, however, to return to the mundane world, so Chu Chung built him a neat little apartment on the grounds of the Upper Tien Chu and took care of all his wants. Every ten days he would go there to visit his father and four times a year he would be accompanied by his wife on these visits. The old man Chin lived to be over eighty before he passed away without illness.

As for Chin Chung (for our hero had again assumed his original name after his reunion with his father) and his wife, they both lived to old age. They had two sons, who both studied and passed the examinations. To this day a man expert in the art of *pang ch'en* is nicknamed "Little Master Chin" or "the oil peddler" by those wise in matters concerning breeze and moonlight.

The Three Brothers

Anonymous

16TH CENTURY

Mark well the reunion under the branches of the Judas tree
Forget not the communal quilt in the Cherry Hall;
Keep in mind always the virtue of brotherly love,
And thus avoid the shame of the bean-stalk poem.

This poem was composed to urge upon people the importance of fraternal love. It contains three allusions, which I shall now explain to the reader one by one.

The first line alludes to the story of the three Tien brothers. These three brothers had lived together from their childhood. The oldest married a wife known as Tien Ta-sao,[1] the second married a wife called Tien Erh-sao.[1] They both lived in sisterly harmony with never a quarrel between them. When the third brother grew up he married a wife called Tien San-sao.[1]

Now San-sao was not a very virtuous woman, and because she had a small dowry of her own and wanted to use it to satisfy her own greed for delicacies and luxuries, she was distressed to see the family cook their rice in a common pot and eat their meals at a common table, and to find that none of them had any money or a steelyard of his own. And so she nagged her husband day and night saying, "Your brothers are in charge of the family purse and the family acres and you know nothing of the income and outgo. They know everything, while you are kept in the dark. How are you to know whether they do not say that they have spent ten parts when they have really spent only one, or a hundred

[1] The names mean first, second, and third sister-in-law, respectively.

when they have spent only ten? You are now living together but the day will come when you will have to separate. If the family fortune should decline, you, being young and inexperienced, will be the one to lose. I think it is best for you to divide up the inheritance now and each to live your own life."

Under this constant nagging Tien San was brought around to his wife's point of view and broached the subject to his brothers through some relatives. At first Tien Ta and Tien Erh were unwilling but at last they yielded to the persistent importunities of Tien San and his wife. They divided everything up into equal parts and each took one. But they did not know what to do with an ancient Judas tree that had brightened their courtyard for generations and which was even then in full bloom. Tien Ta, being a very just and scrupulous man, suggested that they should cut the trunk into three equal sections and weigh out the branches and twigs into three equal groups. The other brothers agreed and they waited only for the morrow to cut down the tree.

When they went out the next morning to cut down the tree, they were astonished to see that it had withered overnight. Moreover, when Tien Ta touched it with his hand it fell, exposing all its dried roots. At this Tien Ta burst out crying. "Why do you grieve so for a mere tree?" the other two brothers asked. "It is not for the tree that I grieve," the eldest brother said, "but for what it symbolizes, for just as we are born into the same clan and of the same parents so are the branches and leaves of this tree sprung from the same trunk and roots. Now the tree has died because its branches and leaves do not want to be separated. It can only portend that we, too, cannot flourish apart. It is for this reason that I grieve."

Tien Erh and Tien San were greatly moved by what their brother said, for how could it be that a man should be less virtuous than a tree? They embraced one another and cried and decided that they would not separate after all.

The sound of their crying had brought the wives to the scene. Ta-sao and Erh-sao were overjoyed when they learned the cause and the turn of events, but San-sao grumbled because she was thwarted. Tien San wanted to divorce his wife but was dissuaded from it by his brothers. San-sao was ashamed and went back to her own room and hanged herself. This is what the Sage meant when he said that he who calls disaster upon himself will perish by it.

When Tien Ta went to look at the Judas tree again, he found, to his even greater astonishment, that it had righted itself, the branches had come back to life and the flowers bloomed more gorgeously than ever. He summoned his brothers to see the miracle and they both marveled at it. Thereafter the Tien family lived together generation after generation, and people paid tribute to them in the following poem:

> Under the Judas tree one tells the story of the three Tiens,
> Whose separation and reunion were reflected by the flowers.
> For branches from the same roots cannot be cut asunder
> And in family affairs one must not listen to women.

The Cherry Hall mentioned in the second line was built by Emperor Hsuan Tsung[2] of the T'ang Dynasty as a private retreat for himself and his brothers, whom he loved dearly. He named it Cherry Hall because the flower of that tree was used as a symbol of brotherly love in one of the *Songs*.[3] He also had a huge bed made and had it furnished with a long pillow and a broad quilt, so that he and his brothers might sleep together after their frequent feasts. Because of his exemplary conduct, posterity composed the following poem in honor of him.

> The sheepskin drum rumbled and the jade flute piped
> As the feast was done in the painted halls.
> The palace ladies lit their candles and waited till dawn,
> Little dreaming that the Ruler would not return for the night.

[2] Reigned 713-755. Better known as Ming Huang, consort of the ill-fated Kuei-fei.

[3] The *Shih Ching* or *Book of Poetry*. The first stanza, as translated by Waley, reads:

> The flowers of the cherry-tree,
> Are they not truly splendid?
> Of men that now are,
> None equals a brother.

The fourth line alludes to the story of Ts'ao Pe'i,[4] the son of the infamous Ts'ao Ts'ao, who after his father's death usurped the throne of Han and established the Dynasty of Wei. Ts'ao P'ei had a younger brother by the name of Ts'ao Chih, who was talented above every one else in the land and was so beloved by his father that there were times when it appeared that he would be named his heir. Ts'ao P'ei was jealous of him and when he assumed power, he wanted to have him put out of the way on some pretext. One day he summoned Tzu-chien[5] and said to him, "The late Emperor used to praise your talents and quick wit. We should like to see it for ourselves. Now we want you to compose a poem in the space of seven steps. If you cannot do so, we shall have you punished for deceiving the late Emperor."

Tzu-chien finished the poem before he had walked seven steps.

> To boil beans one lights the bean stalks.
> While the beans wept, they made this appeal:
> "Since we are born of the same roots
> Why must you burn us with such zeal?"

Ts'ao P'ei was moved to weeping when he heard the poem and decided to forget his old jealousy. Posterity composed the following poem about this incident:

> From earliest times jealousy has ruled the noble and great;
> How little time do seven steps provide!
> How sad that bean and bean stalk continued their enmity
> And that fratricide raged throughout the Six Dynasties.[6]

Do you wonder why I, the story teller, am telling you these three stories today? It is because I want to tell the story known as "The three brothers who achieved fame by their fraternal love." My story does not deal with heroes as talented as Ts'ao Chih or as exalted as Ming Huang and his brothers but it teaches a lesson

[4] A.D. 188-227.
[5] Derived name of Ts'ao Chih.
[6] Roughly, third to sixth centuries, inclusive.

as cleverly as the story of the three Tiens of Judas tree fame. It is hoped that after hearing this story, brothers lacking in harmony will take heed and try to emulate these three brothers.

The couplet says well:

> If one wants to know things that happen in this world
> One must read the books of the ancients.[7]

The events of this story took place during the reign of Ming Ti (A.D. 58-75) of the Eastern Han Dynasty. At that time the empire was tranquil and the people happy in their pursuits; the court echoed with the song of the phoenix and the "mountains and forests"[8] were not disturbed by the sighs of unemployed talents. Now in the Han Dynasty the officials were not picked through a system of examinations as is done today, but through the recommendations of the provincial authorities. Although there were such categories of candidates as Learned Scholars and Righteous Worthies, the most esteemed title was that of Filial-and-Honest. For one who is filial to his parents is bound to be loyal to his prince, and he who is honest is bound to be just and benevolent to the people under his charge. During the Han Dynasty a man who was recommended for this esteemed title was immediately given an official post to fill. If things had been the same during that ancient time as they are nowadays, when even in the district examinations thousands of letters of recommendation are received by the examiners, the coveted title would have gone to young men of rich and noble families, and those who were poor would have had no chance whatsoever, were they as filial as Tsengtzu or as scrupulously honest as Po Yi. But this was not the case in the Han Dynasty because of a wonderful system they had. If a man recommended turned out to be good and capable, not only was he promoted rapidly himself but the recommending official was also rewarded. Conversely, if the recommended man turned out to be worthless and corrupt, not only was he dismissed or punished according to his desert but his

[7] Two lines frequently introduced by story tellers.
[8] As opposed to the "court."

sponsors were also dealt with in like manner. Because of this, no one dared to make indiscriminate recommendations, and consequently justice prevailed and the officials' ranks were kept clean and unblemished. But we can't dwell on these thoughts now.

There was a man by the name of Hsu Wu, a native of Yanghsien district, province of Kuaichi. His parents died when he was fifteen, leaving in his care two younger brothers named Hsu Yen and Hsu Pu, aged nine and seven respectively. Hsu Wu led his servants and slaves in the work of the fields by day and studied under the lamp light in the evening. Though his brothers were too young to work in the fields, Hsu Wu made them watch the proceedings so that they would learn to appreciate the produce of the land. In the evening, however, he would study with them and explain the text to them himself, instructing them in the requirements of proper conduct and encouraging in them the qualities esteemed in man. If they failed to attend his instructions, he never reprimanded them but would, kneeling in the ancestral temple, weep and reprove himself for his lack of inspiring example, until his brothers were stricken with shame and promised to mend their ways.

Thus time went on and his younger brothers soon reached manhood, and the family fortune prospered. Hsu Wu was urged by his friends to marry but Hsu declined, saying, "If I marry I shall have to give up sharing the same bed with my brothers. I cannot bear to sacrifice brotherly love for the sake of conjugal happiness." And so together they went on plowing by day and studying by night, eating out of the same vessels and sleeping in the same bed. His fame grew. He became known as Hsiao-ti Hsu Wu, or Hsu Wu the filial and fraternal, and his virtues were celebrated in the following saying:

In Yanghsien Hsu Wu is the shining light,
Who plows by day and studies by night.
More parent than brother is he;
Rare indeed such fraternity!

His reputation reached the ears of the provincial authorities, and recommendations poured into the Court. He was appointed a counselor, and the provincial authorities were instructed to apprise him of his appointment. Hsu Wu then made preparations to go to the capital. He instructed his brothers to carry on their plowing and studying just as they had been doing under his supervision and commanded the servants and slaves to serve and obey their younger masters well. After having given these and other instructions, he got together his baggage and, refusing the government carriage provided for him, hired his own conveyance and set out for the capital with one single servant. After some days he reached Changan and there assumed his post.

At the capital his reputation had preceded him and people flocked to his house to make his acquaintance. He was esteemed at court and renowed throughout the empire. When the high officials at court found that Hsu Wu was not yet married, they all wanted to marry their daughters to him. Thereupon Hsu Wu thought to himself thus: "It would not be right for me to marry before my brothers do. Moreover, we are of a poor plowing-and-reading[9] family and it is only by luck that I now serve at court. If I were to marry the daughter of a rich and noble family, it is likely that I'll find her spoiled and unsuited to a simple family like ours. She would, too, have difficulty in getting along with the future wives of my brothers; I must be on my guard against this."

Thus he thought to himself but of course he could not give such a reason for refusing the offers of marriage. He simply said that he was already engaged and that he could not break a marriage contract made in the days of his poverty. This enhanced his reputation. He was frequently consulted on questions which the great ministers could not decide, and, being well versed in the teachings of the sages, he never failed to give them good counsel. He became more and more valued at court and in a few years' time rose to a high position.[10]

In the meantime he had not forgotten about his brothers. One

[9] *Keng-tu,* the great middle class from which the administrative officials are recruited through the examination system.

[10] Up to this point I have translated the story more or less in full. I have cut the remainder of the story to about half its original length by omitting all superfluous padding.

day, suddenly realizing that they had not yet been recommended, he decided that he would return to his native home and see how they were progressing with their studies. He presented a memorial to the throne and asked for leave, which was granted.

Once he reached home, however, Hsu Wu decided to retire from official life altogether. Then he summoned his brothers to him and questioned them on the progress they had made in their studies. They pleased him greatly by answering with ease and fluency. He looked into their joint patrimony and found that it had prospered under his brothers' management.

Then Hsu Wu solicited the respectable families in the region and made suitable matches for his brothers. Not until then did he himself marry. His brothers' weddings followed. A few months went by, and then one day Hsu Wu said to his brothers: "I have read that brothers should set up separate establishments after their majority. Now that you and I are all married, we should each set up his own house." His brothers obeyed, and on a selected day they prepared wine and invited the elders of the village to their house. After a few rounds of wine, Hsu Wu told the elders of his prosposal to separate from his brothers. He summoned the servants and slaves and listed the family inheritance. He took for himself the larger buildings, saying to his brothers, "I must have these in order to keep up appearances suitable to my position; you can have the more modest huts, since your positions do not require anything more elaborate." He took for himself the more fertile land, saying, "I shall need these more productive parcels to provide me the wherewithal to entertain my large circle of friends; the sterile pieces will do for you if you practice proper industry." Then finally he took for himself the better servants and slaves and gave a similar reason for his action.

Now the elders gathered were surprised by Hsu Wu's behavior, for they had expected him, with his reputation for brotherly love, to ask little for himself and give more to his brothers and never dreamed that he would take everything desirable for himself and leave to his brothers the equivalent of barely half the estate. Some of the more righteous guests left abruptly in great indignation.

Some of the more impetuous were about to reprove Hsu Wu to his face but they were prevented from doing so by the more discreet guests present.

Now those guests that advised silence had good reasons for their action. They said, "The hearts of rich and aristocratic people are different from those of us poor. Hsu Wu has changed since he has served at Court. Moreover, outsiders should not try to stir up dissension in the family. You and I are, after all, outsiders and should not meddle in their affairs. It probably would not be of any use, but would only serve to make the younger brothers conscious of the injustice done to them, whereas now they are willing to obey their eldest brother without a murmur. If they were unwilling, they would speak up for themselves. It is now too late to put in our word for them."

The couplet says well:

> Take not upon yourself what is not your own affair
> Speak not to those who are of a different mind from your own.

The younger brothers did not show the least inclination to dispute their eldest brother's disposition of their family inheritance, for they had been taught well the importance of brotherly love and believed implicitly in their eldest brother's judgment.

Thenceforward Hsu Wu occupied the central rooms, while his brothers lived in the smaller rooms to either side. The latter continued to lead the servants and slaves in the labor of the fields and spent their spare moments in studying. When they encountered passages that they could not understand they would take their problems to Hsu Wu and ask for his elucidation. The wives, too, emulated the example set by the brothers and lived in sisterly harmony.

Then the elders of the district began to say among themselves that Hsu Wu was a fraud but that Hsu Yen and Hsu Pu were truly filial and honest. They composed a jingle in which they set forth the circumstances of the disposal of the Hsu family inheritance and bemoaned the fact that true merit should have been without reward. The fame of Hsu Yen and Hsu Pu spread so that when Ming Ti ascended the throne and issued an order to the provincial authorities to seek out new talents for the court they were enthusiastically recommended. At first they were loath to leave behind their simple life and the tutelage of their eldest brother, but the latter urged upon them the duty of serving their sovereign and sent them to court, where in due time they rose to high positions and earned reputations for themselves only slightly less eminent than the one their brother had earned before them. Then one day they suddenly received a letter from Hsu Wu, which read as follows:

> For a commoner to receive summons from the court and to rise among the ranks of the nine ministers is the highest honor that can come to a man. Yet the two Shus said well: 'He who knows contentment will not suffer humiliation; he who knows when to stop will avoid disaster.' Since you two have no unique talents that raise you above the rest of mankind, it is best for you to show courage in retirement and vacate your positions for more worthy men.

Upon receipt of this letter Yen and Pu immediately sent in their resignations, which the Emperor twice refused but accepted the third time. Then the brothers hastened home by traveling night and day and presented themselves before their eldest brother. The day following their arrival Hsu Wu prepared a feast to which he invited all the elders of the village and at which he revealed certain things which proved the truth of the poem:

> Just as the quail knows nothing of the roc,
> And the river god of the capacities of the oceans,
> So would the anxieties of the Sages' minds
> Be beyond the surmise of the vulgar multitude.

Even before he spoke, Hsu Wu's tears began to flow, to the bewilderment of his neighbors and his younger brothers. The latter knelt before him and asked, "Brother, why do you grieve?" and Hsu Wu answered: "I have something which I have kept to myself for several years and of which I must speak now." And then, pointing to his brothers, he continued: "It was because you two did not achieve fame that I had to resort to steps against my heart and thus brought disgrace on the ancestors and made myself the object of scorn in the eyes of our neighbors—it is because of this that I weep." Then he took out the family register in which was entered the family holdings and the receipts of grains and cloth and silks during the past years and passed it around the company present. They, however, still could not understand his intention. Hsu Wu continued: "I tried to instruct my brothers so that they might achieve fame and bring honor to our ancestors, but unfortunately I won before they did an undeserved name and was elevated to official ranks while they continued to work in the fields and to pursue their studies. I had thought of emulating Ch'i Hsi of antiquity[11] who did not hesitate to recommend members of his own family through any fear that people might impute to him favoritism, but I did not dare do it because I was afraid that it might stain my brothers' good names for the rest of their lives. Therefore I proposed division of the family inheritance and appropriated for myself the best of everything, knowing full well that my brothers, well schooled in brotherly love and self-denial, would not dispute with me over such worldly possessions. Thus I braved the foul path of greed so that my brothers might earn a reputation for generosity. Indeed it was as I had calculated: they did in fact receive the kind and just recommendations of you, my good neighbors, and rose to the ranks of the officials. My wish has been fulfilled and I am, therefore, turning over everything to my brothers, as is only just, and also in order that you, my neighbors and elders, may know what I have hidden in my heart during these past years."

Only then did Hsu Wu's neighbors and elders of the district learn what had been the real purpose behind Hsu Wu's apparent greediness and they were filled with shame for their own ill-founded suspicion and filled with admiration for Hsu Wu's ex-

[11] First half of the sixth century B.C. When, on his retirement, he was asked to name some one to take his place, he first recommended one of his enemies and then, when the latter died before taking office, his own son.

traordinary conduct. His brothers had begun to weep during the course of his recital; now they fell on their knees before their brother and thanked him for the sacrifices that he had made on their account. They refused, however, to accept Hsu Wu's offer, insisting that the increased value of the family fortune was justly his own since it was owing to his able management that the estate had prospered. Hsu Wu, on his side, insisted that all was his brothers' due, and thus the brothers pushed the register back and forth until finally the neighbors intervened and the family inheritance was divided under their supervision into three equal shares among the brothers. Hsu Wu, however, was determined to redeem his past action by some act of self-denial. He proposed, therefore, to set aside half of his share of the estate for the relief of the poor of the district. Not to be outdone, Yen and Pu did the same, much to the universal admiration of the inhabitants of the region.

The elders of the district then reported in detail these deeds of brotherly love to the provincial authorities, who in turn presented the case to the Emperor. An edict was issued to give formal recognition of the meritorious conduct of the Hsu brothers by erecting an arch at the head of the street where they lived. Henceforth it became known as the Street of Brotherly Love. As for the brothers, they all lived to a great age and enjoyed the never failing delights of their simple lives.

Bibliographical Note

The most comprehensive collection of Chinese tales of the literary or *ch'uan-ch'i* type in English is to be found in *Chinese Prose Literature* by E. D. Edwards (2 vols. London, 1937-38), particularly in Vol. II, where the reader will also find Miss Edwards's versions of tales Nos. 2-12, and 14-15, besides numerous others. For later imitations of tales of this type and of anecdotes in the Six Dynasties tradition, see *Liao Chai Chih Yi,* by P'u Sung-ling (1640-1715), translated by H. A. Giles under the title *Strange Stories from a Chinese Studio* (2d ed. Shanghai, 1908). The most accessible English translations of tales of the popular or *p'ing-hua* type are: E. B. Howell, *The Inconstancy of Madame Chuang* (London, 1925) and *The Restitution of the Bride* (London, 1926); George Soulié de Morant, *Chinese Love Tales* (New York, 1931), containing seven tales from the *Hsing Shih Heng Yen;* Harold Acton and Lee Yi-hsieh, *Glue and Lacquer* (London, 1941), containing four tales from the same source. None of the tales in these volumes have been duplicated in mine.

Notes on the Tales

HSU YEN'S STRANGE ENCOUNTER

The Indian origin of this tale is obvious. It is based on the parable of Buddha's hair, wherein each hair is said to give forth an infinite number of rays of light, each enveloping an image of Buddha, of ordinary size and complete down to the last hair. For two Western discussions of this theme, see Charles B. Maybon, "Un conte chinois du Vie siécle," *Bulletin de l'École Française d'Étrême Orient,* VII (1907), 360-63, and comment on it by Edouard Chavannes in the *T'oung Pao,* Ser. II, Vol. 9 (1908), pp. 599-601. A tale almost identical with Wu's version first appeared in the *Ling Kuei Chi* of a fourth-century writer. The only difference is that in the earlier version, the miracle was supposed to have been performed by a foreign priest, while in Wu's version the magician had become Sinicized.

Wu Chün was a well known poet of his time and is known to have compiled a history of the Ch'i dynasty. The present tale is taken from the *Hsü Ch'i Hsieh Chi,* which as we have it today represents only portions recovered from the *T'ai P'ing Kuang Chi* and other sources.

THE ANCIENT MIRROR

This may be regarded as the earliest of the tales known as the ch'uan-ch'i type, though it is difficult to draw the line between it and the earlier anecdote. Actually it is no more than a series of mirror lore (that is, anecdotes about the magic quality of ancient mirrors), loosely strung together by the device of the first-person narrative. The author is, according to his own account, the elder brother of Wang Chi, the poet, and therefore the younger brother of Wang T'ung, author of a philosophic treatise known by his preferred name *Wen Chung Tzu.* His name is given as Wang Ning in the biography of Wang Chi in the *New T'ang History.* "The Ancient Mirror" is his only extant work.

THE WHITE MONKEY

There are four principal types of monkey legend in Chinese literature. By far the most ancient in origin is the legend of the monkey as the kidnaper of beautiful women, of which "The White Monkey" is one of the best examples. Some writers have attempted to connect this legend with the *Ramayana,* but as far as this early version is concerned I am more inclined to think that the similarity is purely coincidental. Another type of legend makes the white monkey an elusive messenger of the gods, whose specialty is to deliver the "book of heavenly stratagems" to the right person at the proper time. In a third type the monkey is described as a river demon of prodigious strength in a tale by Li Kung-tso (author of "Hsieh Hsiaowo" entitled "Ku Yueh Tu Ching.") The best-known monkey legend is of course about a monkey who became a god (The Great Sage, Equal of Heaven), the hero of one of the longest Yuan plays (Wu Ch'ang-lin, *Hsi Yu Chi*) and one of China's best known novels. The latter has been translated by Arthur Waley and published under the title *Monkey* (New York, 1943).

THE DISEMBODIED SOUL

The notion of an errant soul is an ancient and universal one; so is the notion that ghosts and spirits may take corporeal form and live among men. The idea that an errant soul, that is, a soul that wanders off from its body, can have a corporeal existence while its corpus is still more or less in a working condition, such as we find in this story, is rare if not unique. This probably explains the fact that in later elaborations of this theme (take, for instance, T'ang Hsien-tsu's famous play *Mu Tan T'ing,* translated into German by Vincenz Hundhausen under the title *Die Rückkehr der Seele,* Leipzig, 1937) prefers the variation in which the unhappy heroine languishes and dies, visits the lover as a corporeal ghost, and then comes back to life when her body (which has in the meantime been miraculously saved from disintegration) is exhumed.

Besides Edwards' translation, the reader will also find a version by Lin Yutang in *The Wisdom of China and India.*

THE MAGIC PILLOW

It may be instructive to compare the better known variations of this rather trite theme ("Life is but a dream") for such a comparison will demonstrate concretely the difference between the Six Dynasties anecdote and the T'ang tale and show how the traditional fiction writer is essentially an elaborator.

The direct ancestor of Shen's tale is a legend recorded by Kan Pao (fl. 290-320) in his *Sou Shen Chi* or *Quest of the Gods,* which runs as follows:

"In a temple at Tsiaohu there is a jade pillow with a crack on it. Once Yang Lin, a merchant of Shanfu, went to the temple to pray. 'Would you like to have a good marriage?' the temple attendant asked him, and on Yang Lin's answering that he would, the attendant conducted him to the pillow, whereupon he crawled into the crack and found therein painted halls and gem-studded chambers. There he met a high official named Chao, who gave his daughter to him in marriage. Six sons were born to him and they all became scribes in the imperial secretariat. For more than thirty years he lived in that land of illusion and had no thought of returning. Then he suddenly woke up and found himself by the pillow as before. He was greatly moved by his experience."

Shen's story is many times longer, but it is essentially only an elaboration. When Li Kung-tso made use of this theme, however, he introduced what we might call the device of objectification, that is, he undertook to prove that the dream was more than a dream. In his tale (known as "The Governor of the Southern Branch") the hero discovers, after waking from a long, long dream life, that the country he visited is in fact a colony of ants in an ancient tree not far from his house, that there is in fact a province of Nan K'o or Southern Branch, and that there had been indeed a war between this colony of ants and another colony some distance away. In short, every significant detail in the dream was corroborated after he woke up.

Now let us take a big jump in time and examine the variation on this theme by P'u Sung-ling of the late seventeenth century.

He frankly called his tale "Hsü Huang Liang" or "A New Version of the Yellow Millet Theme," and in the first part of his story he paralleled Shen's version fairly closely except that he made something of a villain of his hero. In the second part, however, he made the villain die, suffer the tortures of hell, and live another life of misery (as an abused concubine) to atone for his crimes. As a climax, he (as the concubine) was falsely accused and convicted for the murder of his master, and woke up crying out his innocence.

The dream theme has also been made use of extensively by Yuan and Ming dramatists. Ma Chih-yuan (fl. 1230-60) made use of Shen's tale in his *Yellow Millet Dream,* while T'ang Hsien-tsu (1550-1617) made use of both Shen's story (*On the Road to Hantan*) and Li Kung-tso's variation of it (*The Southern Branch*).

JENSHIH

Fox legends outnumber all other animal lore in popular Chinese mythology, not excluding the all-pervading dragon. In the *T'ai P'ing Kuang Chi* there are nine chapters devoted to fox fairies and only eight to the dragon. In P'u Sung-ling's collection the fox figures in from a quarter to a third of the total of around 400 anecdotes and tales. "Jenshih" is by no means the earliest tale of this type—there is, as a matter of fact, a story by Liu Yi-ch'ing of the fifth century (preserved in the *Fa Yuan Chu Lin,* chapter 31) which bears the same relation to "Jenshih" as Kan Pao's tale bears to Shen Chi-chi's "The Magic Pillow."

THE DRAGON'S DAUGHTER

Except for a few flaws pointed out in the footnotes, this is to my mind one of the best tales in the literary tradition. There are no serious contradictions in motivation, as in the case of "Li Yahsien" and "Ying Ying," and it contains some passages of lofty prose (Liu Yi's defiant speech when the Lord of Ch'ien T'ang told him to marry his niece or else—) rarely encountered in this branch of Chinese literature.

For a brief discussion of this theme and the plays derived from it, see Edwards, II, 86. Nothing is known of the author, and this tale is apparently his only extant work.

HUO HSIAOYÜ

Li Yi, the villain of this story, was a well-known poet of his time, though little of his verse has come down to us. It is recorded in the *Kuo Shih Pu* by Li Chao that Li Yi had a suspicious nature and it may well be that the story was founded on fact.

LI YAHSIEN

One of the most celebrated faithful-courtesan stories, from which stem at least two plays (see Edwards, II, 154). There are also several variations on this theme in tales of the popular tradition. In the original the hero is simply referred to as *Sheng* (the student, the young man) and the heroine *Wa* (the girl). To simplify matters I have, following the example of the anonymous author of "The Oil Peddler," referred to them by the names given to them by the Yuan dramatist Shih Chün-pao.

It is not without trepidation that I have decided to include this and the story of Ying Ying, for both of them have already been translated with skill and grace by Arthur Waley (*More Translations*). I have ventured to do it partly because I want to bring together, for the convenience of students of Chinese fiction, the most representative tales in one volume, and partly because those interested in the problems involved in translating from the Chinese may find it instructive to compare Mr. Waley's versions and mine.

Po Hsing-chien is the younger brother of Po Chü-i, the poet. He is also the author of a series of three short tales entitled "San Meng Chi," or "Three Dreams." (See Edwards, I, 209-11.) Hsing-chien's dates as I have given are based on pertinent material in Po Chü-i's collected works.

THE STORY OF YING YING

Chang Sheng (the student Chang) and Ying Ying may be described as the Romeo and Juliet of Chinese literature. Yet what a cad Chang Sheng is and how the story must reflect on the Chinese idea of love! In extenuation it might be pointed out that Chang does not appear quite as black in Wang Shih-fu's play *The Western Chamber* (of which there are two English translations: S. I. Hsiung, *The Western Chamber;* Henry H. Hart, *The West Chamber*), as he does in Yuan Chen's story, and that it is the play rather than the story that has made Chang Shen and Ying Ying the ideals of would-be Talented Youths and Beautiful Maidens. In the play, Ying Ying does not lecture Chang Sheng one day and then suddenly gives herself to him without apparent reason the next, but relented only when Chang was dying of lovesickness; neither did Chang Sheng betray Ying Ying as he does (again without any apparent reason) in the story.

It has been suggested that this story is based on an autobiographical incident, but I have found no plausible, much less conclusive, evidence for it. Besides the versions by Mr. Waley and Miss Edwards, the reader will find still another version by Mr. Hsiung, included in his translation of the play.

The cause for the mutiny of the garrison at Puchou is rather obscure. What I have translated as "One of his lieutenants—Ting Wen-ya by name—had mistreated his troops" may in all likelihood mean something like this: "There was a eunuch named Ting Wen-ya [who had been placed over the army of the region as a confidential observer for the emperor] who was unpopular with the troops."

HSIEH HSIAOWO

The art of telling fortune by analyzing the component parts of a character as shown in this story is still practiced in China today. The fortune teller's equipment consists of a number of selected characters written on small pieces of paper rolled into loose cylinders, from which the client would pick out one at random. A more skilled practitioner of the art may allow the client, if the latter is literate, to write down the first character that happens to come into his head and proceed to analyze it *ex tempo*. This requires, of course, a greater degree of skill than is necessary if one limited oneself to a selected number of characters rehearsed beforehand. It might be pointed out that the analysis is more often ingenious than etymologically correct.

THE KUNLUN SLAVE

Tuan Ch'eng-shih (d. 863) is sometimes given as the author of this tale but most recent authorities are inclined to accept it as the work of P'ei Hsing. The *T'ai P'ing Kuang Chi* gives a work known as *Ch'uan Ch'i* as the source for this and the story of Yinniang, together with twenty-two other tales, but it is impossible to tell with certainty whether P'ei Hsing was the author, compiler, or both of these tales.

YINNIANG

For the story of another swordswoman, see "Hung-hsien chuan," Edwards, Vol. II, pp. 123-27. In the nineteenth century the swordsman theme and the *kung-an* or trial theme were combined in a number of popular novels, wherein crime detection depends on the ability of the guardians of peace to "fly along the eaves and jump over walls." The heroes of these novels do not, as a rule, exhibit any magic power as Yinniang does; their accomplishments are more in line with that of the Kunlun slave.

A PREDESTINED MARRIAGE

In popular mythology the role of matchmaker is shared by "The Old Man with the Red Cord" and "The Old Man under the Moon." However, both are supposed to dwell in sunnier regions than this tale makes out.

TU TZU-CHUN

This tale is again of Indian origin. In Hsuan Tsang's *Ta T'ang Hsi Yü Chi* it is recorded, in a slightly simpler form, as a legend explaining the name of a pond east of the "deer forest" in the country of P'o-lo-ni-ssu. See Samuel Beal, *Buddhist Records of the Western World* (London, n.d., popular ed.), II, 55-59.

THE JADE KUANYIN

This, together with the "Judicial Murder of Tsui Ning," is one of few stories of popular origin which have not suffered much retouching in the hands of later editors. For anyone who can read these two tales in the original, it is impossible not to notice the earmarks of their Sung or Yuan authorship on almost every page. Note the suspense at the end of Part I. One can almost hear the story teller say after he had recited the couplet, "If you want to know what happened next, come to our next session and I will tell you." Later in printed versions of popular novels the formula is modified to: "If you want to know what happened next, read the following chapter."

THE JUDICIAL MURDER OF TSUI NING

For another translation of this tale, see the *T'ien Hsia Monthly* April, 1940, where it appears under the title "The Tragedy of Tsui Ning." Stories of this type are known as *kung-an* or trial stories; they are the equivalent for detective fiction in the West.

THE FLOWER LOVER

This tale may be of Sung origin but bears unmistakable evidence of having been polished by Feng Meng-lung (b. 1574-5; d. 1645-6), editor of the *Hsing Shih Heng Yen.* I have abridged some of the more repetitious passages, which are hardly necessary in a printed version since one doesn't have to contend with an audience that drifts in and out, as the oral story tellers had to.

THE OIL PEDDLER

Possibly of Sung origin, told by story tellers not long after the events took place. However, it probably contains accretions of the intervening centuries, to say nothing of elaborations by the editor of the *Heng Yen.* It is considered by Hu Shih, among others, as one of the finest stories of its type. Here again (as in the story "Ying Ying") we find the Chinese attitude toward love different from the Western: no Western hero would want to be accepted by his lady fair out of gratitude. I have cut the story down to about one half of its original length, but I have left out nothing that is not either superfluous or downright repetitious. As far as I know, there is no other translation of this tale in English.

THE THREE BROTHERS

The story of Hsu Wu is based upon the first part of a brief biography of his grandson Hsu Ching in the *History of the Later Han,* section 106. It is not unlikely that this represents an original composition by Feng Meng-lung after the manner of the story teller's story; it is inconceivable that a story teller would use the stilted language in which the dialogues are often couched or impose on his audience a letter in the literary style like the one Hsu Wu wrote to his brothers urging them to resign.

It might be pointed out that modern writers have remarked about the calculating and low cunning shown by Hsu Wu; he has been cited as a symbol of the deplorable state that Confucianism had fallen into by the latter part of the Han dynasty. It was such men as Hsu Wu, it has been argued, that made the Six Dynasties reaction against Confucianism inevitable.